THE

ANNALS

OF

ROGER DE HOVEDEN

COMPRISING

THE HISTORY OF ENGLAND

AND OF

OTHER COUNTRIES OF EUROPE

VOLUME ONE, THE FIRST PART

A.D. 732 TO 1154

ISBN 1 897853 39 4

First published, London, 1853.
Facsimile reprint 1994
by Llanerch Publishers,
Felinfach.

THE
ANNALS
OF
ROGER DE HOVEDEN
COMPRISING
THE HISTORY OF ENGLAND
AND OF
OTHER COUNTRIES OF EUROPE
VOLUME ONE, THE FIRST PART
A.D. 732 TO 1154

TRANSLATED BY
HENRY T. RILEY

A FACSIMILE REPRINT

Also published by Llanerch:

ROGER OF WENDOVER'S FLOWERS OF HISTORY in four paperbacks of which two have been published to date (June, '94).

A HISTORY OF THE KINGS OF ENGLAND by Florence of Worcester.

THE CULDEES OF THE BRITISH ISLANDS by William Reeves.

THE TOMBS OF THE KINGS: AN IONA BOOK OF THE DEAD by John Marsden.

NORTHUMBRIAN CROSSES OF THE PRE-NORMAN AGE by W. G. Collingwood.

THORSTEIN OF THE MERE: A SAGA OF THE NORTHMEN IN LAKELAND by W. G. Collingwood.

SYMBOLISM OF THE CELTIC CROSS by Derek Bryce.

TALIESIN POEMS by Meirion Pennar.

For a complete list of small-press editions and facsimile reprints, 100+ titles, write to LLANERCH PUBLISHERS, FELINFACH, LAMPETER, DYFED, WALES. SA48 8PJ.

PREFACE.

THE only printed version of this valuable Chronicle is that contained in the " Scriptores post Bedam" of Sir Henry Saville, London, 1596, and reprinted at Frankfort in 1601. The typographical errors and omissions in both these editions are almost innumerable; so much so, that of necessity the more onerous duties of an Editor* devolve in a considerable degree upon the Translator of any of the authors contained in the volume.

In the present Translation the text has been carefully examined throughout, and the greater portion, it is believed, of the errors corrected; in many instances on the safest of all grounds—reference to the works of contemporary writers. Attention is called in the Notes to the more important of these

---

* This was sensibly felt to be the case by Mr. Sharpe, in his translation of William of Malmesbury. Archbishop Nicolson says, in his " English Historical Library," p. 59, " Hoveden's History was published by Sir H. Saville; but (as Sir H. Spelman observes in his Glossary, on the word *Frithborga*) there are many errors in that foreign Edition of this, and all our other Historians, and, therefore, he well cautions the English reader attentively to consider the spelling of such words as are of our own growth, as very frequently mistaken by printers, that are strangers to our country and language." It is but just to remark that, in the present instance, the errors in the English edition are almost as numerous as in the foreign one.

corrections, in cases where they are a matter of question.
It has been thought advisable to retain the ancient names of
places where they differ materially from those of the present
day, and to add the latter in the Notes.

Of the author of this work but little is known. He is sometimes spoken of as a native of York, but it is more probable
that he was born at Hoveden, now Howden, a vill in the
East Riding of Yorkshire, which belonged to the bishops of
Durham, and where they occasionally resided. Frequent
mention is made of this place in the Annals, in connection
with those powerful prelates.* It has been suggested by some
writers that our author is the person mentioned by Robert of
Gloucester as " Hew of Howdene."† Among the various
offices held by him, he is said to have been a professor of
Theology at Oxford, and to have been employed, perhaps
at a later period of his life, by Henry II., in the capacity
of chaplain. Like many of the more learned clergy of his
day, uniting the study of the Law‡ with that of Divinity,

* For the first time, at p. 389 of this Volume. We learn from our author
that Hugh de Pusaz, or Pudsey, bishop of Durham, died at Howden.

† Mr. Hardy says, in the Introduction to the " Monumenta Britannica," p. viii., " The Burton Annals (Gale I.) mention a Hugh Hoveden,
as does Robert of Gloucester, but Roger is certainly the person intended.
The mistake arose probably from the practice of indicating an author's
name by the initial letters only, and the scribe hastily inserted H instead
of R." The lines of Robert of Gloucester alluded to are the following, (he
is speaking of Richard I.) :

> " But who so wole of his chevalrie, know or wyte,
> Rede he in the cornycles that ben of him wryte,
> That Mayster Hew hath of Howdene ywrouzte."

If in these lines he refers to our Chronicler, it is pretty clear that he is the
same person who wrote the life of Richard I., mentioned by Bishop Tanner
as said to be among the Digby MSS. in the Bodleian Library.

‡ This will probably account for the vast amount of information on
legal matters which is to be found in the latter part of the work. Tanner
seems to think that Hoveden devoted himself to the law when in mid-

he acted as one of the clerks* or secretaries of that king ; and, probably in such capacity, was employed in visiting monasteries on the death of the abbats or priors, for the purpose of receiving such portions of the revenues thereof as accrued to the crown. This fact will account for the great number of letters, charters, papal rescripts, bulls, and other matters relative to the Ecclesiastical history of his time, which are to be found in his work ; while his connection, through the place of his birth, with the sees of York and Durham, will explain why the affairs of those sees are so abundantly treated of.

Hoveden has been charged by Leland with surreptitiously borrowing from Simeon of Durham, the great Chronicler of Northumbria ; but it is not improbable that he enjoyed opportunities of free access to the materials from which Simeon compiled his Chronicles, and, as Archbishop Nicolson remarks,† if he did copy anything from him, he has greatly improved his narrative by carefully identifying the chronology of many matters confusedly related by that author. That in some instances he has closely followed Simeon of Durham and other preceding Chroniclers, cannot, however, be questioned ; but the evident universality of the practice among the Annalists of his times, shews that the censure of Leland is misplaced, and that Hoveden was actuated by no sordid motive, or wish to assume the credit of the labours of his predecessors.

The exact periods of his birth and death are unknown ; but Tanner, following Leland, thinks that he did not commence

life, and subsequently entered the Church. He informs us that Walter of Coventry states in his Annals that Hoveden was in the number of the domestics of Henry II. ; that he was sent to Norwich by that king, on a visit to the abbey there, for the purpose of auditing the expenditure of the monks, and of superintending the election of a new abbat ; and that his duties of a similar nature extended to other places.

* Benedictus Abbas mentions him as " Unus de clericis regis."

† Engl. Hist. Library, pp. 59, 60.

writing his Annals till after the death of Henry II., in 1189; when probably he devoted himself entirely to literary pursuits.* It is not improbable that he survived till the time of Henry III.

That he was a man of considerable learning, and, for his time, of extensive knowledge, is evident from his work. We find him frequently, and in some cases† appositely, quoting Virgil, Ovid (who seems to have been his favourite author), Lucan, and other Latin poets; but it is a curious fact, that he on no occasion mentions the name of the author from whom he quotes, or, indeed, of any Classical writer whatever. Like most of the learned Ecclesiastics of his day, he appears to have found peculiar charms in the jingle of the Leonine or Latin rhyme; a taste which had been recently introduced into this country by its Norman conquerors. His work also bears abundant proof that he was versed in the legal and theological lore of those times.

On the other hand, it is clear, from his easy credulity, that his mind was not at all in advance of his age. Miracles (some of them of a very trifling and silly nature), portents, omens, prophecies, and astrological predictions, are readily, and as a matter of course, copied into his pages; while visits of the Devil in person would almost appear to be considered by him as everyday occurrences. Jews, Saracens, heretics, and Pagans are summarily dealt with in his pages; and amid the pious ejaculations which on some few occasions he utters when depicting the miseries or frailties of mankind, we find not a word of sympathy wasted on their sufferings.

The Annals of Hoveden are not merely a Chronicle of En-

---

* We may here remark, that the passage in p. 247 of this Volume, in which he appears to assert that he was eye-witness to an event that happened in 1144, is copied almost literally from Henry of Huntingdon, who was probably the alleged witness of the miracle.

† See vol. ii. p. 42, where he mentions Tully.

glish affairs, but (in the latter part especially) form a history of the events of the then known world. Scotland, France, Germany, Norway, Denmark, Spain, Portugal, Italy, Constantinople, Asia Minor, and the Holy Land, all come under his notice, and he sometimes treats of their affairs at considerable length. On two occasions* he gives an episodical account of the then existing state of Geographical knowledge respecting the West and the South of Europe, which, in spite of the lamentably defective state of the text, cannot fail to be read with interest.

The work is divided into two Parts; the First of which, professing to be a continuation of Bede's Ecclesiastical History, commences in 732 and concludes in 1154. The Second Part commences in 1155, and breaks off in 1201, the third year of the reign of king John. Why this division was made, it is impossible with certainty to say; but it will readily be perceptible to the reader that events are treated in the First Part with much greater conciseness than in the second. This circumstance would perhaps warrant the conclusion that he marked the beginning of the reign of Henry II., in 1155, as the commencement of a period the events of which had passed under his own personal notice. In the concluding portion of the work, from the year 1192, his circumstantiality is such that we might almost imagine ourselves reading a newspaper account of events which happened nearly seven hundred years ago.†

By some writers, among whom Bishop Tanner may be mentioned, his style has been considered defective, but it is nevertheless remarkable for its simplicity and freedom from affectation. From his peculiar position there is no doubt that

* Under the reign of Richard I.

† As a proof of this, we may remark, that while the events of the period from 1155 to 1201 are compressed by Roger of Wendover and Matthew Paris into less than 250, the narrative of Hoveden, relative to the same period, extends to more than 800, pages.

he was able, and from the internal evidence offered by his
work, he clearly was desirous, to resort to the most authentic
sources of information within his reach ; consequently, though
his method of compilation is occasionally crude and defective
in arrangement, much is to be found, especially in the latter
portion of his work, which may be safely depended upon, and
which is to be met with in no other of the Chronicles of those
times.   This high estimate of his authority appears to have
been formed at an early period ; for we learn from Archbishop
Nicolson,* on the authority of Pitts, that in the year 1291,
Edward I. caused diligent search to be made in all the libraries
of England for copies of his Annals, for the purpose, on their
evidence, of adjusting the disputes as to the homage due to
him from the crown of Scotland.   In later times, Sir Henry
Saville, Selden, Archbishop Nicolson, and others of the learned,
have concurred in bearing testimony to his diligence and
fidelity as a historian, and, according to Leland, notwithstand-
ing the censure in another place so undeservedly pronounced
upon him, he is superior to all the chroniclers who preceded
him.

His Annals are his only work the genuineness of which is
undisputed.   Vossius, however, asserts that he was the author
of a History of the Kings of Northumbria, and a Life of
Thomas à Becket.   In his Annals, he enters fully into the
disputes between king Henry and à Becket, and appears,
though in a very guarded manner, to sympathize with the
sufferings of that prelate, while at the same time he seems
desirous to exculpate his royal master from the crime of having
been accessary to his base assassination.

The remarks which he makes upon the characters of the
illustrious personages of his times are few and cautious ;
still, the prominence which he gives to certain circumstances

* Brit. Hist. Library, pp. 59, 60.

and characteristics disclose the bias of his thoughts. It is evident that he considered Henry II. a great king, and he manifests a probably sincere sympathy for him in the numerous afflictions, caused to him by the unprincipled conduct of his sons, Henry, Richard, and Geoffrey. After the accession of Richard, Hoveden seems to hint that boundless sensuality. was his great failing, and, though in words he does not say so, he affords sufficient grounds for the conclusion that treachery, meanness, and avarice, were in his opinion the striking features of the character of king John. His history does not come down to the time of the death, or "disappearance," as Roger of Wendover thinks proper to call it, of Arthur, duke of Brittany. He evidently dislikes the crafty and unprincipled Philip Augustus, king of France; and the zest with which he relates, on numerous occasions, how that monarch turned his back in flight before the prowess of Richard is highly amusing.

We may remark, in conclusion, that among the most interesting portions of the work, may be reckoned the following; the account of the contests between king Henry and Thomas à Becket; the first persecution of the Albigenses; the Assizes of Clarendon and Northampton; the Laws* of William the Conqueror, as re-enacted by Henry II.; the Coronation of Richard I.; the Journal of that king's voyage to the Holy Land, and of his adventures during his stay in Sicily; the contest between Hugh, bishop of Coventry, supported by the other prelates, and the chancellor, William, bishop of Ely; and the lengthened disputes between Geoffrey, archbishop of York, and his dean and chapter; which latter are not yet brought to a conclusion, when the work somewhat abruptly ends.

* Here the text is in such a corrupt and mutilated state that it entirely defies successful management. The Translation has therefore been made from the more correct text of the same Laws, which is found in the " Leges Anglo-Saxonicæ" of Dr. Wilkins. London, 1721.

The following remarks, relative to this Chronicler, are ex-
tracted from the Introduction to the "Monumenta Britannica,"
commenced by the late Mr. Petrie, and recently published
under the care of Mr. Hardy :

"Hoveden's Annals extend from A.D. 732 to A.D. 1201.
Pars Prima: from A.D. 732 to A.D. 1154. From the commencement to the death of Egbert, in 837, his history is
taken from Simeon of Durham, sometimes literally transcribed,
at others condensed. Occasionally, however, Hoveden changes
the collocation, and makes slight verbal alterations. He then
returns to 751,* and takes up Henry of Huntingdon, who is
followed, with a few verbal changes, to the death of Ethelred I., in 872. Then follows a recapitulation † of the history of the West Saxon Kings from Cerdic, continued to
Henry I. ; not always, however, agreeing with Huntingdon's
History. He then returns to the year 849,‡ and again transcribes or abridges Simeon of Durham to the year 1122,§
making a few insertions from other sources. From 1122 to
1148, Huntingdon's History is again resorted to, abridged
or transcribed, with a few additions. From 1148‖ to 1154
Hoveden's History is very brief and confused, and that part
of it relating to Scotland is apparently derived from the same
source as the Chronicle of Melrose.

"*Pars Secunda:* from A.D. 1154 to A.D. 1201. From 1154¶
to 1164** it is of the same character : thence to 1170†† it

---

* See p. 20 of this Volume, where he seems to revert to the year 749
in taking up Henry of Huntingdon. This change of the text will account
for the apparent oversight noticed in p. 20, n. 68. According to Simeon
of Durham's text, Hoveden makes Egbert to reign thirty-six years and six
months, while, following Henry of Huntingdon, he gives him a reign of
forty years, representing him as dying in 840 or 842.

† See p. 39 of this Volume.   ‡ See p. 40.   § See p. 216.
‖ See p. 250.   ¶ See p. 253.   ** See p. 259.   †† See p. 325.

chiefly relates to à Becket, inserting twenty-eight of his
epistles, three of which are not found in Lupus's edition.
From Christmas 1169 to 1192, Hoveden either abridges or
transcribes Benedictus Abbas, or had access to the same
materials. When he abridges, it is by compression, or by
changing the order of the transaction, relating the events belonging to the same transaction connectedly ; whereas Benedictus Abbas, by observing a stricter chronological arrangement, frequently separates them. Hoveden, however, has
inserted entire many letters and charters which are either
omitted or abridged by Benedictus Abbas ; and when he gives
the journal of the expedition of Richard the First's fleet to
Messina, he appears to have had the original document before
him, as his account is fuller than that of Benedictus Abbas.
He also speaks in the first person, as if he were transcribing
the narrative of one that was present, which is not the case
with Benedictus Abbas. Hoveden has also exclusively several
particulars relating to Spain, Portugal, and Scotland. Under
the year 1192 he gives an account of Richard the First's captivity and deliverance, with a journal of his transactions from
his return to England in March, to his landing in France in the
following May. From that period to the conclusion, his History is very diffuse, containing many papal bulls and letters,
chiefly Ecclesiastical, relating, as might have been expected, to
the province of York,' or to the Northern parts of England,
regulations for courts of law, &c.

" * Some persons have thought that Hoveden continued his
History to the year 1226 ; but this mistake seems grounded
on the continuation which has been ascribed to Walter of
Coventry, who borrowed both from Hoveden and Benedictus
Abbas, and yet refers to Hoveden alone.

* This appears in the " Monumenta" as a Note to the above extracts.

"It is remarkable that Benedictus Abbas should twice (pp. 93, 108) mention Hoveden, and that Hoveden, although he appears to transcribe or abridge Benedictus, should omit all mention of himself."

H. T. R.

THE ANNALS

OF

ROGER DE HOVEDEN.

INTRODUCTION.

At the beginning of this work, I propose to trace the genealogical line of the kings of Northumbria,* down to the times of those, who, coming after the death of the most venerable Bede, have not hitherto been treated of.

Ida held the sovereignty twelve years;[1] after whose death Glappa reigned one year. He was succeeded by Adda, whose reign lasted eight years; on whose decease Ethelric became king, and reigned seven years. Theoderic succeeded him, and, after a reign of four years, lost his life and left the kingdom to Fridubuld. He, having reigned one year, was succeeded by Huscus,[2] who, after a reign of seven years, lost his kingdom and his life. Ethelfred, the most distinguished for valour among these kings, was the eighth in succession, and reigned for a period of twenty-eight years. He was succeeded by King Edwin, who having embraced Christianity, as king and martyr ascended to heaven, after a reign of seventeen years. After him, Oswald, a most Christian king, reigned over Northumbria for a period of seven years. He having ascended to the mysterious realms of heaven, Oswy succeeded him as king, and held the government twenty-eight years. He being

---

* It is worthy of remark, that the account here given of the Northumbrian kings, differs very materially from that of Bede, William of Malmesbury, and the Anglo-Saxon Chronicle.

[1] V. r. Eleven years.

[2] V. r. Hussus.

removed to the realms of bliss, Egfrid received the sovereignty, and after a reign of fifteen years was slain by the Picts, because he had unrighteously ravaged Ireland.[3]

In his room, his brother Alfred became king, and was succeeded by his son, Osred, who being slain, Choenred ascended the throne, and was succeeded by Osric, whose successor was Ceolwulph, the brother of Choenred. It was to him that Bede, the historian, dedicated his history of the English.

Having enumerated these, it is my intention to adopt the history of the most holy and learned Bede as the foundation of this work, commencing at the last sentence thereof; and, recording the years of our Lord, carefully reviewing in their order the reigns of the kings, and briefly, to the best of my ability, remarking upon the life and miracles of the rest of the faithful, it is my earnest desire, together with them, to receive from Christ the reward of everlasting salvation.

Come, thou benign Spirit, who without thine own aid art never imparted; bestow thy bounty on my tongue, thou who in thy bounty dost bestow tongues.[3*]

THE FIRST PART.

In the year from the incarnation of our Lord 732, as Bede informs us, Bretwald, archbishop of Canterbury, departed this life, and was buried in the church of St. Peter. In this year, Tatwin was consecrated archbishop of Canterbury, it being the fifteenth year of the reign of Ethelbald, king of Mercia. In the same year, also, king Ceolwulph was taken prisoner, shorn, and sent back into his kingdom. He was imbued with a wonderful love for the Scriptures, as the truthful chronicler, Bede, states in the beginning of his Preface. In the same year, bishop Acca was expelled from his see,[4] and Cynebert, bishop of Lindesey,[5] died.

In the year 733, having received his pall from the Apostolic See, Tatwin ordained Alwin and Sigfrid bishops. An eclipse

---

[3] In A.D. 684, he had sent his general, Beort, with an army to lay waste Ireland; and in the following year, having himself led his troops against the Picts or Britons at Strath Clyde, he was slain at Drumnechtan, in the county of Forfar,

[3*] This is said in reference to Acts ii. 3, 4.

[4] Of Hexham.   [5] In Lincolnshire.

of the sun took place on the nineteenth day before the calends of September, about the third hour of the day, insomuch that the face of the sun seemed to be almost entirely covered with a very black and horrible shield.

In the year 734, on the second day before the calends of February, the moon was covered with a redness like blood for nearly a whole hour, at about the time of cock-crow; a darkness then coming on, she returned to her usual brightness. In the same year, Tatwin, the new archbishop of Canterbury, died. The first bishop of this city was Augustine, that famous instructor of the whole kingdom, and excellent founder of the Christian faith and religion, to whom, in their order, succeeded Laurentius, Mellitus, Justus, Honorius, Deusdedit, the most learned Theodore, and Bretwald, whom Tatwin followed, as I have already mentioned. In the same year, Fridebert was ordained bishop of Hagustald.[6]

In the year 735, Nothelm was ordained archbishop of Canterbury, and Egbert, bishop of York, was ordained to the archbishopric of the Northumbrians, being the first who, since Paulinus, had received the pall[7] from the Apostolic See. In this year the learned Bede departed this life at Jarrow.[8]

In the year from the incarnation of our Lord 736, Nothelm, having received the pall from the pope of Rome, ordained three bishops, namely, Cuthbert, Eordwald, and Ethelfrid.

In the year 737, bishop Aldwin, who was also called Wor, departed this life, and in his room Witta[9] and Tota were consecrated bishops of the Mercians[10] and the Mid-Angles.[11] In the same year, in place of Ceolwulph,[12] Eadbert, his uncle's son, received the kingdom of Northumbria.

In the year 738, Swetbrit,[13] king of the East Saxons, died. In the following year, Ethelherd, king of the West Saxons, departed this life, on which his brother Cuthred was appointed king in his room. In the same year, archbishop Nothelm died, four years after having received the archbishopric, and Adulph, bishop of Rochester, departed this life.

[6] Hexham, in Northumberland.
[7] Without it he was not entitled to the title of archbishop.
[8] In Durham.   [9] Or Winta.
[10] Witta was consecrated bishop of Lichfield.
[11] Tota was the first bishop of Leicester.
[12] He resigned his crown, and embraced the monastic life.
[13] Called Selred by Roger of Wendover, and others.

In the year 740, Ethelwald, bishop of Lindisfarne, departed to the Lord, and Kinewulph was appointed to that see. In the same year of sacred memory, bishop Acca was removed to the realms of the living, after having held the bishopric of Hagustald twenty-four years, at the east side of which church his body was honorably interred : afterwards, when more than three hundred years had elapsed from his burial, in consequence of a divine revelation, he was removed by a certain priest, and placed in a coffin within the church, with due honor, where to the present day he is held in great veneration; as a merited proof of his sanctity before all men, the chasuble, tunic, and sudarium,[14] which had been deposited in the earth with his most hallowed corpse, preserve even unto this day, not only their original appearance, but even their original strength of texture.

In the same year in which the holy bishop Acca departed to the realms of heaven, Arwin, the son of Eadulph, was slain, on the ninth day before the calends of January, being the sixth day of the week. In the same year, Cuthbert received the archbishopric of Canterbury, being the eleventh archbishop ; and, in succession to Adulph, Dun became bishop of Rochester.

In the year 741, the monastery in the city of York was burnt, on the ninth day before the calends of May, being the first day of the week.

In the year 744, a battle was fought between the Picts and the Britons; and in the following year, fiery strokes were beheld in the air, such as no men of that generation had ever seen before, and were visible throughout almost all the night of the calends of January. In the same year also, according to some accounts, the second Wilfrid, bishop of York, departed to the Lord on the third day before the calends of May; but it is my opinion, that before Bede had completed his history, this Wilfrid had been already translated to the realms of heaven. In these days died Inguald, bishop of London, and at this time flourished Saint Guthlac.

In the year 749, died Elfwald,[15] king of East Anglia, upon which Hunbenna and Albert divided the kingdom between them. In the following year, that is to say, in 750, king Eadbert

[14] This may either mean a peculiar head-dress worn by the priesthood, or the " fanon " or " mappula," a small handkerchief, a napkin, worn over the left wrist.   [15] Called Athelwold by Roger of Wendover.

brought bishop Kinewulph prisoner to the city of Bebba,[16] and caused the church of St. Peter, in Lindisfarne, to be besieged.[17] Offo, the son of Alfred, was unthinkingly running with all haste towards the relics of Saint Cuthbert, the bishop, when he was dragged out of the church, without his weapons, and almost famished with hunger.

In the same year, bishop Allwich died, and Ardulf, a deacon, was ordained to the bishopric.[17*] Cuthred, the king of the West Saxons, rose against Ethelbald, king of Mercia.

In the year from the incarnation of our Lord 752, on the day before the calends of August, an eclipse of the moon took place.

In the year 753, Boniface the archbishop, who was also called Winfrid, with fifty-three others, was crowned with the martyrdom of the Franks. In the following year, Cuthred, king of the West Saxons, died, the sceptre of whose kingdom was received by Sigebert.

In the year 756, being the fifteenth [18] year of his reign, king Eadbert, with Unnust, king of the Picts, led an army to the cities of Alclutit,[19] and there received the Britons of that neighbourhood under their subjection, on the first day of August; but, on the tenth day of the same month, almost the whole of the army which he led from Deouama,[19*] was destroyed at Niwambirg, that is at the new city. In the same year Baltere, the anchorite, attained the life of the righteous, and departed unto the Lord. On the eighth day before the calends of December, the moon, on her fifteenth day, being about her full, appeared to be covered with the colour of blood, and then, the darkness decreasing, she returned to her usual brightness; but, in a wondrous manner, a bright star followed the moon, and, passing across her, preceded her when shining, at the same distance at which it had followed her before she was darkened.

In the year 757, Ethelbald, king of Mercia, was treacherously slain by his own allies.[20] In the same year a civil war

[16] Now Bamborough, in Northumberland.

[17] " Basilicam " here is probably a wrong reading for " basilicâ;" if so, the meaning will be, that Eadbert ordered Kinewulph to be confined in the church of St. Peter, at Lindisfarne, which agrees with the account given by Roger of Wendover.   [17*] Of Sidnancaster, or Lindesey.

[18] V. r. Eighteenth.   [19] Supposed to be Dumbarton, in Scotland.

[19*] Holinshed calls this place Ouan. Probably the reading in his MS. was " De Ouania," instead of " Deouma," as in the printed copy.

[20] This is probably said in reference to Cuthred, king of the West

arose among the Mercians, and Beornred being put to flight, king Offa was victorious.

In the year 758, king Eadbert voluntarily resigned the kingdom, which he had received from God, to his son Osulph, who held it but one year and then lost it, having been treacherously slain by his own servants near Mechilwongton, on the ninth day before the calends of August.

In the following year, Ethelwald, who was also called Moll, began to reign on the nones of August. At the beginning of the third year of his reign a most severe battle was fought, near Edwin's Cliff, on the seventh day before the ides of August, in which, after a fight of three days, Oswin was slain, and thus king Ethelwald gained the victory. This took place on the first day of the week. In the same year, Unnust, king of the Picts, departed this life.

In the year 762 king Ethelwald took Etheldreda for his queen, on the calends of November, at Cataract.[21] In the third year from this, that is to say in 764, there was a great snow with intense frost, not to be compared with any in former ages. It covered the earth from the beginning of winter almost until the middle of spring, and through its rigour the trees and vegetables mostly withered away, and many marine animals were found dead. In the same year, likewise, Ceolwulph, formerly king, and afterwards a servant of our Lord Jesus Christ and a monk, departed this life.

It was to this king that the truthful Bede wrote the epistle which begins thus: "To the most glorious king, Ceolwulph, Bede, servant of Christ, and priest. I formerly, at your request, most readily transmitted to you the Ecclesiastical History of the English Nation, which I had newly published, for you to read and give it your approbation; and I now send it again to be transcribed, and more fully considered at your leisure." The king himself, after renouncing the world, became a monk in the church of Lindisfarne, and there struggled for a heavenly kingdom. His body being afterwards brought to the

Saxons, who, having made a treaty of peace with Ethelbald, attacked and slew him at Seekington; or it may allude to the version of the story that he was slain by his own subjects, headed by the rebel Beornred. Lambarde reconciles the two versions by suggesting that Cuthred, king of Wessex, invaded Mercia, and conspired with some of Ethelbald's subjects, of whom Beornred was chief.   [21] Catterick, in Yorkshire.

church at Norham, according to the accounts given by the inhabitants of that place, became famous for working many miracles.
Through the influence of this king, after he had become a
monk, licence was granted to the monks of the church of Lindisfarne to drink wine or ale; for before, they were in the
habit of drinking only milk or water, according to the ancient
rule prescribed by Saint Aidan, the first bishop of that church,
and that of the monks who, coming with him from Scotland,
had received there a settlement by the munificence of king
Oswald, and rejoiced to live in great austerity, with a view to
a future life.

In the same year, many cities, monasteries, and towns, in
various places, and even kingdoms, were laid waste by sudden
conflagrations; such, for instance, as the city of Sterburgwenta,[22]
Homunic,[23] the city of London, the city of York, and Doncaster;
many other places also, the same calamity overtook.

In the same year died Frehelm the priest and abbat, and
Tocca,[24] bishop of the Mercians, on which Eadbert was ordained
bishop in his room. At this period, also, Frithwold, bishop
of Whitherne, departed from this world, and Pechtwin was
appointed in his stead.[25]

[22] This is most probably an error, the name of two places being made
into one. Lambarde in his Dictionary, quoting from Simeon of Durham,
mentions in place of this name, Stretbourgh and Winton, and adds, " by
which order of speech it seemeth that he took it for a great town ; how-
beit, I have not hitherto found it." Holinshed (whether quoting from
Roger de Hoveden, or Simeon of Durham, does not appear,) mentions
here Stretehu and Geivento, places, not improbably, as imaginary as the
Sterburgwenta of our text.

[23] It is not clear what place is meant by this name. Holinshed mentions it as Alnwick.

[24] V. r. Totta.

[25] In the text, " Candida Casa," or "the White House." The bishopric
of Whitherne was also called that of the Picts, Abercorn, or Galloway.
Its establishment is thus related by Bede, Eccles. Hist. B. iii. c. 4.
" In year of our Lord 565, when Justin the younger, the successor of
Justinian, had the government of the Roman empire, there came into Britain
a famous priest and abbot, a monk by habit and life, whose name was
Columba, to preach the word of God to the province of the northern
Picts, who are separated from the southern parts by steep and rugged
mountains ; for the southern Picts, who dwell on the side of those mountains, had long before, as is reported, forsaken the errors of idolatry, and
embraced the truth, by the preaching of Ninias, a most reverend bishop
and holy man of the British nation, who had been regularly instructed at

In the year 765, fiery strokes were seen in the air, such as formerly appeared on the night of the calends of January, as I have already mentioned.[26] In the same year Ethelwald lost[27] the kingdom of Northumbia at Wincanheale,[28] on the third day before the calends of November, and was succeeded in the kingdom by Alcred, who was a descendant, as some say, of king Ida. Hemeli, bishop of the Mercians, also departed this life. Cuthred was ordained bishop of Lichfield; and at the same period archbishop Bregwin died, and had Lambert for his successor; bishop Aldulph also dying, Ceolwulph succeeded him in the diocese of Lindesey.

In the year 766, Egbert, archbishop of York, rested in the peace of Christ, on the thirteenth day before the calends of December, it being the thirty-fourth year of his episcopate; and in the same year Saint Frithebert, bishop of Hagustald,[29] departed this life.

In the year 767, Albert was consecrated bishop of York, and Alcmund bishop of Hexham, on the eighth day before the calends of May. In the same year Albert was ordained bishop of the East Saxons, and Ceolwulph was consecrated bishop of Lindesey. In this year also, Etha, the anchorite, died happily at Cric,[30] a place distant about ten miles from the city of York.

In the year 768, being the tenth year after the abdication of his kingdom, Eadbert happily breathed forth his spirit, being a member of the priesthood, and devoted to the service of God. In the same year died Pepin, king of the Franks, and Hadwin was ordained bishop at Macuhi.[31]

Rome, in the faith and mysteries of the truth; whose episcopal see, named after St. Martin the bishop, and famous for a stately church (wherein he and many other saints rest in the body), is still in existence among the British nation. The place belongs to the province of the Bernicians, and is generally called the ' White House,' because he there built a church of stone, which was not usual among the Britons."

[26] Under the year 745.

[27] This seems to imply that he was deprived of it by treachery or violence. Holinshed says, " After that Moll had reigned six years, he resigned his kingdom. But others write that he reigned eleven years, and was in the end slain by treason of his successor Altred."

[28] Probably Finchale, in Durham; though Lambarde suggests that Wighal, near Thorpebares, in Yorkshire, is the place here spoken of.

[29] Hexham.   [30] Probably Crecca, or Crake, near York.

[31] Probably Saint Mesmin de Mici, in the province of Orleans, in France.

In the year 769, Cataract[31] was burnt by the tyrant Carnred, and by the judgment of God, he himself perished by fire in the same year.

In the year 771, Offa, king of Mercia, subdued in war the nation of the East Angles. In the same year, Carloman, the king of the Franks, being attacked by a sudden disease, departed this life, on which his brother Charles,[32] who had before possessed half his father's kingdom, acquired the sovereignty of the whole, and afterwards, by his invincible bravery, obtained the chieftainship of all the peoples of the Franks.

In the year 772, Charles, the king of the Franks, having collected a powerful army and assembled the warlike forces of his kingdom, invaded the nation of the Saxons, and after having lost many of his principal and most noble men, betook himself home.

In the year from the incarnation of our Lord 773, bishop Hadwin[32*] departed this life, and Leuthfrid was appointed bishop in his room. Wulfeth also, abbat of Beverley, died, and Albert, the archbishop of York, received the pall that had been sent to him by pope Adrian.

In the year 774, duke Eadwulph died, and Alcred being deprived of the counsel and assistance of his own family and his chief men, exchanged the dignity of a crown for exile, and with a few companions of his flight, first betook himself to the city of Bebba,[33] and afterwards to the king of the Picts whose name was Cynoth. The city of Bebba is an extremely well fortified place, of no great size, but extending over the space of about two or three fields, having a single approach, hollowed out [of the rock], and in a wonderful manner raised on high and ascended by steps; it has, on the summit of a hill, a church most beautifully built, in which is a precious shrine, wherein, wrapped in a pall, lies the right hand of the holy king Oswald, uncorrupted, as Bede, the historian of this nation, relates. There is on the western side, and in the highest part of the city, a fountain

---

[31] Catterick, in Yorkshire.   [32] Known in history as Charlemagne.
[32*] The words in the original are " Episcopus Migensis." It is not improbable that the bishopric of Orleans is here alluded to; probably the same that is mentioned under the year 768.
[33] Bamborough.

hollowed out in a marvellous fashion, the water of which is
sweet to drink, and most limpid to the sight.

Ethelred,[34] the son of Ethelwald, reigned in his father's
stead, and, as will appear in the sequel, held the government hardly five years.   At the same period, Charles, the most
invincible king of the Franks, after having harassed it with a
siege, took Ticinum, the most noble city of the Lombards,
together with king Desiderius himself, and gained possession
of the whole of Italy.

In the year 775, Cynoth, king of the Picts, departed this
life, and duke Eadulph was fraudulently taken prisoner by
stratagem, and after a short time slain, buried, and forgotten.
Abbat Ebbi also died, and king Charles, as I have already
observed, the most warlike of the Franks, being attended
and supported by, and glorying in, the entire might of his
army, entered the country of the Saxon in battle array, and
accompanied by his legions.   This district, raging with fire and
sword, he laid waste by most severe conflicts ; inflamed with
furious anger, with a mighty arm he succeeded in adding to
his own supreme empire the cities of Sigeburg and Aresburg,[35]
and the province of Bohwer,[36] which had been previously overrun by the Franks.

In the year 777, Peewin, bishop of Whitherne, departed to
the Lord, and was succeeded by Ethelbert.

In the year 779, Ethelred being expelled from the throne,[37]
and driven into exile, was forced to undergo great trials.   On
the expulsion of Ethelred, Elfwald, the son of Osulph, received the kingdom of Northumbria, and held it ten years.   He
was a pious and just king, as a future circumstance will prove.

In the year 780, dukes Osbald and Ethelherd, having collected
an army, burned Bearn, the king's patrician,[38] at Seletune,[39]
on the ninth day before the calends of January.   In the same
year, archbishop Albert departed from this world unto Christ,
Eanbald, while he was yet alive, having been appointed to the

[31] By some called Ethelbert.   [35] Probably Arensberg, in Westphalia.
[36] Probably a mistake for Roer, or Rohwer, a river of Westphalia, the
allusion being to the province through which it flows.
[37] Of Northumbria.   [38] See the note under year 788.
[39] Lambarde says, " I take this place to be Salton, now in Yorkshire,
and yet the conjecture were not unreasonable to think it Salston, in
Nottinghamshire."

same see. Bishop Kinewulph[40] also, having laid aside the cares of the world, this year gave up the government of his church, together with the management of all his household,[41] to Higbald. In the same year also, bishop Eanbald, having received the pall which had been sent him from the Apostolic See, was solemnly invested as archbishop.

In the year 781, Alcmund, bishop of Hagustald, a man of remarkable piety and of great virtues, departed to Christ, in the third year of the reign of the glorious king Elfwald, on the seventh day before the ides of September; Saint Gilbert[42] succeeded him.

In the year 783, being the third year of the righteous king Elfwald, Werburg, who had formerly been queen of the Mercians, but was then an abbess, departed this life, to live eternally with Christ. At the same period, bishop Kinewulph departed to the realms of heaven in the fortieth year of his episcopate.

In the year 786, being the eighth year of king Elfwald, Bothwin, the venerable abbat of the church of Ripon, in the sight of his brethren who were present, departed to the kingdom of heaven, and Albert was elected in his room and ordained. In the same year Aldulph was consecrated bishop by archbishop Eanbald, and bishops Gilbert and Higbald, at Corbridge.[43] In these days, Rictrith, who was formerly a queen, and afterwards an abbess, departed unto the Lord. At the same period, Kinewulph, king of the West Saxons, was murdered in a dreadful manner by the perfidious tyrant Kinebard, and the cruel assassin, himself, was without mercy slain by duke Osred, the avenger of his master; upon which, Brithric received the kingdom of the West Saxons. At this time, legates from the Apostolic See were sent to Britain (the venerable bishop George being the chief among them) by pope Adrian, to renew among us the ancient ties of friendship and the catholic faith, which Saint Gregory the pope had taught through Saint Augustine : having been honorably received by the kings and archbishops or primates of this country, they returned home in peace, with great presents, as was befitting.

In the year 787, a synod was held at Wincanheale,[44] on the

[40] Bishop of Lindisfarne.
[41] " Familiæ ;" alluding probably to the community of monks at Lindisfarne.
[42] Roger of Wendover says Tilbert.
[43] In Northumberland.
[44] See under the year 765.

fourth day before the nones of September; at this period, Albert, abbot of Ripon, died, and Sigred succeeded him.

In the year 788, a conspiracy having been formed, king Elfwald was slain by a shocking death, by his patrician[44*] Sigga, the ninth day before the calends of October, at a place called Siltecester near the wall.[45] The body of this excellent king was carried by great crowds of monks to the church of Hagustald, attended with the chaunts of the clergy, and was honorably buried there, in the church of Saint Andrew. He was succeeded by his nephew Osred, the son of king Alcred, who reigned one year. In the place where the good king Elfwald was murdered, a light sent down from heaven, is said to have been seen by great numbers of people. A church was built there by the faithful of that place, and consecrated to the honor of God, and of the saints, Cuthbert the bishop, and Oswald the king and martyr.

In the year 790, Ethelred was recalled from exile, and again, by the grace of Christ, seated on the throne of his kingdom. But king Osred, having been betrayed by the treachery of his nobles, was deprived of his kingdom and shorn in the city of York, and afterwards, compelled by necessity, went into exile. In the second year of his reign, duke Eardulph was taken prisoner, and was taken to Ripon, and there slain without the gate of the church by the above-named king. The brethren having carried his body to the church with Gregorian chaunts, and then placed it in a tent outside thereof, after midnight he was found alive within the church.

In the same year Baldwulph was ordained bishop of Whitherne, at the place which is called Hearrahaldh, which may be translated "the place of the lords." For in the preceding year, bishop Ethelbert left his own see,[47] on the death of Saint Gilbert, and received the bishopric of Hagustald, as his see.

In the year 791, the sons of king Elfwald were dragged away by force from the city of York, and, having been enticed from the principal church by false promises, were shockingly slain by king Ethelred, at Wonwaldremere;[48] their names were

[44*] The Patricians of the Anglo-Saxon kings were probably nobles of high rank, attached to the royal household.

[45] The wall of Severus is alluded to. The author of the chronicles of Durham and Lindisfarne calls the place Thirlwall. Perhaps Benwell, in Northumberland, is the place alluded to.   [47] Of Whitherne.

[48] Said by Lambarde to be Winandermere, near Kendal, in Westmoreland.

Elf and Elfwin. In this year also, Lambert, archbishop of Canterbury, departed to the Lord ; Ethelherd, abbat[49] of the monastery of Lhudu, was elected his successor and consecrated archbishop.

In the year 792, Charles, king of the Franks, sent to Britain a book containing articles agreed upon in a synod, which had been sent to him from Constantinople; in which book, oh shame ! there were found many things repugnant and contrary to the true faith, and especially that it had been unanimously agreed to by three hundred, or even more, of the various bishops of the East, that images ought to be worshipped, a thing that the Church of God utterly abhors. Against this Albinus wrote an epistle, wonderfully confirmed by the authority of the Holy Scriptures, and presented it with the same book, in the name of our bishops and princes, to the king of the Franks.

In the same year also, Osred, relying upon the oath and fidelity of certain nobles, came secretly from Eufania,[50] the place of his exile; and then, being deserted by his soldiers, was taken prisoner by the said king Ethelred, and by his order slain at a place called Dingburg, on the eighteenth day before the calends of October. His body was carried to Tynemouth,[51] and buried in the royal tomb, in the noble monastery there. In the same year king Ethelred took as his queen Elfleda, the daughter of Offa, king of Mercia, at Cataract, on the third day before the calends of October.

In the year 793, being the fourth year of the reign of King Ethelred, dreadful prodigies alarmed the wretched nation of the English, for terrific lightnings, and dragons in the air, and strokes of fire were seen hovering on high and shooting to and fro; which were ominous signs of the great famine and the frightful and ineffable slaughter of multitudes of men which afterwards ensued. In the same year also, duke Sigga, who slew king Elfwald, died a merited death, and his body was carried to the island of Lindisfarne, on the ninth day before the calends of May.

Lindisfarne is a large island, eight miles or thereabouts in circumference. In it was a noble monastery, where the illus-

[49] Roger of Wendover says, that he was previously bishop of Winchester.
[50] Probably either the Hebrides, a name of which was Evania, or the Isle of Man, which was called Ebonia.   [51] In Northumberland.

trious bishop Cuthbert was interred,[52] together with other bishops who most worthily succeeded him. With respect to them, the words of the chaunt may be appropriately repeated— " The bodies of the saints are buried in peace." [53] Lindis is the name of a river which, two feet in width, runs into the sea. When it is "Ledon," or low tide, the river can be seen ; but when it is "Malina," or the high tide of the sea, then the Lindis cannot be seen. The tide of the ocean follows the moon, and, as though by its inhaling, is raised to high water, and then, by its breathing forth, is driven back again. It seems to flow and to ebb twice a day, later each time by three quarters and[54] half an hour, as Bede testifies. Farne is the name of an island on which the most blessed Cuthbert passed the life of a hermit. It is not so large as Lindisfarne, but is situate out at sea, and is buffeted day and night by huge billows.

In the same year, the pagans,[55] coming from the northern regions to Britain with a naval armament, made descents in all quarters, plundering, ravaging, and slaughtering, like most cruel wolves, not only beasts of burthen, oxen and sheep, but priests and Levites as well, and multitudes of monks and nuns. They came, as I have observed, to the church of Lindisfarne and laid waste all places with dreadful havoc, trod down holy places with their polluted feet, undermined the altars, and carried off all the treasures of the holy church. Some of the brethren they slaughtered ; some they carried off with them in chains ; a very great number, loaded with abuse, they thrust out naked, and some they drowned in the sea. With respect to them, the words may be appropriately quoted : " Fortune bears hard upon the lot of the guiltless. Evil is the due punishment of wickedness. The wrong-doers are seated after their wont on a lofty throne, and the guilty in an unjust manner are treading upon the necks of the righteous. Bright virtue lies concealed in obscure shades, and the just suffer the penalties of the wicked."

[52] " Positus erat " may either mean that they were located there during their lives, or that they were buried there. Probably the latter is the meaning.

[53] " Corpora defunctorum in pace sepulta sunt."

[54] In the original it is " et." " Aut," " or," would seem to be a more appropriate reading. The whole passage is involved in considerable obscurity.   [55] The Danes.

These having retired, congratulating themselves on their booty and their wicked deeds, I shall recount what misfortunes the succeeding year brought.

In the year 794, the pagans above mentioned having laid waste the harbour of king Egfrid, plundered the monastery of Donum.[56] But Saint Cuthbert did not permit them to depart without punishment; for their chief was there slain by the English, and died a cruel death; and, after the interval of a short time, the violence of a tempest wrecked, destroyed, and foundered their ships, and overwhelmed a vast number in the sea. Upon this, some of them were thrown upon shore, and soon dispatched without mercy; and this justly befell them, for they grievously injured those who had not injured them. At that time Ethelherd died, who was formerly a duke, but then a priest in the city of York. In the same year the venerable pope Adrian[57] departed unto the Lord on the seventh day before the calends of January. He held the See twenty-six years, ten months, and eleven days. He was buried in the church of Saint Peter, the prince of the Apostles, and over his tomb a tablet of marble, fixed against the wall, recounted his good works, in verses written by the command of king Charles[58] in letters of gold.

In the year 795, the same most valiant king Charles, having laid waste their country, with a strong hand, by his arms subdued the nation of the Huns. Their prince having been put to flight, and their army worsted or cut to pieces, he carried away thence fifteen waggons filled with gold, silver, and precious vestments made entirely of silk, each of which was drawn by four oxen. All these the same king, on account of the victory which had been granted him by the Lord, ordered to be divided among the churches of Christ and the poor, returning thanks together with all those who had fought together with him.

In the year 796, being the seventh year of King Ethelred, Alric, who was formerly a duke, but then a priest in the city of York, departed this life; and shortly afterwards, that is

---

[56] This passage is evidently corrupt. The words are " Portum Egfredi regis vastantes, Monasterium Doni annis prædarerunt." The corresponding passage in the Anglo-Saxon Chronicle is, " and plundered Egfert's monastery at the mouth of the Wear."

[57] The First.   [58] Charlemagne.

to say, on the fifth day before the calends of April, an eclipse of the moon took place between the time of cock-crow and daybreak. In the same year, king Ethelred was slain at Cobre, on the fourteenth day before the calends of May. On this, Osbald, a patrician, was chosen king by some of the nobles of that nation ; and after twenty-seven days, being deserted by all the royal household and the nobles, and banished and expelled from the kingdom, he retired with a few followers to the island of Lindisfarne, and went thence with some of the brethren by ship to the king of the Picts.

Then Eardulph, whom I have previously mentioned, the son of Earnulph, having been recalled from exile, received the crown, and on the seventh day before the calends of June, was consecrated at York, in the church of Saint Peter, before the altar of Saint Paul, where that nation had first received the blessings of baptism. Not long after this, that is to say, on the seventh day before the calends of August, Offa, the most mighty king of the Mercians, departed this life, after having reigned thirty-nine years, and was succeeded in the kingdom by his son Egfrith, who died the same year.

Upon this, Kenulph, the father of Kenelm, received the crown of the kingdom of Mercia, and gloriously held it in the invincible power of his might ; in the same year also Ceolwulph died at Lindesey, and shortly after, that is to say, on the fourth day before the ides of August, Archbishop Eanbald died at the monastery called Edete, and his body was carried, with a vast concourse accompanying it, to the city of York, and honorably buried there, in the church of Saint Peter the Apostle. Immediately thereupon, another Eanbald, a priest of the same church, was elected archbishop, and consecrated at Sochesburg[69] by bishops Ethelbert, Higbald, and Baldwulph.

In the year 797, this last Eanbald, having received the pall from the Apostolic See, was solemnly confirmed in the archbishopric of Northumbria, on the sixth day before the ides of September, being the nativity of Saint Mary; with regard to which day, the poet says : "With honor shines the day on which Mary the good virgin, proceeding from the line of king David, was born unto the world."

In the same year died Ethelbert, bishop of Hagustald, whom

[69] Socburgh, in the diocese of Durham.

Eadred succeeded, and was ordained by archbishop Eanbald and bishop Higbald at a place which is called Widford.

In the year 798, a conspiracy having been entered into by the murderers of king Ethelred, Wada, the leader in the plot, together with the others, fought a battle against king Erdulph, at a place which is called by the English Billingahon, near Wallalalege, and after many were slain on either side, earl Wada with his men was put to flight, and king Erdulph bravely gained a victory over his foes. In the same year, London was destroyed by a sudden conflagration, together with a vast multitude of people.

At this period, Kenulph, king of the Mercians, with all the strength of his army, entered the province of Kent, and laid it waste with dreadful slaughter. At the same time, Eadbert, king of Kent, was taken prisoner, and the king of the Mercians ordered his eyes to be put out, and his hands to be cut off without mercy, as a punishment for their pride and treachery ; then, having obtained the suffrage of the Lord, he added the rule of his kingdom to his own sway, placing the crown upon his head and the sceptre in his hand. In the same year also, being the third year of the above-named king Kenulph, a synod was held at the place which is called Wincanhele,[60] under the presidency of archbishop Eanbald, many ecclesiastics and men of princely dignity attending thereat. They devised many things for the benefit of the Holy Church of God, and of the nation of Northumbria and all the provinces, as to the observance of Easter, feasts, and judgments, both holy and secular. These enactments rendered those days distinguished for just kings, virtuous nobles, and holy bishops, and other wise men, namely, priests and monks; through the foresight and justice of whom, and their holy deeds, the state of the kingdom of Northumbria sent forth a sweet fragrance in those times. The lord archbishop Eanbald commanded the profession of faith in the articles of the five synods to be repeated, concerning which it is thus written in the history of the English : " We do agree to the holy and universal decrees of the five synods of the fathers, holy and acceptable to God, in such form as the text of the present book contains," &c.

In the year 799, in the British seas a very great number of ships were tossed and wrecked, or dashed against each other, and sunk, together with a vast multitude of men. In the same

[60] Finchale, in Durham.

year, Brorda, a prince of the Mercians, who was also called Hyldegils, departed this life. An abbat also, whose name was Altilthegno,[61] was murdered by his deputy, and died a shocking death. At this period, Osbald, who was formerly an exile and a patrician, and king for a time, but afterwards an abbat, departed this life, and was buried in the church at York. Earl Aldred, the murderer of king Ethelred, was slain by earl Thormund, in revenge for his master the said king.

In the year 800, Heardred, bishop of Hagustald,[62] died in the third year of his episcopate, and was succeeded by Eanbrith. At the same period also, on the ninth day before the calends of January, the day before the Nativity of our Lord, a mighty wind blowing either from the south or the west, by its indescribable force destroyed very many cities, houses, and towns in various places, and levelled them with the ground; innumerable trees were also torn up from the roots, and thrown to the ground. In the same year an inundation took place, the sea flowing beyond its ordinary limits. An extensive murrain also prevailed among the cattle in various places.

In the year 801, Edwin, also called Eda, who had formerly been a duke of Northumbria, but was at that time, by the grace of the Saviour of the world, an abbat, being firmly rooted in the service of God, breathed his last, in the presence of his brethren, on the eighteenth day before the calends of February. At this time, Eardulph, king of Northumbria, led an army against Kenwulph, king of Mercia, because he had entertained his enemies; the latter also collected an army, and obtained very considerable aid from other kingdoms. A long war having been waged between them, at length, by the advice of the bishops and chief men among the English on both sides, and through the intervention of the king of the Angles,[63] they agreed to a truce; and a most solemn treaty of peace was concluded between them, which, by oath upon the gospel of Christ, both kings ratified, taking God for their witness, and giving sureties, that all their days, so long as they should live and be invested with the insignia of royalty, there should remain between them lasting peace and true friendship, unshaken and inviolate.

In the same year Hathubert, bishop of London, departed this life, and shortly after a great part of the city itself was de-

[61] This passage is probably corrupt.   [62] Hexham.
[63] Probably this alludes to the king of East Anglia.

stroyed by a sudden conflagration.   In this year Charles, the
most mighty king of the Franks, was declared supreme emperor
at Rome, by all the senate, the imperial crown being placed
upon his head by our lord the pope.

In the year from the incarnation of our Lord 802, Brithric,
the king of the West-Saxons, who had most gloriously reigned
over that nation for seventeen years, departed this life, and
was succeeded by Egbert.   The said king Brithric had taken
in marriage Eadburga, daughter of Offa, king of the Mercians,
who ordered the great dyke to be made between Britain[64] and
Mercia, that is to say, from sea to sea.   Now this Eadburga,
being the daughter of a king and surrounded with much pomp,
was inspired with wonderful ambition, and, after the manner
of her father, began to live in a tyrannical manner and to
despise all men, insomuch that she was hated not only by nobles
and magistrates, but even by all the people.   She did not cease
uttering accusations continually against all the religious before
the king, and by her evil speaking so wrought upon her husband
by means of her blandishments, that those whom she accused,
she caused to be put to death or banished the realm; and if
she was unable to effect this, she did not hesitate secretly to
take them off by poison.

There was at that time a certain illustrious youth, very
dear to the above-named king, and greatly beloved by him,
whom, when she wished to accuse him to the king, and could
not accomplish it, with wicked intent she cut off by poison,
the king in ignorance having tasted which, he expired.   But she
had not purposed to give the poison to the king, but to the
youth, whereas the head of all the nobles partaking of it first,
they both drank of the deadly draught, and both perished
through the extremely bitter taste thereof.   He being slain by
reason of this wicked deed, this most wicked poisoner was
smitten with fear, and crossing the seas in her flight with innumerable treasures, repaired to Charles, the most famous king
of the Franks.

As she stood before him in his chamber, and offered the
king precious gifts, he thus addressed her; " Choose, Eadburga,
which of the two you would prefer, myself or my son, who is
standing with me in the room;" on which she, without any deliberation, foolishly made answer and said; " If the option were

[64] Meaning Wales.

c 2

given me, I would sooner choose your son than yourself, because he seems to be the younger;" on which king Charles is
said to have replied:—"If you had chosen me, you should
have had my son, but inasmuch as you have chosen him, you
shall have neither me nor him for your own." However, on
account of her wickedness, the king conferred on her a most
excellent monastery, in which, laying aside her secular dress,
and hypocritically assuming the garb of the nuns, she spent a
very few years. For as this execrable woman lived wickedly
in her own country, so much more the miserably and wickedly
was she discovered to have been living in a foreign land. For, a
short space of time having elapsed, while by some she was
supposed to be performing her appropriate duties, she was debauched by a certain low fellow of her own nation. "Let
cloudy error give way before justice; let it cease, in fact, to
seem a wondrous thing, that a woman should be taken in
adultery." There is nothing for one to wonder at; "Nothing
is there concealed which shall not be known."

After this, by order of the emperor Charles the Great, she was,
with great weariness and anguish of mind, expelled from her
holy monastery, and, exposed to the reproaches of all, passed
the rest of her life in poverty and misery; attended to the last
by one poor servant, and begging daily at houses and castles
and in cities, she died miserably at Pavia.[65]

Brithric, the glorious king of the West-Saxons, being dead,
king Egbert succeeded him in the rule and sway, and, springing from the royal stock, placed the diadem of the whole kingdom on his head, being encircled with a most ample crown.
For he was a most active man, and, distinguished for his
power, he subjected many realms to his dominion. He reigned
thirty-six years and seven months.

To Egbert succeeded his most mighty son Ethelwulph,
who by his noble wife had four sons, whose names were Ethelbald, Ethelbert, Ethelred, and Alfred, all of whom in turn
succeeded to the kingdom.

Cuthred, therefore,[66] the above mentioned king of Wessex,
after having conquered the most valiant earl Edelhun,[67] as I
have already[68] mentioned elsewhere, when, in the thirteenth

---

[65] Asser says that he had conversed with persons who had seen her
begging there.   [66] He now reverts for a period of about fifty years.
[67] Or Adhelm.
[68] This is an error, as he has not mentioned the victory over Edelhun.

year of his reign, he was no longer able to endure the exactions
and insolence of Ethelbald, king of Mercia, met him, with his
troops ranged under their banners, at Bereford,[69] having post-
poned all hopes of surviving to liberty. He also brought with
him Edelhun, the above-named warlike earl, who was then
reconciled to him, and relying on whose valour and counsel
he was enabled to incur the hazards of war. On the other
hand, Ethelbald, the king of kings, together with the Mercians,
had brought the men of Kent, and the West Saxons, and
numerous forces of the Angles. The armies, therefore, being
drawn up in battle array, marching straight onward, were drawing close to each other, when Edelhun going before, and bearing
the standard[70] of the king of Wessex, which was a golden
dragon, pierced the enemy's standard-bearer. On this, an
outcry arising, the party of Cuthred was greatly encouraged,
and immediately thereupon the hostile ranks closed, and
rushed on to mutual slaughter, with dreadful blows and a
terrific crash.

In this battle, with all their pride, the Mercians were so
humbled, that for a long series of succeeding years fortune rendered them subject to Wessex. Any one, who had just before seen
the ranks shining with coats of mail, bristling with helmets,
rough with lances, variegated with standards, and resplendent
with gold, might shortly afterwards have seen them steeped in
blood, with lances broken, scattered in ruin, bespattered with
human brains, and frightful to look upon. With determined obstinacy, and displaying the greatest bravery, they rallied beneath
their standards, and waged the combat with swords and battle-
axes, and with direful intent line rushed on against line, each
side having an assured hope of victory. There was no thinking
of flight; the Mercians were urged on by the swelling pride of
their proud dominion, the men of Wessex were inflamed by the
dread of slavery. But in every direction Edelhun, the above-
named earl, penetrated the ranks, and a road lay open, strewed
with ruin, while in the dreadful carnage his battle-axe was
hewing through both bodies and armour.

Ethelbald, the most valiant king of the Mercians, rushed on
in every direction, and slaughtered the enemy, while to his

[69] Burford.   [70] Roger of Wendover makes a mistake in representing
Edelhun (whom he calls Athelun) as the standard bearer of Ethelbald,
the king of the Mercians.

most unconquerable sword arms were only like garments, bones like flesh. When, therefore, (just like two fires set in different places, which consume every thing that intervenes) it came to pass that the king and the earl met face to face, each terribly and franticly gnashed his teeth at the other and shook his right hand and put himself on his guard, and with mighty blows they both provoked the attack. But the God who opposes the haughty, depressed the wonted confidence of mind of the haughty king. When, therefore, he could neither recover his spirit nor his strength, while his own men were still engaged, in a fit of terror he took to flight, and from that day to the time of his death, God granted him no prosperity whatever. For, four years after this, again engaging[71] at Secandune,[72] after a dreadful slaughter of his army, disdaining flight, he was slain, and was buried at Repandun;[73] and thus this most mighty king, after he had reigned forty-one years, paid the penalty for his immoderate pride.

From this period, the kingdom of Wessex, being greatly strengthened, did not cease to increase till it had reached perfection. In the fourteenth year of his reign, Cuthred fought against the Britons,[74] who, vainly opposing him who had conquered king Ethelbald, speedily took to flight, and deservedly suffered a very great slaughter, without any loss to the enemy. In the following year, Cuthred, the high and mighty king, illustrious for so many successes and victories, departed this life.

Sigebert, a relation of the above-named king, succeeded him, but held the sovereignty for a short time only; for growing haughty and insolent, by reason of the exploits of his predecessor, he became intolerable even to his own domestics, as he ill-treated them in all manner of ways, and either perverted the common laws of the kingdom to his own advantage, or disregarded them for his own profit; on which, Cumbra, his earl, a most noble man, at the entreaty of the whole people, acquainted the cruel king with their complaints; but when he exhorted him to act with more moderation, and to treat the people with kindness, and laying aside his wonted inhumanity, to show himself amiable to God and man, the king immediately ordered him to be killed by an unrighteous death, and becoming more cruel and more intolerable to his people, proved himself a still

[71] With Cuthred.   [72] Seckington ; Lambarde, however, conjectures Saxwold, in Lincolnshire.   [73] Repton, in Derbyshire.   [74] The Welsh.

greater tyrant. In the second year of his reign, having persisted in his intolerable pride and wickedness, the nobles and
the people of the whole kingdom met together, and upon mature
deliberation, by the universal consent of all, king Sigebert was
expelled from the kingdom.

On this, Kinewulph, a virtuous young man of royal descent,
was elected king. The impious Sigebert on being banished
by his people, fearing the death that was the due of his
wickedness, took to flight, and concealed himself in a great
wood which is called Andredeswald,[75] where a certain swineherd
of earl Cumbra, who, as I have mentioned, had been iniquitously
slain, found the king in his concealment, and recognized him
when thus found, and becoming the avenger of his master, slew
him when thus recognized. Behold the manifest judgments of
God! behold how, not only in a future world, but even in this,
he worthily recompenses our deserts. For choosing bad kings
for the merited chastisement of their subjects, one He permits
to rage for long, in order that both a wicked people may long be
harassed, and he, a still more wicked king, may suffer the greater
torments in eternity; as, for instance, Ethelbald, the above-
named king of Mercia. But another one He cuts short with
a speedy end, lest his people, weighed down with excessive
tyranny, may not be able to take breath, and by reason of the
immoderate wickedness of the ruler, may deservedly incur the
speedy retribution of the eternal vengeance; as, for instance,
this Sigebert of whom we are speaking, who in as great a degree
as he proved himself wicked, was as disgracefully slain by a
swineherd, and passed from one calamity to another. For
which reason, to the eternal justice be praise and glory, now
and for ever!

In the first year of king Kinewulph, Beornred succeeded
Ethelbald, king of Mercia, in the kingdom, but only for a short
time. For in the same year Offa expelled him, and reigned
over Mercia thirty-nine years. Offa, a most noble youth, was the
son of Winfred, the son of Kanwulph, the son of Osmod, the son
of Epa, the son of Wippa, the son of Creada, the son of Kine-
wald, the son of Cinbba, the son of Hycis, the son of Comer,

[75] This wood is considered by Lambarde to have been in Kent, and the
part which is now called the Weald of Kent. The place, however, at
which Sigebert was slain is mentioned as Privet's-flood, and is supposed to
be the same as Privett, in Hampshire.

the son of Ageltheu, the son of Offa, the son of Wermund, the son of Widaet, the son of Woden.[76]

Offa was a most warlike king ; for he conquered the people of Kent in battle, and vanquished in war the people of Wessex and the Northumbrians. He also shewed himself a pious man, for he transferred the bones of Saint Alban to a monastery which he had built and greatly enriched, and gave to the pope of Rome, the vicar of St. Peter, a fixed tribute for ever, from each town in his kingdom.[77]

In the third year of king Kinewulph, Eadbert, king of the Northumbrians, seeing the unfortunate lives and unhappy ends of the above-named kings, (namely, Ethelbald and Sigebert,) and at the same time the praiseworthy life and glorious end of his predecessor Ceolwulph, chose that better part which could not be taken away from him. For having resigned his kingdom, he assumed the tonsure of his head, destined to produce for him an everlasting crown, and put on the dark-coloured clothes that were to confer on him an ethereal splendour. He was the eighth of those kings who of their own accord gave up their kingdoms for Christ, or rather, to speak more truth-fully, exchanged them for an eternal kingdom ; which eight are in the everlasting enjoyment of the multiplied delights of unspeakable blessings, and their blessed example is worthy of imitation.

He was succeeded in the kingdom by his son Osulf; who after he had reigned one year, was infamously betrayed by his own household, and slain.

After him, Mollethelwald[78] reigned nine years. About this time archbishop Cuthbert[79] died.

In the sixth year of the reign of king Kinewulph, Ethelbert, king of Kent, departed this life. In the same year, Ceolwulph, who, having resigned his earthly kingdom, had become a monk, departed unto a heavenly one. In the following year,

[76] Roger of Wendover differs considerably in the names, and gives two more ancestors to Offa before Woden. His words are, " the son of Ware-mund, who was the son of Withleg, who was the son of Wagon, who was the son of Frethegeath, who was the son of Woden."

[77] This is the Rome-scot, or St. Peter's pence, which consisted of a penny from each house, payable on the festival of Saint Peter. According to some accounts, it was Ina who made the first grant of it to the Papal see.

[78] This is the same king whom he has already mentioned under the year 759, by the name of Ethelwald, surnamed Moll.

[79] Of Canterbury.

Lambert was made archbishop of Canterbury. After having reigned six years, Mollethelwald resigned[80] the kingdom of Northumbria; after him Aelred reigned eight years, in the second year of whose reign, Egbert, archbishop of York, departed this life, after having enjoyed the archbishopric for a period of thirty-six years: Frithebert, bishop of Hagustald,[81] also died, after having been bishop thirty-four years.

Archbishop Egbert was succeeded by Adelbert,[82] and Alcmund succeeded bishop Fridebert.

In the fourth year of king Aelred, died Pepin, king of the Franks, Stephen, pope of Rome, and Eadbert,[83] the son of Hecta, a most famous duke of [East] Anglia.

In the year of grace 769, in the fifteenth year of king Kinewulph, a wondrous mutation first began to take place.[84] For the Roman empire, which had for so many years continued to enjoy pre-eminence, became subject to Charles the Great, king of the Franks. This took place after thirty years of his reign, which first commenced in this year,[85] and from that time forward, down to the present day, it has belonged to his successors.

In the twentieth year of king Kinewulph, king Offa and the Mercians fought against the people of Kent at Ottanforde,[86] and after a dreadful slaughter on both sides, the illustrious Offa was crowned with success. In the same year, the Northumbrians expelled their king Aelred from Eworwic,[87] in Easter week, and chose for their king, Ethelred, the son of Mollethelwald, who reigned four years. In this year were seen dreadful signs in the heavens after sunset, of a red color;[88] and, to the great astonishment of people, serpents were seen in Sussex.

In the second year after this, the Ancient Saxons, from whom

[80] He says previously, under the year 765, that this king lost his kingdom at Wincanhele.

[81] Hexham.   [82] Before called by him, Albert.

[83] The Anglo-Saxon Chronicle calls him a king, but it does not appear of what place.

[84] This is a paraphrase for the words in the text, "Incepit fieri mutatio dexteræ excelsi;" which literally translated, would make perfect nonsense. The text is evidently corrupt.

[85] This is wrong; he has previously said that his reign began in the year 771.

[86] Otford, in Kent.   [87] York.

[88] Ethelwerd, in his Chronicle, says, that it was the sign of the Lord's cross.

the English nation is descended, were converted to the faith, and in the same year, Withwin,[89] bishop of Whitherne, departed this life, in the twenty-fourth year[90] of his episcopate.

In the twenty-fourth year of his reign, Kinewulph fought against Offa, near Benetune;[91] being humbled by the fortune of war, he retreated,[92] and Offa reduced that fortified place to subjection. In the same year, Ethelbert was consecrated at Eworwic,[93] bishop of Whitherne.

In the following year, Ethelbald and Herebert, earls of the king of Northumbria, rebelled against their master, and slew Aldulph, the son of Bose, general of the king's army, in a pitched battle at Kingesdiwe;[94] and afterwards in a great battle, the same generals slew Kinewulph and Egga, the king's earls, at Hilatirn. Upon this, the above-named king Ethelred, having lost his generals and his hopes, fled from before them, and they elected Alfimod[95] king, who reigned for a period of ten years. In the following year, the nobles and high-reeves of Northumbria burned a certain earl and justiciary of theirs,[97] who had shown himself more severe than was befitting. In the same year, archbishop Esbert[99] died at Cestre,[1] and was succeeded by Enbalo. In this year, Kinebald was made bishop of Lindisfarne. In the same year also, a battle took place between the Franks and Ancient Saxons, the Franks being the conquerors.

In the next year, Alfinild, king of Northumbria, sent to Rome for the pall, and gave it to archbishop Embald.[2] At the same period, Gilbert succeeded Alcmund, bishop of Ha-

[89] Under the year 777, he previously calls him Pechtwiu.

[90] This is probably incorrect; he held the bishopric but fourteen years, according to the Saxon Chronicle.

[91] Benson, or Benington, in Oxfordshire.

[92] "The various reading, "loco secessit,"seems far preferable to that in the text, "jocose cessit;" "he jokingly," or "good humouredly yielded."

[93] York.

[94] The various reading is Kingsclive. Roger of Wendover calls this place Cuneaclive, and the Anglo-Saxon Chronicle Kings-cliff.

[95] Under the year 779, he is previously called Elfwald. A various reading makes the name "Alfimold." Below he is called Alfinild.

[97] The fate of the patrician Bearn is previously related under the year 780.

[99] Of York. He is previously called Albert. The Saxon Chronicle says that he died at York.   [1] Probably Chester-le-street, in Durham.

[2] Also called Eanbald and Enbalo.

gustald,[3] who had lately died. About this time, there was a synod held at Ade.[4] After Kinewulph had reigned twenty-six years, and, being victorious, had gained many battles against the Britons,[5] and subdued them on every side,[6] at length, he determined on banishing a certain young man, named Kineard, the brother of Sigebert. Upon this, he attacked the king at Meretune,[7] whither he had privately gone to visit a certain female. On finding this to be the case, the king stoutly defended himself at the door, until he caught sight of the youth, upon which he rushed out and wounded him, whereon all his confederates turned upon the king, and slew him On the uproar being heard, the king's soldiers, who were in the town, ran towards the youth, and refusing gifts of lands and money that were offered by him, all died bravely fighting, with the exception of one Briton, who was severely wounded, and taken as a hostage. In the morning, the soldiers of the king, who were near at hand in waiting,[8] when the king was slain, hemmed in the young man and his confederates; on which he thus said to them; " Your kinsmen are on my side; I will give you lands and money to your hearts' content, if you will not fight against us ; I made the same offer to your companions, and refusing it they perished !" To this they made answer, that no money was dearer to them than their lord, and that they would avenge the death of their king and their com-rades ; and then rushing on, after a severe combat at the door, they slew the young man and eighty-four others who were with him. The only one left was a little son of the young man, and he received a wound. Kinewulph was buried at Winchester, in the thirty-first year of his reign, the young man at Acsminster.[9]

Brithric, who also sprang from king Cerdic so often mentioned,

---

[3] Hexham.

[4] Evidently a mistake for Acle, or Aclea, or Ockley, in Surrey ; which is mentioned in the Anglo-Saxon Chronicle as the place where the synod was held in 782.   [5] The Welsh.

[6] The various reading, " Ex omnia parte," has been adopted, as it seems preferable to the words of the text, " Ex Dei parte."

[7] Merton, in Surrey.   [8] " In atrio," literally, " in the court."

[9] Axminster, in Devon. William of Malmesbury, and Roger of Wendover, however, agree in stating, that he was buried at Repandun, or Repton, in Derbyshire. Kinewulph, in reality, reigned only nine and twenty years.

succeeded Kinewulph, and reigned over Wessex sixteen years. In his second year, pope Adrian sent legates into Britain, to renew the faith which Augustine had preached. Being honorably received by the kings and the people, they raised a fair edifice upon a firm foundation, the mercy of Christ co-operating with them. They held a council at Cealtide,[10] where Iambert[11] resigned a portion of his episcopate; there also Higbert was elected[12] by king Offa. In the same year, Egfrid was consecrated king of the province of Kent.[13]

In the following year, being the year of grace 786, there appeared a sign[14] upon people's clothes, which may be justly deemed marvellous to be mentioned and to be heard of. Whether this took place as a forewarning of the movement relative to the recovery of Jerusalem, and the assumption of the cross,[15] which happened three hundred and eleven years after this period, in the time of William[16] the younger, or whether it was rather intended for the correction of the people, lest they should not view the plague of the Danes with which they were shortly afterwards afflicted, in the light of a chastisement, I will not rashly undertake to settle, but, the mysteries of God I leave to God.[17]

In the fourth year of his reign, Brithric took to wife Eadburga, the daughter of Offa, king of Mercia. Strengthened on the throne by this alliance, he gave way to pride. In these days, the Danes came to Britain, with three ships, for the sake of plunder; the king's reeve in that province, seeing this, went to meet them without taking due precautions, in order that, having captured them, he might carry them to the king's town;[19] for he was ignorant who they were, or for what purpose they had come; but, being immediately surrounded by them, he was slain. He was the first person of the English nation slain by

---

[10] Lambarde makes this place to be Chalkhythe, but does not say in what county.   [11] Archbishop of Canterbury.

[12] To be Archbishop of Lichfield, the portion of his province which the Archbishop of Canterbury had resigned.

[13] Which he held jointly with his father Offa.   [14] The sign of the cross.

[15] By the Crusaders as their emblem.   [16] William Rufus.

[17] The note of interrogation in the text after "relinquimus" seems misplaced.

[18] "Præpositus regis;" the king's bailiff or reve, or steward of the shire; holding the office of the present sheriff.

[19] "Castrum;" literally, "fortified town."

the Danes, and after him many thousands of thousands were slaughtered by them at different periods; these too were the first ships of the Danes that arrived here.

In the following year, a synod was held in Northumbria, at Wincanhele.[20]

In the sixth year of king Brithric, a synod was held at Aclea.[21] By infamous treachery, Sigga slew Alwulph, the good king of Northumbria. In the same spot where this king, the beloved of God, was slain, a heavenly light was often beheld; his body was buried in the church of Hagustald. After him, Osred began to reign, but in the following year was betrayed, and expelled from the kingdom.

Ethelred, the son of Mollethelwald, was then restored to the kingdom; and in the fourth year of his reign, having collected forces for the purpose, Osred was on his return, in order that he might expel Ethelred from the kingdom, by whom he himself had been expelled. On his route he was captured and put to death, and buried at Tynemouth. How just then his remark, who said, " Oh, how blind to the future is the mind of man !" For when the above-mentioned youth Osred, dancing and elated with joy, was made king, how little did he think that in the second year from that time, he should be deprived of his throne, and in the fourth, of his life ! For which reason, let us ever be thoughtful in prosperity, being ignorant how near at hand adversity may be.

At this time, Offa, king of the Mercians, ordered the head of Saint Ethelbert[21*] to be cut off, and in these days, Lambert, archbishop of Canterbury, departed- this life, and abbat Ethelred was elected in his room archbishop of Canterbury. Eanbald, archbishop of York, consecrated Badulph,[22] bishop of Whitherne.

In the tenth year of king Brithric, there were seen fiery dragons flying through the air, which tokens were followed by two plagues; first, a dreadful famine, and then the pagan nations coming from Norway and Denmark. These first ravaged the kingdom of Northumbria in a frightful manner, and then, in the district of Lindisfarne, on the ides of January, dreadfully destroyed the churches of Christ, together with the inhabitants; at which period also, died Sigga, the perfidious duke who had acted the traitor towards the righteous king Elfwald.

[20] Finchale.   [21] Ockley, in Surrey.   [21*] King of East Anglia.
[22] A mistake for Eadulph. He was the last bishop of Whitherne.

In the eleventh year of king Brithric, that is to say, in the year of grace 795, the Northumbrians slew their king, Ethelred, who, in the same year in which king Osred was slain, becoming elated with pride, had forsaken his own wife and taken a new one, little thinking that he himself was destined to be slain within two years from that time. After him Herdulph obtained the kingdom of Northumbria, and was consecrated king by archbishop Embald,[23] bishop Ethelbert and bishop Hingbald, and bishop Baldulph, and ascended the throne at York.

In these days pope Adrian and the great king Offa, departed this life; this Offa reigned with mighty sway in Mercia, during a period of thirty-nine years. He subdued Kenulph, king of Wessex, and the people of Kent and Northumbria.

King Offa was succeeded by his son Egfrith, who reigned one hundred and forty-one days, and then died; he was succeeded by Kenulph, the father of Kenelm, a most powerful king.[24] In the same year, Eadbert, who also bore the name of Pren, obtained the kingdom of Kent. The pagan nations laid waste Northumbria, and sacked the monastery of Egfrid at Tynemouth; they were there met by the most noble of the English, men extremely well inured to war, and, their chieftains being slain, the barbarians were overcome, and betook themselves to their ships. When they had reached the sea, they continued their flight with their ships, on which some of them were wrecked by a tempest, and many of them drowned; but some of them coming ashore were taken, and were beheaded near the sea-shore.

Not long after this, Kenwulph, king of Mercia, laid waste the province of Kent, and captured Pren, who was not a match for him in might, and had consequently concealed himself in hiding-places and out-of-the-way spots, and carried him back with him in chains.

In the fourteenth year of king Brithric, the Romans cut out the tongue of pope Leo, and put out his eyes, and expelled him from his see; but he, as written documents inform us, through the grace of Christ, was enabled again to see and to

[23] Eanbald.
[24] The word "maris" seems out of place here, as no definite meaning can be attached to it, unless it is meant to say that Kenelm was a man, which seems quite superfluous.

speak, and once more became pope. Three years after this, king Charles was made emperor, and having been consecrated by the same pope Leo, condemned those to death who had ill-treated the pope, but afterwards, by reason of the pope's entreaties, he saved their lives, and sent them into exile.

Three years after this, Brithric, king of Wessex, also departed this life, after he had most gloriously reigned over that nation seventeen years, having in ignorance taken some poison, which his wife Eadburga, the daughter of king Offa, had prepared for a certain young man; in consequence of which, they both died, as I have mentioned more at large above. At this time a great battle was fought in Northumbria, at Wellehare,[25] in which perished Alric, the son of Herbert, and many others with him. The extreme perplexity that would result, necessarily prevents me from entering into a full description of the circumstances, fluctuations, and results of the wars; for the nation of the English was naturally hardy and proud, and in consequence incessantly engaged in intestine warfare.

Egbert[25*] therefore, in the year of grace 800, or, according to some, 802, being the eighth in order of ten most valiant kings, whom I have elsewhere remarked, as pre-eminently distinguished for their singular merits, on the death of Brithric succeeded to the throne, and reigned thirty-seven years and seven months over the kingdom of Wessex. At a youthful age, his predecessor Brithric, and Offa, king of Mercia, had banished him from this country. He was in exile three years at the court of the king of France, but behaved himself nobly and discreetly. On the death of the above-named king, he returned and gained the kingdom. On the same day, earl Ethelmund returned from Wicum,[26] and, coming to Kinemeresforde,[27] met earl Wistan with the men of Wiltshire, and there they fought, and both earls being slain, the Wiltshire men gained the victory.

[25] This is probably an error for Wellham, or Wylam, in Northumberland. Lambarde says, "In the beginning of the reign of King Egbert, one of the great monarchs of this realm, there was a great battle fought at a place in the north country, called then Welham, which I take to be now called Wyllom in Coupland."

[25*] He now resumes the narrative where broken off in p. 20.

[26] The country of the Wiccii, who inhabited Worcestershire and Gloucestershire.

[27] Kempsford. Lambarde suggests that this may be Comberford, near Calne.

In the fourth year after this, died Ethelred, archbishop of Canterbury, and was succeeded by Wilfred, and two years after, Cuthred, king of Kent, departed this life.

In the following year, Hardulph, king of Northumbria, was expelled from his kingdom.

In the fourteenth year of his reign, Egbert overran the territories of the Britons[28] from east to west, and there was no one who could even attempt to make resistance to his prowess.

In the year after this, Charles, king of the Franks and emperor of the Romans, departed this life; and in the following year, Saint Leo, the pope, having died, Stephen succeeded him, who in his turn was succeeded by Paschal.

Shortly after this, Kenwulph, king of Mercia, departed this life, and was succeeded by Ceolwulph; but in the third year after this, he lost his kingdom, and Beornwulph gained possession of it.

In the fourteenth[29] year of his reign, Egbert fought a battle with Beornwulph, king of Mercia, at Ellendune,[30] by reason of which, an old saying mentions that, "The river Ellendune was red with gore, choked up with carnage, and stinking with putrefaction." . After a very great slaughter there of both nations, Egbert was the melancholy conqueror. After this, pursuing his successes, he sent his son Ethelwulph, who afterwards became king, and bishop Alcstan,[31] and earl Wulhard, with a great army, into Kent; on which they drove Balred, the king, beyond the Thames. King Egbert then received the people of Surrey, and Kent, and Sussex under his subjection, of whom his kinsman, Pren, had formerly been unjustly deprived. In this year also, the king of East Anglia, together with his people, acknowledged king Egbert as his protector; and after this, in the same year, the East Angles slew Bernulph, king of the Mercians, who was succeeded by Ludecen.

In the same year there was a very great battle between the Britons[32] and the people of Devonshire, at Gavelford,[33] where many thousands of men were slain on both sides.

In the following year, Ludecen, king of Mercia, and five earls, were slain.

<hr/>

[28] The people of North Wales.   [29] This should be " twenty-fourth."
[30] Supposed to have been near Winchester, though Highworth, in Wiltshire, and Hillingdon, in Middlesex, have been suggested.
[31] Of Sherborne.   [32] The Welsh.   [33] Camelford, in Cornwall.

In the twenty-seventh year of his reign, Egbert expelled Wilaf, king of Mercia, who had succeeded king Ludecen, and possessed himself of the kingdom. As he had now gained possession of all the kingdom on the south side of the Humber, he led an army to Dore[34] against the Northumbrians; on which, submissively offering concord and obedience to the great king, they were peacefully reduced to subjection.

In the following year, king Egbert led an army into North Wales, and subjected it by force of arms.

In the succeeding year, Wilfred, archbishop of Canterbury, died, and was succeeded by Ceolnoth.

In the thirty-eighth[35] year of king Egbert, an army of Danes returned to England; and shortly after, they were vanquished at Danemute,[36] and put to flight. Shortly after this, they ravaged Sepey,[37] on which king Egbert with his forces fought against them, they having come thither with thirty-five very large vessels. In the following year he fought against them at Carra,[38] and there the Danes gained the victory, and two bishops, Herefred[39] and Wilfred,[40] with two dukes, Dudda and Osmod, were slain.

In the following year, a naval force of the Danes came into West Wales, on which the Welsh united with the Danes and made an attack upon king Egbert. The king, however, enjoying success, gloriously repulsed them, and, valiant as they were, bravely routed them at Hengistendune.[41]

In the year after this, Egbert, the great king and monarch of Britain, departed this life, after having made his sons heirs to the kingdoms of which he was in possession, appointing Ethelwulph king of Wessex, and Ethelstan king of Kent, Sussex, and Essex. But as we have now come to the mo-

[34] Lambarde suggests, that it may possibly be Darton, or Darfield, in Yorkshire.   [35] This should be "thirty-fifth."
[36] A various reading gives Donemuth. Lambarde thinks that this place stood at the confluence of the rivers Don and Trent, not far from the town of Kingston-upon-Hull.
[37] The isle of Sheppey, at the mouth of the Thames.   [38] Charmouth.
[39] He appears to have been bishop of Winchester.
[40] He was bishop of either Sherburne or Selsey.
[41] Lambarde says, "I take this to be the same place that is at this day called Henkston Doune, in Cornwall; for the fall is easy from Hengistdune to Hengstdune, and so to Hengston; and it is most apparent that it was either in Cornwall, or not far off."

narchies of England, and to the frightful plague which afflicted us in the descents of the Danes, the book may be made appropriately devoted to a new subject.

At the beginning[41] of my history, I have mentioned that Britain was afflicted with five plagues; the fourth of which, namely, that caused by the Danes, I shall treat of in the present book, and the more so, as this was far more dreadful and caused far more bloodshed than the others. For the Romans kept Britain under their subjection during only a short period, and ruled it gloriously by the laws of the conquerors. Again, the Picts and the Scots made frequent irruptions into Britain on the northern side, but, still, they did not attack it in every quarter, and on being sometimes repulsed with loss, they not unfrequently paused in their invasions. Again, the Saxons, using all their endeavours, gradually gained the land by warfare: when gained, they kept possession of it; when in their possession, they built upon it; when built upon, they ruled it with their laws. The Normans also, who speedily and in a very short time subdued this country, granted to the conquered their lives, their liberty, and the ancient laws of the realm, upon which matters I shall enlarge at the proper time.

On the other hand, the Danes continually and perseveringly harassed the land, and in their incursions shewed a desire not to keep possession of it, but rather to lay it waste, and to destroy everything, not to obtain rule. If at any time they were overcome, no benefit resulted therefrom, for on a sudden a fleet and a still greater army would make its appearance in another quarter; and it was a matter for astonishment how, when the kings of the English would march to fight with them on the eastern side, before they approached the troops of the enemy, a messenger would come in haste and say, "O king, whither are you going? An innumerable fleet of the pagans on the southern side has taken possession of the coasts of England, and, depopulating cities and towns, has ravaged every place with fire and sword;" on the same day another would come running and saying, "O king, whither are you flying? A terrible army has landed on the western side of England; if you do not quickly turn and make head against them, they will think that you have taken to flight, and will

[41] He has not previously made any such remark: this and some other passages would lead us to infer that some portion of the work is lost.

pursue you with flames and carnage." On the same day or the succeeding one, another messenger would come running and out of breath, and say, "Whither, ye nobles, are you going? The Danes, leaving their northern regions, have already burnt your houses, already carried off your property, tossed your children on the points of their spears, and committed violence on the wives of some, while those of others they have carried away with them."

Thus then, both king and people, being distracted by so many evil rumours and sinister reports, were relaxed both in hands and heart, and pined away with consternation of mind. Consequently, not even when they were victorious, did they experience any joy, as usually is the case, nor did they entertain any assured hopes of safety. The following is the reason why the justice of God raged so fiercely, and his wrath was so greatly inflamed against them.

In the primitive church of the English, religion shone forth with most brilliant lustre, inasmuch as kings and queens, nobles and princes, as well as bishops of churches, being inflamed with ardent desire for a heavenly kingdom, sought either the walls of the monastery or voluntary exile, as I have already shown. But in process of time all traces of virtue waxed so faint in them, that they would allow no nation to be their equal for treachery and wickedness, a thing which is especially notorious in the history of the kings of Northumberland; for just as their impiety has been described in my account of the actions of the kings, in the same way did men of every rank and station persist in a course of deceit and treachery, and nothing was esteemed disgraceful except piety, while innocence was considered most deserving of a violent death. In consequence, the Lord Almighty sent down upon them, like swarms of bees, most bloodthirsty nations, who spared neither age nor sex, such as the Danes and the Goths, the Norwegians and the Swedes, the Vandals and the Frisians; who, from the begining of the reign of king Ethelwulph down to the time of the arrival of the Normans and of king William, that is to say, for a period of three hundred and thirty years, dreadfully afflicted this country, and laid it waste with desolation far and wide. Sometimes also, in consequence of the nearness of Britain, as the avengers and scourges of God for the misdeeds of the people, they invaded the country of France; but, having made

D 2

these observations, it is time to return to the thread of my narrative.

In the first year of his reign, Ethelwulph made head against these enemies in one part of his kingdom; and, as multitudes of the pagans increased on every side, he sent earl Wulfred, with a part of his army, to attack some Danes, who, with thirty-three ships, had effected a landing at Hampton;[42] on there meeting with them, after an immense slaughter of the enemy, gained a glorious victory. King Ethelwulph also sent earl Ethelhelm, with the levies of Wessex, to attack another army at Port;[43] an engagement taking place, after an obstinate battle the earl was slain, and the Danes were victorious.

In the following year, earl Herbert fought against them at Merseware,[44] and the Danes being the conquerors, his own men were put to flight, and he was slain. In the same year, an army of the pagans marched through the eastern parts of England, namely, Lindesey, East Anglia, and Kent, and slew an innumerable multitude with the sword.

In the next year after this, coming further inland, the army of the Danes slew an immense number of people in the neighbourhood of Canterbury, Rochester, and London.

In the fifth year of his reign, Ethelwulph, with a part of his army, fought against the crews of thirty-five ships at Carre,[45] and the Danes were victorious. For, although the

---

[42] Southampton.   [43] The isle of Portland.

[44] Instead of naming the place, the Anglo-Saxon Chronicle says: "This year Herebert, the ealdorman, was slain by the heathen, and many with him, among the Marshmen." In Ethelwerd's Chronicle the place is called Merswarum, and Romney Marsh is supposed to be intended under that name. Lambarde has the following quaint note on this passage: "Henry Huntingdon, in the Fifth Book of his History, speaking of the conflicts had with the Danes under the reign of Ædelwulfe, reports, amongst other things, that Herebert, an earl, fought with them, at a place which he called Marseware, and was slain. Matthew Westminster repeateth the same, and instead of Marseware, setteth down 'apud Marsunarum.' So that both these, and so many others as have followed them, take the name Mersewar for a place, and not for a number of persons. In which, through ignorance of the Saxon tongue, they have foully erred; for the Saxon books say that Herebert was slain, ' and with him many of the Mercians, or men of Mercia.' So that the history describeth of what country they were that were slain, but not in what place the slaughter was committed."

[45] Charmouth.

number of the ships was but small, still the number of men on board of them was considerable.

In the fifth year after this, the venerable bishop Alstan and duke Ernulph with the men of Somerset, and duke Osred with the men of Dorset, fought against an army of Danes at Pendredesmuthe,[46] and by the aid of God, slew many of them, and obtained the glory of a triumph.

In the sixteenth year of his reign, Ethelwulph and his son Ethelbald, having collected all their forces, fought with a large army of the barbarians, who had come with two hundred and fifty[47] ships to Thames-mouth, and had destroyed those cities, famous and renowned for ages, London and Canterbury, and put to flight Bretwulph, king of the Mercians, together with his army; who never afterwards enjoyed success, and dying in the following year, was succeeded by Burrhed. After this, the Danes growing still bolder, all their forces were collected in Surrey, and they met the king's troops at Akelea.[48] In consequence, a battle was fought between these two great armies, so mighty and so severely contested, that no person had ever before heard of such a battle being fought in England. You might behold warriors sweeping onward on either side, just like a field of standing corn, rivers of blood flowing and rolling along in their streams the heads and limbs of the slain; but it would be an act of excessive and over-nice fastidiousness to attempt to describe individual exploits. In short, God granted the fortune of war to the faithful, and those who put their trust in him, but to his enemies and contemners defeat and indescribable confusion. King Ethelwulph therefore, being conqueror in this mighty battle, gained a glorious triumph.

In the same year, Ethelstan, king of Kent, and duke Ealred[49] fought a naval battle against the Danes at Sandwich, and having made a great slaughter of the enemy, captured nine of their ships, on which the rest took to flight. Earl Cheorl, also, with the men of Devonshire, fought against the pagans at Wienor,[50] and having killed a great number of them, was victorious. Consequently, this year was one of good fortune to the

[46] The mouth of the river Parret, in Somersetshire.
[47] Another reading is 315; but the other historians make the number 350.   [48] Ockley.
[49] The Anglo-Saxon Chronicle and Ethelwerd's Chronicle call him Elchere: he is also so called in p. 42.   [50] Wembury, near Plymouth.

English nation. This, however, was the first year in which the army of the pagans remained throughout the whole of the winter, which they did in the isle of Teneit.[51]

In the eighteenth year of his reign, Ethelwulph materially assisted Burrhed, king of the Mercians, in subjugating the people of North Wales, and gave him his daughter in marriage. He had four sons, who were all kings in succession, namely, Ethelbald, Ethelbert, Ethelred, and Alfred. This Alfred his father sent, when he was a child five years old, in the year above-mentioned, to Rome, to the court of pope Leo; the same pope afterwards pronounced his blessing on him as king, and treated him as his own son. This year, duke Ealhere, with the men of Kent, and Huda, with the men of Surrey, fought against an army of the heathens in Teneit, and a great multitude on either side was slain, or perished by shipwreck, and both the above-named dukes lost their lives.

Ethelwulph, the illustrious king of Essex, in the nineteenth year of his reign, set apart a tenth of all the lands in his realm, and bestowed it upon the church, for the love of God, and for his own salvation. Afterwards, he went to Rome in great state, and took with him his son Alfred, whom he loved more than the others. There he remained one year, and on his return thence, took the daughter of Charles the Bald, king of France, to wife, and brought her with him into this country; after having lived with her two years, he died, and was buried at Winchester. He had at first been bishop of that city, but on the death of his father, Egbert, being compelled by necessity, he was made king, and, having married a noble wife, became father of the four sons above-named. About this period, the pagans passed the whole winter at Sepey, that is to say, "the island of sheep."

The above-named king, on his decease, left to his son, Ethelbald, his hereditary kingdom of Wessex, and to Ethelbert, another son, the kingdom of Kent, with Sussex and Wessex. Both the brothers being young men of excellent natural disposition, held their kingdoms without the slightest molestation as long as they lived.

Ethelbald, the king of Wessex, after he had reigned peacefully for five years, was cut off by a premature death.

---

[51] Thanet. The Anglo-Saxon Chronicle mentions the isle of Sheppey here, and makes it some years later.

All England bewailed the youthful age of Ethelbald, and there was great mourning for him; he was buried at Sherburne, and England was afterwards sensible what a loss she had experienced in him.

Ethelbert, the brother of the above-mentioned king, reigned after him in Wessex, having been previously king of Kent. In his days a naval force came, and having attacked Winchester, destroyed it; thus "fell the ancient city that for many a year had borne the sway."

Ethelbert, dying ten years after, was succeeded by Ethelred, who, after reigning six years, was succeeded by king Alfred, whose reign lasted twenty-eight years. His genealogy, together with his actions and the events of his time, are described below.

THE KINGS OF WESSEX.

CERDIC reigned five years.

KENRIC, his son, reigned twenty-six years.

CHENLING, his son, reigned thirty-one years.

CHELRIC reigned six years.

CHELWULPH reigned fourteen years.

KINIGLIS, who was a Christian, reigned one year. He was baptized by Saint Birinus.

KENWALD, his son, reigned thirty-one years.

SEXBURGA, the queen, reigned one year.

ESCWIN reigned two years.

KENTWIN reigned nine years.

CEDWALLA reigned two years; and died at Rome, while wearing the white garments.[52]

INA reigned thirty-six years, and afterwards died at Rome.

ADELARD reigned thirteen years.

CHUTRED reigned sixteen years.

SIGEBERT, a cruel man, reigned one year, and was expelled.

KINEWULPH reigned twenty-six years, and was afterwards slain.

BRITHRIC reigned sixteen years. In his reign the Danes first came to England.

EGBERT reigned thirty-five years. He was monarch of all England.

ETHELWULPH reigned eighteen years.

[52] The white or initiatory garments of the novice, or intended monk.

ETHELBALD reigned five years.

ETHELBERT reigned six years.

ETHELRED, his brother, reigned five years.

ALFRED the Learned reigned twenty-nine years.

EDWARD reigned twenty-four years.

ATHELSTAN, his brother, reigned sixteen years.

EDMUND reigned six years and one day.

EDRED reigned nine years and one day.

EDWIN reigned three years and nine months.

EDGAR the Just reigned sixteen years.

EDWARD the Martyr reigned four years.

ETHELRED, his brother, reigned thirty-eight years.

EDMUND Ironside reigned nine months.

CANUTE, the Dane, reigned nineteen years.

HAROLD, his son, reigned five years.

HARDICANUTE reigned two years.

EDWARD the Just reigned twenty-four years.

HAROLD reigned nine months.

WILLIAM the Bastard reigned twenty-one years.

WILLIAM RUFUS reigned thirteen years.

HENRY, the Lion of Justice, reigned thirty-five years and three months.

In the year from the incarnation of our Lord 849, Alfred, king of the Anglo-Saxons, was born in the district called Berkshire;[53] the following is the order of his genealogical line. King Alfred was the son of king Ethelwulph, who was the son of Egbert, who was the son of Ealmund, who was the son of Eafeo, who was the son of Eoppa, who was the son of Ingild. Ingild, and Ina, the famous king of the West Saxons, were two brothers; this Ina went to Rome, and there ending this life, entered a heavenly country, there to reign with Christ. They were the sons of Coenred, who was the son of Ceolwald, who was the son of Cutha, who was the son of Cuthwin, who was the son of Ceaulin, who was the son of Cynric, who was the son of Creda, who was the son of Cerdic, who was the son of Elesa, who was the son of Elta, who was the son of Gewis, from whom the Britons call all people of that nation by the name of Gewis;[54] he was the son of Wig, who was the

---

[53] At Wantage.

[54] He probably alludes to the West Saxons, or people of Wessex, who were called Gewissæ.

son of Freawin, who was the son of Freoderegeat, who was the son of Brand, who was the son of Bealdeag, who was the son of Woden, who was the son of Friderwald, who was the son of Frealaf, who was the son of Friderwulph, who was the son of Fingoldulph, who was the son of Geta, (which Geta the pagans long worshipped as a god,) who was the son of Cetua, who was the son of Bean, who was the son of Sceldua, who was the son of Heremod, who was the son of Itermod, who was the son of Hathra, who was the son of Wala, who was the son of Beadwig, who was the son of Shem, who was the son of Noah, who was the son of Lamech, who was the son of Methusaleh, who was the son of Enoch, who was the son of Malaleel, who was the son of Canaan, who was the son of Enos, who was the son of Seth, who was the son of Adam.

The mother of Alfred was named Osburg, an extremely pious woman, noble by nature, noble too by birth; she was the daughter of Oslac, the famous butler of king Ethelwulph; who was a Goth by nation, inasmuch as he was descended from the Goths and Jutes, of the seed of Stuf and Withgar, two brothers and earls; who, having received possession of the isle of Wight from their uncle, king Cerdic, and his son Cinric, their cousin, slew the few British inhabitants they could find in that island, at a place called Withgaraburgh;[55] for the rest of the inhabitants of the island had been either slain or had escaped into exile.

In the year 851, Cheorl, earl of Devonshire, with the men of Devon, fought against the Danes and defeated them. In the same year a great army of the pagans came with three hundred and fifty ships to the mouth of the river Thames, and sacked Dorobernia, that is, the city of Canterbury, and put to flight Bretwulph, king of the Mercians, who had come to oppose them.

After this, the Danes growing more bold, all their army was collected in Surrey. On hearing this, Ethelwulph, the mighty warrior, with his son, Ethelbald, collected an army at the place which is called Akelea,[56] and, engaging with the pagans, he defeated them with unheard-of slaughter.

In the year 852, Berthwulph, king of the Mercians, departed this life, and was succeeded by Burrhed. In the same year,

[55] It is supposed that this may have been Carisbrook, in the isle of Wight.   [56] Ockley, in Surrey.

king Ethelstan and earl Elchere, conquered a great army of the
pagans at Sandwich, and after slaying nearly all of them, took
nine of their ships.

In the year 853, Burrhed, king of the Mercians, supported by
the assistance of king Ethelwulph, attacked the Mid-Britons,[57]
and having conquered them, reduced them to subjection.   In
the same year, king Ethelwulph sent his son Alfred, who was
then five years old, to Rome with a great escort of nobles ; on
which, Saint Leo, the pope, at the request of his father, ordained
and anointed him for king, and, receiving him as his own adopted
son, confirmed him, and sent him back with his blessing to his
father.

In the year 854, Wulfred, having received the pall, was
confirmed in the see of York, Osbert being king of Northumbria; Eardulph also received the bishopric of Lindisfarne.   At
this period, earl Alchere with the men of Kent, and duke
Wada, with the men of Surrey, fought a severe battle in the isle
of Tened[58] against the pagans, and after routing them at the
first onset, at length, after very many had fallen on either side,
both the noblemen were slain.   This year, Ethelwulph, king
of the West Saxons, gave his daughter in marriage to Burrhed,
king of the Mercians, at the royal town which is called Cyp-
panhame,[59] with a great profusion of all kinds of riches.

In the year 855, a great army of the pagans passed the whole
of the winter in the isle of Sceapeye,[60] that is to say, "the
island of sheep."   In the same year, king Ethelwulph released
the tenth part of the whole of his kingdom from all royal
service and tribute, and with an everlasting pen[61] at the cross
of Christ, offered it up to the One and Triune God, for the redemption of his soul and those of his predecessors.   He also
proceeded with great pomp to Rome, and taking with him
his son Alfred, whom he loved more than his other sons, and
whom he had before sent to Rome, now for the second time,
remained there a whole year, on the completion of which, he
returned to his own country, bringing with him Juthina,[62] the
daughter of Charles, king of the Franks.   After his return
from Rome he lived two years.

Among the other good works that he did, he ordered every

[57] The Welsh, on the borders of England.   [58] Thanet.
[59] Chippenham, in Wiltshire.   [60] Sheppey.
[61] Graphio. "Graphium," was properly the "stylus," or iron pen of the
ancient Romans.   [62] Her name was really Judith.

year to be taken to Rome three hundred mancuses of money; a hundred in honor of Saint Peter, for the purchase of oil, with which all the lamps of that church might be filled at the vigils of Easter, and likewise at cock-crow; a hundred also, in honor of Saint Paul, for the same purpose; and a hundred mancuses for the Catholic Pontiff, the successor of the Apostles.

He being dead, and buried at Winchester, his son Ethelbald, during two years and a half after the reign of his father, governed the West Saxons, and with disgraceful wickedness took to wife, Judith, the daughter of king Charles, whom his father had married. At the same period, the most holy Edmund, who sprang from the race of the ancient Saxons, ascended the throne of East Anglia.

In the year 860, king Ethelbald departed this life, and was buried at Sherburne, and his brother Ethelbert succeeding him, held Kent, Surrey,[63] and Sussex as his kingdom; in his days a great army of the pagans came up from the sea, and having hostilely attacked the city of Winchester, destroyed it. As they were returning towards the sea, laden with great booty, Osric, earl of Hampshire, with his men, and earl Ethelwulph, with the men of Berkshire, stoutly confronted them, and, an engagement taking place, the pagans fell on every side, the rest being dispersed in flight.

Ethelbert, also, having governed his kingdom peacefully, and with the love of all, for five years, died amid the great regrets of his people, and was buried at Sherburne, near his brother, in the year 863. In this year also, Saint Swithin, bishop of Winchester, departed unto the Lord.

In the year 864, the pagans wintered in the isle of Tened, and made a firm treaty with the men of Kent, who agreed to give them money for observing their compact. In the meantime, however, just like foxes, the pagans secretly sallied forth from their camp by night, and, breaking their covenant, in hopes of greater gain, ravaged all the eastern coast of Kent.

In the year 866, Ethelred, brother of king Ethelbert, undertook the government of the kingdom of the West Saxons. In the same year, a great fleet of the pagans came from Danubia to Britain, and wintered in East Anglia, where that force in a great measure provided itself with horses.

[63] The reading clearly ought to be " Suthrigiam," but the text has it " supremam."

In the year 867, the above-mentioned army of the pagans removed from East Anglia to the city of York, and laid waste the whole country as far as Tynemouth. At this period a sedition arising among the people of Northumbria, they expelled Osbert their lawful king from the kingdom, and raised a certain tyrant, Ella by name, who was not of royal birth, to the supreme power ; but, on the approach of the pagans, this discord was for the common good in some measure allayed, on which Osbert and Ella united their forces, and having collected an army, marched to York.   On their approach, the pagans at once took refuge in the city, and endeavoured to defend themselves within the walls.   The Christians, perceiving their flight and dismay, began to pursue them even within the walls of the city, and to destroy the ramparts; but when the ramparts were now levelled, and many of the Christians had entered the city together with the pagans, the latter, urged by despair and necessity, making a fierce onset upon them, slaughtered and cut them down, and routed them both within and without the city ; here the greater part of the Northumbrians fell, the two kings being among the slain ; on which, the remainder who escaped made peace with the Danes.   Over them the pagans appointed Egbert king, in subjection to themselves ; and he reigned over the Northumbrians beyond the Tyne six years.   This took place at York on the eleventh day before the calends of April, being the sixth day of the week, just before Palm Sunday.   In the same year Elfistan, bishop of Sherburne departed this life, and was buried at that place.

In the year 868, a comet was distinctly seen.   Alfred, the venerated brother of king Ethelred, asked and obtained in marriage a noble Mercian lady, daughter of Ethelred, earl of the Gaini,[64] who was surnamed " Mucil," which means " the great."   Her mother's name, who was of the royal family of Mercia, was Eadburga ; she was a venerable woman, and for very many years after the death of her husband, lived a life of extreme chastity, as a widow, even to the day of her death.

In the same year, the above-mentioned army of the pagans, leaving Northumbria, advanced to Nottingham, and wintered

[64] This is "Gamorum," in the text, but it ought to be " Gainorum, of the Gaini ;" who were the inhabitants of Gainsborough, in Yorkshire.

in that place ; on which Burrhed king of Mercia made a treaty with them.

In the year 869, the above-mentioned army of the Danes again advanced to Northumbria, and remained there one year, ravaging and laying waste, slaughtering and destroying a very great number of men and women.

In the year 870, many thousands of Danes collected together under the command of Inguar and Hubba, and coming to East Anglia, wintered at Teoford.[65] At this time king Edmund was ruler over all the realms of East Anglia, a man holy and just in all things, and in the same year, he, with his people, fought valiantly and manfully against the above-mentioned army, but inasmuch as God had predetermined to crown him with martyrdom, he there met with a glorious death. In the same year Ceolnoth, archbishop of Canterbury, departed this life, and was succeeded by Ethelred.

In the year 871, the above-mentioned army of the pagans entered the kingdom of the West Saxons, and came to Reading, on the southern banks of the Thames, which is situate in the district called Bearocscira.[66] There, on the third day after their arrival, two of their earls, with a great multitude, rode forth to plunder, while the others, in the meantime, were throwing up a rampart between the two rivers Thames and Kennet, on the right hand side of that royal town.[67] Ethelwulph earl of Berkshire with his men, encountered them at a place which in English is called Englefield,[68] that is to say, "the field of the Angles," where both sides fought bravely, until, one of the pagan earls being slain, and the greater part of their army destroyed, the rest took to flight, and the Christians gained the victory.

Four days after this, king Ethelred and his brother Alfred, having collected an army, came to Reading, killing and slaying even to the very gates of the castle as many of the pagans as they could find beyond. At length, the pagans sallying forth from all the gates, engaged them with all their might, and there both sides fought long and fiercely, till at last the Christians turned their backs, and the pagans gained the day; there too, the above-named earl Ethelwulph was slain.

Four days after this, king Ethelred with his brother Alfred,

[65] Thetford in Norfolk.   [66] Berkshire.   [67] Reading.
[68] Englefield about four miles from Windsor.

again uniting all the strength of their forces, went out to
fight against the above-mentioned army, with all their might
and a hearty good-will, at a place called Eschedun,[69] which
means "the hill of the ash." But the pagans divided themselves into two bodies, with equal close columns, and prepared
for battle. For on that occasion they had two kings and
many earls; the centre of the army they gave to the two kings,
and the other part to all the earls. On seeing this, the Christians also, dividing their army into two bodies, with no less
alacrity, ranged them front to front; after which Alfred more
speedily and promptly moved onward to give them battle;
whereas, just then, his brother Ethelred was in his tent at
prayer, hearing mass, and resolutely declared that he would not
move from there before the priest had finished the mass, and
that he would not forsake the service of God for that of men.
This faith on the part of the Christian king greatly prevailed
with God, as we shall show in the sequel.

Now the Christians had determined that king Ethelred, with
his troops, should engage with the two pagan kings; and that
his brother Alfred, with his men, should take the chance of war
against all the nobles of the pagan army. Matters being thus
arranged, while the king, still at his prayers, was prolonging
the delay, the pagans, fully prepared, advanced rapidly towards
the place of combat; on which, Alfred, who then held but
a subordinate authority, being unable any longer to cope with
the forces of the enemy, unless he either retreated, or made
the charge before his brother came up, at length, with the
courage of a wild boar, manfully led on the Christian troops
against the army of the enemy, and, relying on the divine aid,
his ranks being drawn up in close order, immediately moved
on his standards against the foe. At last, king Ethelred having
finished his prayers, on which he had been engaged, came up,
and having invoked the great Ruler of the world, immediately
commenced the battle.

But at this point, I must inform those who are not aware of
the fact, that the field of battle was not equally advantageous
to those engaged. For the pagans had previously taken possession of the higher ground, while the Christians drew up
their forces on the lower. There was also on that spot a thorn

[69] Now Aston, in Berkshire; some, however, think that Ashendon in
Buckinghamshire is meant.

tree, of very stunted growth, around which the hostile ranks closed in battle, amid the loud shouts of all. After they had fought for some time boldly and bravely on both sides, the pagans, by the Divine judgment, were no longer able to bear the onset of the Christians, and the greater part of them being slain, the rest took to a disgraceful flight.

At this place one of the two kings of the pagans, and five of their earls, were slain, and many thousands of them besides who fell at that spot, and in various places, scattered over the whole breadth of the plain of Eschedun. There fell there king Baiseg, and earl Sydroc the elder, and another earl Sydroc the younger, earl Osbern, earl Freana, and earl Harold. The whole army of the pagans pursued its flight all night, until next day, when most who had escaped reached the castle.

In four days [70] after these events, Ethelred, with his brother Alfred, uniting their forces, marched to Basing, again to fight with the pagans, and after a prolonged combat the pagans at length gained the victory. Again, after a lapse of two months, king Ethelred and his brother Alfred, after having long fought with the pagans, who had divided themselves into two bodies, conquered them at Meretun,[71] putting them all to flight; but these having again rallied, many on both sides were slain, and the pagans at last gained the day.

The same year, after Easter, king Ethelred departed this life, after having manfully ruled the kingdom five years amid much tribulation, on which his brother Alfred succeeded him as king, in the year from the incarnation of our Lord 872. He was the most accomplished among the Saxon poets, most watchful in the service of God, and most discreet in the exercise of justice. His queen Elswisa bore him two sons, Edward and Egelward, and three daughters, Egelfleda, queen of the Mercians, Ethelgeva, a nun, and Elethritha.

At the completion of one year [72] from the beginning of his reign, at a hill called Walton,[73] he fought a most severe battle

[70] Asser and Roger of Wendover say fourteen days; which is more probable. [71] Merton.

[72] "One month" is a various reading here, and is supported by Roger of Wendover.

[73] A various reading here, supported by Asser, Roger de Wendover, and the Anglo-Saxon Chronicle, is Wilton, but Brompton calls the place Walton in Sussex.

with a handful of men against the pagans; but, alas! the enemy was victorious; nor indeed is it to be wondered at, that the Christians had but a small number of men in the engagement; for in a single year they had been worn out by eight battles against the pagans, in which one of their kings and nine dukes, with innumerable troops, had been slain.

In the year 872, Alchun, bishop of the Wiccii,[74] having departed this life, Werefrith, the foster-father of the holy church of Worcester, and a man most learned in the holy scriptures, was ordained bishop by Ethered archbishop of Canterbury, on the seventh day before the ides of June, being the day of Pentecost; he, at the request of king Alfred, translated the books of the dialogues of the pope Saint Gregory, from the Latin into the Saxon tongue. At the same period, the Northumbrians expelled their king, Egbert, and their archbishop Wulpher. An army of the pagans came to London, and wintered there, on which the Mercians made a treaty with them.

In the year 873, the said army left London, and first proceeded to the country of the Northumbrians, and wintered there in the district which is called Lindesig,[75] at a place called Torkeseie,[76] on which the Mercians again made a treaty of peace with them. Egbert the king of Northumbria dying, his successor was Reisig, who reigned three years. Wulpher, also, was this year recalled to his see.

In the year 874, the above-mentioned army left Lindesey, and, entering Mercia, wintered at a place which is called Reopadun.[77] They also expelled Burrhed king of Mercia, from his kingdom, in the twenty-second year of his reign. Going to Rome, he died there, and was honorably buried in the church of Saint Mary, in the school of the Saxons. After his expulsion, the Danes reduced the kingdom of the Mercians to subjection, and committed it to the charge of a certain military officer of that nation, Ceolwulph by name, on condition that whenever they chose, without any subterfuge, they might take and keep it.

[74] The inhabitants of Gloucestershire and Worcestershire.

[75] Lindesey in Lincolnshire.

[76] Of this place Lambarde says; " it is a town in Lincolnshire, which, because it stood near the water, and was much washed therewith, obtained the name of an island, for so the latter part of the word, ' eie ' doth signify, the former being the name of some person."

[77] Repton in Derbyshire.

In the year 875, the army of the pagans, leaving Reopadun, divided into two bodies, one part of which, with Alfdan, proceeded to the country of the Northumbrians, and reduced the whole kingdom of Northumbria to subjection. Thereupon Erdulph, bishop of Lindisfarne, and abbat Edred carried away the body of Saint Cuthbert from the island of Lindisfarne and wandered about with it for a period of seven years. The other division of the army with Guder,[79] Osbitel, and Amund, their three kings, wintered at Grantebrige.[80]

King Alfred, in a naval engagement with six ships of the pagans, captured one, and the rest escaped by flight.

In the year 876, the pagan king Halden divided Northumbria between himself and his followers. Reisig, king of the Northumbrians, died, and was succeeded by Egbert the Second. Rollo, the pagan, a Dane by birth, with his followers this year entered Normandy, on the fifteenth day before the calends of December; he was the first duke of the Normans, and on being baptized thirty years afterwards, was named Robert.

The above-mentioned army sallying forth by night from Grantebrige, entered a fortified place which is called Werham.[81] On learning their sudden arrival, the king of the Saxons made a treaty with them, on condition that having first given hostages,[82] they should depart from the kingdom. However, after their usual custom, caring nothing for hostages or oaths, they broke the treaty, and one night took the road to Examcester,[83] which in the British language is called Caer-wisc.[84]

In the year 877, the above-mentioned army left Examcester, and marching to Cyppanham,[85] a royal town, passed the winter there. King Alfred in these days endured great tribulations, and lived a life of disquietude. In the same year also, Inguar and Haldene came from the country of the Demetæ,[86] in which they had wintered, like ravening wolves, after having slaughtered multitudes of Christians there and burned the monasteries, and sailing to Devonshire, were slain there by the

---

[79] The various reading supported by the other chronicles is Guthrum.
[80] Cambridge.   [81] Wareham.   [82] The Danes, namely.
[83] Exeter, " the fortified city on the Ex."
[84] " The city on the river Wisc."   [85] Chippenham.
[86] The original has " De Meticâ regione," which is obviously an error for " de Demeticâ regione." The Demetæ were the people of the coast of South Wales.

most valiant thanes of king Alfred, together with twelve hundred men, at Cernwich,[87] in which place the said king's thanes
had shut themselves up for safety.

King Alfred being encouraged in a vision by Saint Cuthbert,
fought against the Danes, at the time and place where the
saint had commanded him; and having gained the victory, from
that time forward was always invincible and a terror to the foe.
For the king, putting his trust in the Lord, came with an immense army to the place which is called Edderandun,[88] near
which he found the forces of the enemy prepared for battle.
On this, a severe battle being fought, which lasted the greater
part of the day, the pagans were conquered and put to flight; the
rest being hemmed in by the king's army, fearing the rigours
of famine and cold, and dreading the severity of the king, with
tears and entreaties, sued for peace, and offered hostages together with oaths. In addition to this, their king, whose name
was Guthrum, declared that he wished to become a Christian ;
on which, king Alfred having granted all these requests,
the above-named king of the pagans, together with thirty
chosen men of his army, met him at a place which is called
Aalr,[89] and king Alfred, receiving him as his son by adoption,
raised him from the holy font of baptism, and named him Ethelstan, and enriched him and all his companions who had been
baptized with him, with many presents. He remained with
the king twelve days, receiving during that time most honorable
entertainment, and the king bestowed on him East Anglia,
over which Saint Edmund had reigned.

In the year 878, the above-mentioned army of pagans left
Scippanham[90] as they had promised, and coming to Cirencester
remained there one year. In the same year also, an immense
army of the pagans came from the parts beyond the sea to
the river Thames, and joined the forces before-mentioned. In
the same year, an eclipse of the sun took place, between the
ninth hour[91] and vespers.

In the year 879, the army of the pagans, leaving Cirencester,

[87] More properly Kynwith, near Bideford, in North Devon. Hubberstone,
the spot where Hubba was buried, is still pointed out.

[88] Probably Edington, in Wiltshire.

[89] Called also "Alre," or "Aller," near the isle of Athelney, in Somersetshire.   [90] Chippenham.

[91] Three o'clock in the afternoon. This eclipse took place on the 14th
of March, 880.

proceeded to East Anglia, and parcelling out that country, began to take up their abode there. The pagans, who had passed the winter in the island of Hame,[92] began to visit France,[93] and for one year took their quarters at Ghent.

In the year 880, the above-mentioned army of the pagans, having provided themselves with horses, came into the territories of the Franks, on which the Franks engaged them in battle, and came off victorious. The pagans, having now obtained horses, made incursions on every side. In these days, numerous monasteries in that kingdom were demolished and destroyed. In consequence of this, the brethren of the monastery of the abbat Saint Benedict, disinterred his remains from the tomb where they had been deposited, and taking them with them, wandered to and fro.

In the year 881, the above-mentioned army, having towed their ships up the river Meuse, into the interior of France, wintered there one year. In the same year, king Alfred, engaging in a naval fight with the ships of the pagans, overcame them, and took two, after having slain all that were in them. After this, he inflicted numerous wounds upon the commanders of two ships, till at last, laying down their arms, with prayers and entreaties they surrendered to him.

In the year 882, the army of the pagans so often mentioned, took possession of Cundoth,[94] and quartered there one year. The army, which, under the command of Alfdene, the king of the pagans, had invaded Northumbria, had for some time been without a leader, in consequence, as I have already mentioned, of the slaughter of Alfdene and Inguar by the thanes of king Alfred: but now, having subdued the inhabitants of the country, they took possession of it, and began to take up their abode there, and to inhabit the districts of Northumbria that they had before laid waste.

Upon this, Saint Cuthbert, appearing in a vision to abbat Edred, commanded him to tell the bishop and all the army of the English and the Danes, that, paying the price of his redemption, they must redeem Cuthred, the son of Hardicanute, whom

[92] This is the place which the other chroniclers call Fulenham, now Fulham, near London.
[93] Roger of Wendover says that the Danes, who wintered at Fulham, "arrived from the parts of Gaul."
[94] Or "Cundaht," now Condé, in France.

the Danes had sold as a slave to a certain widow at Winting-
ham,[95] and when redeemed must make him their king. This
was accordingly done, in the thirteenth year of the reign of
king Alfred.   Cuthred being thus raised to the throne, the
episcopal see, which was previously in the island of Lindisfarne,
was established at Cestre,[96] anciently called Cuneceastre, seven
years after its removal from the island of Lindisfarne.   At
this time also, the law of peace which Saint Cuthbert had also
enjoined by means of the above-named abbat, (namely, that
whoever should flee to his body, should enjoy peace without
molestation from any one, for thirty-seven days,[97]) both king
Cuthred and king Alfred enjoined as a law of perpetual observance.   In addition to this, the above-named two kings, with
the consent of all, had previously given, in augmentation of
the former episcopal see, the whole territory between the Tyne
and the Tees to Saint Cuthbert, for a perpetual possession : for
long before this period, the bishopric of the church of Hagustald[98] had ceased to exist.   And whatever person, with what
intent soever, should attempt to infringe these provisions, him
with everlasting curses they condemned to the punishments of
hell.

There belonged to the bishopric of Lindisfarne, from early
times, Luguballia,[99] or Luel, and Northam ;[1] all the churches
also, that lay between the river Tweed and the south Tyne, and
beyond the uninhabited land, as far as the western side, at
this period belonged to the above-named church.   These
houses also belonged to the see, Carnhum and Culterham, and
the two Gedewerdes,[2] on the southern bank of the river Tyne,
which bishop Egred built; Meilros[3] also, and Tigbre, and
Tinigham and Colingham, and Brigham, and Tillemuthe, and
Northam, above-mentioned, which was anciently called Ubbanford.   Mercwrede was also in the possession of this
church, having been given with all its appurtenances by king
Ceolwulph.

For this house the king, on renouncing the world, transferred

---

[95] Whittingham, in Northumberland.
[96] Chester-le-street, in Durham.
[97] Roger of Wendover says a month.   [98] Hexham.
[99] Carlisle.   [1] Or Norham, in Northumberland.
[2] There is no doubt that the names of most of these places belonging
to the bishopric of Lindisfarne, are shockingly misspelt in the text.
[3] Melrose, in Roxburghshire.

together with himself to the church of Lindisfarne, of which, he became a monk, and fought for a heavenly kingdom. His body being afterwards brought into the church of the above-named town of Northam, became famous there, according to the report of the inhabitants of the place, for performing many miracles. It was through the agency of this king, after he had become a monk, that licence was granted to the monks of the church of Lindisfarne to drink wine or ale; for before that, they were accustomed to drink nothing but milk and water, according to the ancient tradition of Saint Aidan, the first bishop of that church, and of the monks, who, accompanying him from Scotland, had there, by the liberality of king Oswald, received a refuge, and with great severity of discipline, rejoiced to serve God.

Besides this, the above-named bishop Egred built a church at a place which is called Geinforde, and presented it to Saint Cuthbert; he also built Bellingham in Heorternesse, and two other towns, Becclif and Wigeclif, on the southern bank of the river Tees, which he gave to Saint Cuthbert, for the maintenance and support of his servants; and in like manner, Wodecester, and Whittingham, and Edulfingham, and Ecwlingham,[5] being presented by king Ceolwulph, from an early period belonged to Saint Cuthbert.

In the year 883, pope Marinus, in his love for, and at the earnest entreaty of, king Alfred, obligingly made the school of the Saxons at Rome free from all tax and tribute; he also sent many gifts to that king, among which he gave him a large piece of the holy cross, upon which the Son of God was crucified for the salvation of mankind.

At this time the above-mentioned army of the pagans went up the river Sunne[6] to Amiens, and quartered themselves there one year.

In the time of king Alfred, there came into England one John, a Scot by birth, a man of shrewd intellect and of great eloquence. Having a long time previously left his country, he came to France to the court of Charles the Bald, by whom he was entertained with great respect, and was honored by him with his particular intimacy. He shared with the king both his serious and his more merry moments, and was the sole companion both of his table and his retirement. He was also a man of great facetiousness and of ready wit, of which

---

[5] Probably Eglingham, in Northumberland.   [6] Somme.

there are instances quoted even to this day; as the following, for instance. He was sitting at table opposite the king, who was on the other side of it, and the cups having gone round and the courses ended, Charles becoming more merry than usual, after some other things, on observing John do something offensive to the French notions of good breeding, he pleasantly rebuked him, and said, "What is there between a sot and a Scot?" On which he turned back this hard hit on its author, and made answer, "A table only." What could be be more facetious than this reply? The king had asked him with reference to the different notions of manners, whereas John made answer with reference to the distance of space. Nor indeed was the king offended; for, being captivated by this prodigy of science, he was unwilling to manifest displeasure by even a word against the master, for by that name he usually called him.

At another time, when the servant had presented a dish to the king at table, which contained two very large fishes, besides one somewhat smaller, he gave it to the master, that he might share it with two clerks who were sitting near him. They were persons of gigantic stature, while he himself was small in person. On this, ever devising something merry, in order to cause amusement to those at table, he kept the two large ones for himself, and divided the smaller one between the two clerks. On the king finding fault with the unfairness of the division, "Nay," said he, "I have acted right and fairly. For here is a small one," alluding to himself, "and here are two great ones," touching the fishes; then, turning to the clerks, "here are two great ones," said he, pointing at the clerks, "and here is a small one," touching the fish.

At the request, also, of Charles, he translated the " Hierarchia," of Dionysius the Areiopagite, from Greek into Latin, word for word; the consequence of which is, that the Latin version can be hardly understood from having been rendered rather according to the Greek order of the words than according to our own idiom. He also composed a treatise, which he entitled περὶ φύσεων μερισμοῦ,[7] that is to say, "On the Divisions of Nature;" very useful for solving the perplexity as to some questions, making some allowance, however, for him on cer-

---

7 Roger of Wendover says that the title was περὶ φυσικῶν μερίσματος; meaning much the same thing.

tain points.   In some respects he has certainly deviated from the
track of the Latins by keeping his eyes intently fixed upon the
Greeks; for which reason he has been even considered a here-
tic, and a certain Florus wrote against him.   And, indeed,
there are in his book, περὶ φύσεων, very many things which,
unless they are most carefully examined, seem opposed to the
Catholic faith.   Pope Nicholas is known to have been of this
opinion; for he says, in an epistle to Charles, "It has been
reported to our Apostleship, that a certain man, named John,
by birth a Scot, has lately translated into Latin the work of
Saint Dionysius the Areiopagite, which he eloquently wrote in
Greek, touching the divine names and the celestial orders.
Now, according to the usual custom, this ought to have been
sent to us and submitted to the approval of our judgment;
and the more especially as the said John, though he is stated to
be a man of great knowledge, has been said for some time past
by general report not to be quite sound on certain points."
     In consequence of this discredit he became tired of France,
and came to king Alfred, by whose munificence he was appointed
a teacher, and settled at Malmesbury, as appears from the king's
writings.   Here, some years afterwards, he was stabbed with
their writing instruments[8] by the boys whom he was teaching,
and quitted this life in great and cruel torments; at a period
when, his weakness waxing stronger and his hands shaking, he
had often asked in vain that he might experience the bitter-
ness of death.   He lay for some time with an ignoble burial in
the church of Saint Laurence, the scene of his shocking death;
but, after the Divine favour for many nights had honored him
by a ray of fire, the monks, being thus admonished, transferred
him to the greater church, and placed him at the left side of
the altar.
     In the year 884, the above-mentioned army of the pagans
divided themselves into two bodies; one of which entered East
France, the other returned into Kent, and lay siege to the city of
Rouecestre;[9] but the citizens made a stout resistance, and
king Alfred coming to their aid with his army, compelled the
heathens to raise the siege and return to their ships, leaving
the fortress which they had built there before the gates of the
above named city, besides their spoil, and the men and horses

     [8] The "graphia," or "styli," the iron pens with which they wrote on
wax tablets.   [9] Rochester.

which they had brought with them from France. In this
year also a fleet was sent by king Alfred for the defence of the
places around East Anglia. When they had come to the mouth
of the river Stour,[9*] they found there sixteen ships of the
pirates, which they took, slaying all on board of them. Those
of the Danes, however, who were able to escape, collected their
ships in various bodies in every quarter, and then engaging
with the English in a naval battle, while, with inert supine-
ness, they were asleep, a multitude of them unarmed were
slain, and the Danes came off victorious.

At this period, Carloman, king of the Western Franks, that
is to say, of the Alemanni, was killed in hunting, having been
attacked by a wild boar when unattended, which mangled him
with its tusk. His brother Louis had died the year before,
who was also king of the Franks; for they were both sons of
Louis, the king of the Franks, who had died in the year above-
mentioned in which [10] the eclipse of the sun took place. He
also was the son of Charles, king of the Franks, whose daughter,
Jutthitta,[11] Ethelwulph, king of the West-Saxons, had taken
for his queen.

In this year a great army of the pagans came in ships
from Germany into the country of the ancient Saxons. The
Saxons and the Frisians having united their forces against them,
fought with them twice in one year, and were victorious. In
the same year also, Charles, king of the Alemanni, with the
voluntary consent of all, received the kingdom of the West
Franks and all the territories which lie between the Tyrrhenian
sea and the inlet of the ocean which divides the ancient Saxons
and the Gauls. This Charles was the son of king Louis,
who was brother of Charles, king of the Franks, and father of
the above-named Judith ; these two brothers were sons of
Louis, the son of Charles the Great, that ancient and most wise
sovereign, who was the son of king Pepin.

In the year 885, the above-mentioned army, which had first
entered the kingdom of the East Franks, again returned to
the West Franks, and sailed up the river Seine to Paris ; but
after having besieged the city for a year, the inhabitants
making a stout defence, they were unable to effect an entrance
within the walls.

⁹ * The river which divides Essex from Suffolk.   ¹⁰ A.D. 880.
¹¹ Judith.

King Alfred, after the burning of cities and the slaughter of the inhabitants, rebuilt London with great honor, and made it habitable, and gave it into the charge of Ethered, earl of Mercia. To this king all the Angles and Saxons, who before had been dispersed in all quarters, or were with the pagans[12] but not in captivity, came, and voluntarily submitted to his sway. At this period, Plegmund was archbishop of Canterbury.

In the year 886, the above-mentioned army left Paris, being unable to gain their object, and steered their fleet thence along the Seine, as far as a place called Chezy. There having taken up their quarters for a year, in the year following they entered the mouth of the river Iona;[13] and, making great ravages to the country, remained there a year.

In the same year, Charles, king of the Franks, departed this life, in the sixth week after his expulsion from his kingdom by Ernulph, his brother's son. After his death the kingdom was divided into five parts, but the principal part devolved on Ernulph, to whom the other four, of their own accord, took the oath of fealty; inasmuch as not one of them could be legitimate heir on his father's side, except Ernulph alone: with him, therefore, remained the supreme power.

This, then, was the division of the kingdom: Ernulph received the countries on the eastern side of the river Rhine; Rhodulph the inland parts of the kingdom; Odo the west; and Beorgar and Wido[14] Lombardy and all the lands on that side of the mountains. But these kingdoms, thus divided, afflicted each other with mighty wars, and the kings expelled one another out from their dominions.

In this year Ethelhem,[15] earl of Wiltshire, carried to Rome the alms of king Alfred.

In the year 887, among the numberless good things that king Alfred did, he founded two most noble monasteries; one for monks, at a place which is called Ethelingege,[16] or the "the island of nobles," where, collecting monks of various

[12] Asser seems to say that those submitted "who were in captivity with the heathens." This is clearly wrong, for they had not the opportunity of so doing. The Anglo-Saxon Chronicle and Roger of Wendover agree with our author.
[13] Yonne.   [14] Witha, or Guido.
[15] Roger of Wendover erroneously calls this person Athelm, bishop of Winchester.   [16] Or Athelney, in Somersetshire.

orders, he first appointed John to be abbat, a priest and monk, and an ancient Saxon by birth ; the other a noble monastery also near the east gate of Sceaftesbrig,[17] he erected for the reception of nuns, and over it he appointed as abbess his own daughter Ethelgiva, a virgin consecrated to God.   These two monasteries he enriched with possessions in land, and riches of every kind.

In the year 888, Ethelfrid, archbishop of Canterbury, departed this life, and was succeeded by Plegmund.

In the year 889, king Guthrum, whom, as I have previously mentioned, king Alfred raised from the font, giving him the name of Ethelstan, departed this life.   He, with his people, dwelt in East Anglia, and was the first who held and possessed that province, after the martyrdom of the king Saint Edmund.

In the year 890, Wulpher, archbishop of York, died, in the thirty-ninth year of his archiepiscopate.

In the year 892, Hasting, the pagan king, entered the mouth of the Thames, with eighty piratical ships, and threw up fortifications at Middletun.[18]

In the year 893, Cuthred, king of Northumbria, died.   The pagans of Northumbria ratified the peace with Alfred by oath.

In the year 894, the pagans brought their ships up the river Thames, and after that, up the river Lige,[19] and began to throw up their fortifications near the river, at the distance of twenty miles from London.

In the year 895, in summer time, a great part of the citizens of London, and a considerable number from the neighbouring places, attempted to destroy the fortifications which the pagans had constructed ; but on their making a stout resistance, the Christians were put to flight, and four of the thanes of king Alfred slain.

In the year 896, the army of the pagans in East Anglia and Northumbria, collecting plunder by stealth on the coast, grievously laid waste the land of the West Saxons, and especially by using long and swift ships, which they had built many years before.   To oppose them, by order of king Alfred ships were constructed, twice as long, sharp, and swift, and not so high,[20] by the onset of which, the said ships of the

---

[17] Shaftesbury.   [18] Milton, near Gravesend.
[19] Probably the same as the Limen or Rother, in Kent.
[20] The Anglo-Saxon Chronicle says they were higher.

enemy might be overcome. On these being launched, the king
gave orders to take alive as many as they could, and to slay
those whom they could not take; the result of which was,
that in the same year, thirty ships of the Danish pirates were
captured, some of whom were slain, and some taken to the
king alive, and hanged on gibbets.

In the year 897, Rollo, the first duke of the Normans, with
his army laid siege to the city of Chartres; but Wulzelm, the
bishop of that city, calling Richard, duke of Burgundy, and
Ebalus, earl of Poitou, to his aid, and carrying the tunic of
Saint Mary in his hands, by the Divine will put duke Rollo to
flight, and delivered the city.

In the year 898, Ethelbald was ordained archbishop of
York.

In the year from the incarnation of our Lord 899, king
Alfred, son of the most pious king Ethelwulph, having reigned
twenty-nine years and six months, departed this life, in the
fourth year of the indiction,[21] on the fifth day before the
calends of November, and was buried in the new monastery at
Winchester.

He was succeeded by his son Edward, surnamed the Elder,
who was inferior to his father in his acquaintance with literature, but his equal in dignity and power, and his superior in glory.
For, as will be shewn in the sequel, he extended the limits
of his kingdom much farther than his father did. He also
built many cities, and restored some that had been destroyed;
the whole of Essex, East Anglia, Northumbria, and many
districts of Mercia, of which the Danes had been long in possession, he manfully wrested from their hands. After the
death of his sister Ethelfreda, he obtained possession of the
whole of Mercia, and received the submission of all the kings
of the Scots, the Cumbrians, the people of Strath-Clyde, and
the West Britons.

By Egewinna, a most noble lady, he had Ethelstan, his
eldest son; by his wife Edgiva he had three sons, Edwin, Edmund, and Edred, and a daughter named Eadburga, a virgin most

[21] The indiction was so called from the edicts of the Roman emperors;
and as one such edict was supposed to appear regularly every fifteen years,
the years were reckoned by their distance from the year of each indiction.
From the time of Athanasius downwards, they were generally employed
by ecclesiastical writers in describing epochs.

strictly consecrated to God, with three[22] other daughters; one
of whom, Otho, the eighty-ninth emperor of the Romans, and
another, Charles, king of the West Franks, took to wife; whose
father's sister, that is to say, the daughter of the emperor Charles,
Ethelwulph, the king of the West Saxons, had married; the
third daughter was married to Sithric, king of Northumbria.

In this year, Erdulf, bishop of Lindisfarne, departed this
life, and was succeeded by Guthred; Osbert was also expelled
from his kingdom.

In the year 900, the most valiant duke Athulph, brother of
queen Ealwitha, the mother of king Edward, and Virgilius,
the venerable abbat of the Scots, departed this life; also Grim-
bald, the saint and priest, one of the masters of king Alfred,
attained the joys of the kingdom of heaven.

In the year 902, the people of Kent fought with a great host
of the piratical Danes, at a place which is called Holme, and
came off victorious.

In the year 903, that pious handmaid of Christ, queen
Elswitha, the mother of king Edward, departed this life; she
founded a monastery for nuns at Winchester.

In the year 904, the armies of the pagans of East Anglia
and Northumbria, finding that king Edward was invincible,
made peace with him, at a place which, in the English language, is called Thitingaford.[23]

In the year 905, the city, which is called in the British
tongue, Karlegion,[24] and in the Saxon, Legacestre, was rebuilt
by the command of duke Ethered and Ethelfleda.

In the year 906, the bones of Saint Oswald, the king and
martyr, were removed from Bardonig,[25] into Mercia. The
most invincible king Edward, because the Danes had infringed
the treaty which they had made, sent an army of West Saxons
and Mercians into Northumbria, which, having arrived there,
for nearly forty days did not cease to lay it waste, and slaying a vast number of the Danes, compelled their kings and

---

[22] Roger of Wendover mentions five daughters, besides Eadburga,
whom he calls Eadfleda.

[23] This place in the Anglo-Saxon Chronicle is called Hitchinford.
Lambarde calls it "Itingford," and says, "I find it not so circumscribed,
that I can make any likely conjecture where it should be."

[24] Properly "Caerlirion," the ancient name of Leicester.

[25] Bardney.

leaders to renew the treaty of peace with king Edward, which they had broken.

In the year 907, in the province of Stafford, at a place which is called Teotenhale,[26] a memorable battle took place between the English and the Danes; but the English gained the day.

In the year 908, Ethered, the king's earl of the Mercians, a man of great virtue, departed this life; and after his death, his wife Egelfleda, the daughter of king Alfred, for a long time most ably governed the kingdom of the Mercians, except the cities of London and Oxford, of which her brother, king Edward, retained the government.

In the year 909, Egelfleda, the lady of the Mercians, on the second day before the nones of May, came with an army to the place which is called Sceargate,[27] and there erected a fortified castle, and after that, another on the western bank of the river Severn, at the place which is called Brige.[28]

In the year 910, at the beginning of summer, Egelfleda, the lady of the Mercians, proceeded with the Mercians to Tamuirting,[29] and rebuilt that city. In this year king Niel was slain by his brother Sithric.

In the year 911, Werfred, bishop of the Wiccii, departed this life at Worcester; he was a man of great sanctity and learning, and, as I have previously mentioned, at the request of king Alfred, translated the Dialogues of Saint Gregory the pope into the Saxon tongue; he was succeeded by Ethelhun. Egelfleda, the lady of the Mercians, founded the city which is called Eadesbirig,[30] and at the close of autumn another, which is called Warewic.[31]

In the year 912, the most invincible king Edward went to Bedford, before the feast of Saint Martin, and received the submission of its inhabitants, and having remained there thirty days, ordered a city to be founded on the south side of the river Lea.[32]

In the year 913, Egelfleda, the lady of the Mercians, sent an army into the territory of the Britons,[33] to besiege the castle

[26] Totenhall.   [27] Roger of Wendover calls it "Strengate."
[28] Bridgnorth, in Shropshire.   [29] Tamworth, in Staffordshire.
[30] Eddesbury.   [31] Warwick.
[32] This is probably the river meant; though in the original the river is called "Ose," being evidently a misprint for Ouse. The Anglo-Saxon Chronicle here mentions Hertford, on the south side of the Lea, as being founded by Edward.   [33] The Welsh.

at Bricenamere;[34] having taken the place, they captured the wife of the king of the Britons, with thirty-four men, and brought them prisoners into Mercia.

In the year 914, Egelfleda, the lady of the Mercians, on the day before the calends of August, took Derby by storm, and gained possession of that province; four of her thanes, who were most esteemed by her, were there slain at the city gate, while bravely fighting.

In the year 915, Egelfleda, the lady of the Mercians, a woman of remarkable prudence, justice, and virtue, departed this life, on the nineteenth day before the calends of July, in the eighth year after she by herself had governed the kingdom of the Mercians with a vigorous rule, and left her only daughter Elfwinna, whom she had by Ethered, the king's earl, heiress to her kingdom. Her body was conveyed to Gloucester, and honorably buried in the church of Saint Peter.

In the year 916, king Edward sent into Northumbria an army of Mercians, to liberate the city of Mamcestre,[35] and post there some brave soldiers as a garrison. After this, he entirely deprived his niece Elfwinna of her authority in the kingdom of Mercia, and ordered her to be taken into Wessex. King Sithric also took Devonport by storm.

In the year 917, the king of the Scots, with the whole of his nation, Reginald, king of the Danes, with the Danes and English who inhabited Northumbria, and the king of the Strath-Clyde Britons,[36] with his people, chose Edward the Elder as their father and liege lord, and made a lasting treaty with him.

In the year 918, the Clito Ethelward, brother of king Edward, departed this life, on the seventeenth day before the calends of November, and was buried at Winchester; Ethelstan, the bishop of the Wiccii,[37] also died, and was succeeded by Wilfred.

In the year from the incarnation of our Lord 919,[38] Edward the Elder, the most invincible king of the English, departed this life, at the royal town which is called Fearndun,[39] in the thirty-fourth[40] year of his reign, and the fifteenth of the indic-

[34] Brecknock.   [35] Manchester.
[36] This, no doubt, as we learn from other historians, is the meaning of the word "Strecglendwalli."   [37] Bishop of Worcester.
[38] The other chroniclers say that he died in the year 924.
[39] Faringdon, in Berkshire.
[40] This is an error, as it should be twenty-fourth : though, according to our author's reckoning, it would be in the twentieth.

tion, after having greatly distinguished himself while king. He reigned most gloriously over all the nations that inhabited Britain, both those of the Angles, the Scots, the Cumbrians, the Danes, and the Britons.[41] After his death, he left the helm of state to his son Ethelstan, and his body having been carried to Winchester, was buried with regal pomp at the new monastery there.

Ethelstan was crowned at Kingestun,[42] which means " the royal town," and was consecrated with due honor by Athelin, archbishop of Canterbury. In his time, the illustrious child Dunstan was born in the kingdom of Wessex.

In the year 920, Ethelstan, the illustrious and glorious king of the English, with great pomp and state, gave his sister in marriage to king Sithric, who was of Danish origin.

In the year 921, king Sithric departed this life, and king Ethelstan having expelled his son Cuthred, who had succeeded his father, added his kingdom to his own dominions.   All the kings beside, of the whole of Albion, namely, Huwald,[43] king of the West Britons,[44] Constantine, king of the Scots, and Wuer,[45] king of the Wenti, he conquered in battle and utterly routed.   All of these, seeing that they could not resist his valour, met him on the fourth day before the ides of July, at a place which is called Eamot, and having made the oaths, made a lasting treaty with him.

In the year 922, Wilfred, bishop of the Wiccii, died, and was succeeded by Kinewold.

In the year 923, Frithestan, bishop of Winchester, a man of remarkable sanctity, resigned the bishopric of Winchester, Brinstan, a religious man, being ordained bishop in his stead, and in the following year departed to the Lord.

In the year 924, king Ethelstan ordered his brother Edwin to be drowned in the sea.

In the year 925, Ethelstan, the valiant and glorious king of the English, Constantine, king of the Scots, having broken the treaty which he had made with him, marched with a large army into Scotland, and coming to the tomb of Saint Cuthbert, commended himself and his expedition to his guardianship, and presented to him many and various gifts, such as befitted a

[41] The Welsh.   [42] Kingston-on-Thames.
[43] Howel.   [44] West Welsh.
[45] Roger of Wendover calls him Wulferth. The Wenti were probably the people of Monmouthshire.

king, and lands as well; consigning to everlasting flames those
who should take away any portion therefrom. After this, with
a very large force he subdued the enemy, and with his army
laid waste Scotland, even as far as Feoder and Wertermore,
while with his fleet he ravaged as far as Catenes;[46] in consequence of this, king Constantine, being compelled so to do, gave
up his son to him as a hostage, together with suitable presents;
and the peace being thus renewed, the king returned to Wessex.
In the same year Saint Bristan departed this life.

In the year 925, the religious monk Elphege, surnamed the
Bald, a kinsman of Saint Dunstan, received the bishopric of
Winchester.

In the year 927, Anlaf, the pagan king of Ireland and of
many of the islands, being encouraged by his father-in-law,
Constantine, king of the Scots, entered the mouth of the
Humber with a vast fleet, amounting to six hundred and fifteen
sail; on which he was met by king Ethelstan and his brother
the Clito Edmund, with an army, at the place which is called
Brumanburgh.[47] The battle lasted from the beginning of the
day to the evening, and they slew five minor kings and seven
dukes, whom the enemy had invited to their aid, and shed
such a quantity of blood, as in no battle before that had ever
been shed in England; and, having compelled the kings Anlaf
and Constantine, and the king of the Cumbrians, to fly to their
ships, they returned in great triumph. But the enemy having
experienced extreme disaster in the loss of their army, returned
home with only a few men.

In the year from the incarnation of our Lord 940, Ethelstan, the valiant and glorious king of the English, departed
this life at Gloucester, in the sixteenth year of his reign, and
in the fourteenth of the indiction, on the sixth day before the
calends of November, being the fourth day of the week; his
body was carried to the city of Maidulph,[47*] and was there
honorably interred. His brother Edmund succeeded him in
the eighteenth year of his age.

In the year 941, the Northumbrians proving regardless
of the fealty which they owed to Edmund, the mighty
king of the English, chose Anlaf, king of the Norwegians

[46] Caithness.
[47] Or Brunenburgh; 1 rumley, in Lincolnshire. This battle was the
subject of an Anglo-Saxon poem, which is still in existence.
[47*] Malmesbury.

as their king. The elder Richard became duke of the Normans, and continued so for fifty-two years.

In the first year of the reign of king Edmund, king Anlaf first came to York, and then marching to the south, laid siege to Hamtune;[44] but not succeeding there, he turned the steps of his army towards Tameworde,[45] and having laid waste all the places in the neighbourhood, while he was returning to Legacestre,[46] king Edmund met him with an army; but he had not a severe struggle for the mastery,[47] since the two archbishops Odo and Wulstan, having allayed the anger of both of the kings, put an end to the fight. And thus peace being made, the Watlingastrete[48] was made the boundary of both kingdoms; Edmund having the sway on the southern side, and Anlaf on the northern. Anlaf having pillaged the church of Saint Balther and burnt Tinningham, shortly after perished. After this, the people of York laid waste the island of Lindisfarne, and slew great numbers. The son of Sithric, whose name was Anlaf, then reigned over the Northumbrians.

In the year 942, Edmund, the mighty king of the English, entirely wrested five cities, namely, Lincoln, Nottingham, Derby, Leicester, and Stamford from the hands of the Danes, and reduced the whole of Mercia under his own power. He was a friend[49] of Dunstan, the servant of God, and by following his counsels became renowned. Being loaded by him with various honors the latter was appointed to the abbacy of Glastonbury, in place he had been educated.

In the year 943, when his queen, Saint Elgiva, had borne to Edmund, the mighty king, a son named Edgar, Saint Dunstan heard voices, as though on high, singing and repeating, "Peace to the church of England in the times of the child that is now born, and of our Dunstan." In this year, the same king raised king Anlaf, of whom we have previously made mention, from the font of holy regeneration, and gave him royal presents, and shortly afterwards held Reginald, king of the

---

[44] Southampton.   [45] Tamworth.   [46] Leicester.

[47] On the contrary, Roger of Wendover says that the loss on either side was excessive.

[48] The road which passed from the south of England, through London, into the north.

[49] There is little doubt that the word " summus " here, is an error for " amicus."

Northumbrians when he was confirmed by the bishop, and adopted him as his own son.

In the year 944, Edmund, the mighty king of the English, expelled two kings, namely, Anlaf, son of king Sithric, and Reginald, son of Guthferth, from Northumbria, and reduced it to subjection.

In the year 945, Edmund, the mighty king of the English, laid waste the lands of the Cumbrians, and granted them to Malcolm, king of the Scots, on condition that he should be faithful to him both by land and sea.

In the year from the incarnation of our Lord 946, Edmund, the mighty king of the English on the day of the feast of Saint Augustine, the instructor of the English, while, at a town, which in English is called Pucklecirce,[50] he was attempting to rescue his sewer Leo[51] from the hands of a most vile robber, for fear lest he should be killed, was slain by the same man, after having reigned five years and seven months, in the fourth year of the indiction, on the seventh day before the calends of June, being the third day of the week.   Being taken to Glastonbury, he was there interred by Saint Dunstan, the abbat.

His brother Edred succeeded him in the kingdom, and was consecrated king by Saint Odo, the archbishop, at Kingston.

In the year 947, Wulstan, archbishop of York, and all the nobles of Northumbria, swore fidelity to Edred, the excellent king of the English, at a town which is called Tadenesclif,[52] but they did not long observe it; for they elected a certain man, named Eiric, a Dane by birth, to be king over them.

In the year 948, in return for the unfaithfulness of the Northumbrians, Edred, the excellent king of the English, laid waste the whole of Northumbria; in which devastation the monastery at Rhipum,[53] which was said to have been formerly built by Saint Wilfred, the bishop, was destroyed by fire.   But, as the king was returning homewards, the army sallied forth from York, and made great slaughter of the rear of the king's

---

[50] Pucklechurch, in Gloucestershire.   Matthew of Westminster and Roger of Wendover call the place Micklesbury.

[51] It is more generally represented that the name of the robber was Leof; the name no doubt which is here given to the attendant.

[52] Lambarde takes this place to be the same as Topcliff, in Yorkshire.

[53] Ripon.

army, at a place which is called Chesterford. The king being greatly enraged thereat, wished to return at once and entirely to depopulate the whole of that region; but, on understanding this, the Northumbrians, being struck with terror, forsook Eiric, whom they had appointed king over them, and made compensation to the king for his injuries with honors, and for his losses with presents, and mitigated his anger with no small sum of money.

In the year 951, Saint Elphege, surnamed the Bald, bishop of Winchester, who had graced Saint Dunstan with the monastic garb and the degree of priest, ended this life, and was succeeded in the see by Efsin. In this year also died Oswel,[55] the king of the Britons.

In the year 952, Edred, the renowned king of the English, placed Wulstan, archbishop of York, in close confinement at Withanbrig,[56] because he had been often accused before him on certain charges.

In the year 953, Wulstan, the archbishop of York, having been released from custody, the episcopal dignity was restored to him at Dorchester.

The kings of the Northumbrians having now, as I have mentioned above, come to a close, it is my intention here to insert how and to what earls that province afterwards became subject.

The last of the kings of that province, as I have said a little above, was Eiric, whom the Northumbrians, on violating their plighted faith, which they had sworn to king Edred, made king; for which reason the king, in his anger, ordered the whole province to be utterly laid waste. On this, the Northumbrians having expelled their king and slain Amancus, the son of Anlaf, and with oaths and presents appeased king Edred, the province was given in charge to earl Osulph; who afterwards, in the reign of king Edgar, took Oslac as his associate in the government. After this, Osulph took charge of the parts on the northern side of Tyne, while Oslac ruled over York and its vicinity. He was succeeded by Waltef the Elder, who had, as his successor, his son, Ucthred. When, in the reign of king Edric, king Canute

---

[55] V. r. Owel, or, as we write it, Howel.
[56] The Anglo-Saxon Chronicle says Jedburgh.

invaded Northumbria with a hostile force, being compelled by necessity, he went over with his followers to Canute; and after having taken the oath of fealty and given hostages, he was slain by a certain very wealthy Dane, Thurebrand, surnamed Holde, Canute giving his sanction thereto; and in his place his brother, Eadulph Cudel, was substituted. Earl Ucthred left three sons surviving him, Aldred, Eadulph, and Cospatric. The first two of these were successively earls of Northumbria; the third, who did not enjoy the honor of the earldom, had a son named Ucthred, whose son was Eadulph, surnamed Rus, who, in after times, was the leader of those who murdered bishop Walcher; indeed, he himself is said to have slain him with his own hand. However, shortly afterwards, he himself was slain by a woman, and was buried in the church of Gedeworde; but afterwards such a mass of filth as his body was cast out from there by Turgot, formerly prior of the church of Durham, and archdeacon.

After Eadulph Cudel, Aldred, the son of the above-named earl Ucthred, received the earldom, and slew the murderer, Thurebrand, in revenge for the death of his father. On this, Carl, the son of Thurebrand, and the said earl Aldred, after plotting against the lives of each other, were at last reconciled. But shortly after, Aldred, suspecting no evil, was slain by Carl, in a wood which is called Riscwode, the brother of Aldred having joined in the plot. After the death of his brother, Eadulph became earl of Northumbria; who, being elated with pride, laid waste the country of the Britons—that is to say, of the Welsh—in a most cruel manner. But, in the third year after, when, a treaty having been made, he had come to Hardicanute to be reconciled, he was slain by Siward; who, in succession to him, had the earldom of the whole of that province of Northumbria: that is to say, from the Humber to the Tweed. On his death he was succeeded by Tosti; who, having been banished from England for the great injuries which he had done to Northumbria, his earldom was given in charge by king Edward to Morcar; and, afterwards, by king William. Morcar, finding his attention distracted by weighty matters in other quarters, entrusted the earldom beyond the Tyne to Osulph, a young man, son of the above-named earl Eadulph. Morcar being afterwards taken prisoner and placed in confinement, king William gave the earldom of Osulph to Copsi, who was the uncle of

earl Tosti, a man of wisdom and prudence. He, having made
a vow to Saint Cuthbert, gave to his servants in his church,
namely, that of Durham, these lands :—In Merscum, ten carrucates and a half of land, and the church of Saint Germanus
in the same town ; in Thortuna, two carrucates ; and in Thes-
trota, ten bovates of land ; in Readeclive half a carrucate, and
in Gisburgh one carrucate of land.

On being deprived of the earldom by Copsi, Osulph, after
hiding himself in hunger and destitution in the woods and
mountains, at length collected a band of his companions, whom
the same necessity had brought together, and surrounded
Copsi at Niwebrin ; [57] who, escaping among the confusion that
ensued, concealed himself in the church.   Being however
betrayed, the enemy set fire to the church : whereon he was
compelled to make his way to the door, where he was slain by
the hand of Osulph, in the fifth week after he had received
the earldom, on the fourth day before the ides of March.   In
the ensuing autumn, Osulph himself, rushing headlong upon
a spear which a robber presented at him, was pierced thereby,
and died on the spot.

After his death, Cospatric, the son of Maldred, the son of
Crinan, went to king William, and, for a large sum of money,
made purchase of the earldom of Northumbria ; for, through
his mother's side, the honor of that earldom belonged to him ;
his mother being Algitha, the daughter of earl Ucthred, whom
Elgiva, daughter of king Ethelred, bore to him.   This Algitha her father gave in marriage to Maldred, the son of
Crinan.   After this, Cospatric held the earldom until the king
deprived him of it ; making it a charge against him that he
had with his counsel and assistance aided those who had
slain the earl Robert Cumin with his followers, at Durham,
although he really was not present there ; and also alleging
that he had sided with the enemy when the Normans were
slain at York.   Flying, therefore, to king Malcolm, he shortly
afterwards set sail for Flanders ; and, after some time, on
his return to Scotland, the above-named king gave him Dun-
bar, in Lothian, [58] with the adjacent lands, that with these
he might maintain himself and his people until more fortunate

[57] Probably Newburgh, in Yorkshire..

[58] In the original it is " Londoneio ;" most probably an error for " Lau-
donia."

times. But not long after this, being reduced to extreme infirmity, he sent for Aldwin and Turgot, the monks, who at
this time were living at Meilros,[59] in poverty and contrite in
spirit for the sake of Christ, and ended his life with a full
confession of his sins, and great lamentations and penitence,
at Ubbanford, which is also called Northam, and was buried
in the porch of the church there. He gave them two fair
dorsals,[60] that, in whatever place they might chance to take
rest, they should set them up there in remembrance of him.
These are still preserved in the church at Durham.

This Cospatric was the father of Dolfin, Walthen, and Cospatric. After Cospatric, the earldom of Northumbria was
given to Walthen, the son of earl Siward, who was entitled
to it both on his father's and his mother's side. For he was the
son of earl Siward, by Elfleda, the daughter of Alfred, who
was formerly earl. Some time after, Walthen having been
taken prisoner, the charge of the earldom was entrusted to
bishop Walcher up to the time of his death. After him, the
king conferred that honor on Alfric. He, being unable to
make head against times of difficulty, and having returned to
his own country, the same king made Robert de Mowbray earl
of Northumbria; but he being taken prisoner, king William
the younger, and, after him, king Henry, kept Northumbria
in their own hands.

In the year from the incarnation of our Lord 955, Edelred,[61]
the excellent king of the English, fell sick, in the tenth year
of his reign, and his life was despaired of; on which, speedily
dispatching a messenger, he sent for the father of his con-
fessions,[62] namely, Saint Dunstan, the abbat. While repairing
with all haste to the palace, and when he had now got half way
thither, a voice was distinctly heard by him from above, saying, "King Edelred now rests in peace;" whereupon, the
horse on which he was sitting, not being able to endure the
force of the angelic voice, without any injury to his rider,
fell dead upon the ground. The king's body was carried to

[59] Melrose.
[60] Dorsals were garments, or pieces of tapestry, which were hung against
walls as a screen for the backs of those who sat near them; whence their
name   [61] A mistake for Edred.
[62] The text is probably corrupt in this passage.

Winchester, and received an honorable burial from the abbat Dunstan, at the old monastery there.

His cousin, the Clito[63] Edwin,[64] succeeded him in the kingdom; he was the son of king Edmund, and of Saint Elgiva, his queen. In the same year he was consecrated king by archbishop Odo, at Kingston.

In the year 956, Saint Dunstan, the abbat, was banished on account of his righteousness by Edwin, king of the English, and passing the seas, took refuge, during the period of his exile, in the monastery of Blandigny.[65] On the seventh day before the calends of January, Wulstan, archbishop of York, departed this life, and was buried at Oundle;[66] he was succeeded by Oskitel, a venerable man.

In the year 957, Edwy, king of the English, by reason of his unwise administration of the government, being despised by them, was forsaken by the people of Mercia and Northumbria, and his brother, the Clito Edgar, was chosen king by them, and the rule of the two kings was so separated that the river Thames divided their kingdom. Shortly after this, Edgar, the king of the Mercians, recalled Saint Dunstan, the abbat, from exile, with great honor and distinction. A short time after, Coenwald, the bishop of Worcester, departed this life, a man of great humility, and of the monastic profession. In his place Saint Dunstan was elected bishop, and was consecrated by Odo, archbishop of Canterbury.

In the year 958, Saint Odo, the archbishop of Canterbury, separated from each other, Edwy, king of the West Saxons, and Elgiva, either because, as it is said, she was related to him, or because he loved her instead of his own wife.[67] In the same year, the said archbishop, a man famed for his talents, and commendable for his virtues, endued also with a spirit of

---

[63] "Clito" was a title which was sometimes given to all the king's sons among the Anglo-Saxons, but more generally in especial to the eldest sons. It was probably derived from the Latin "inclytus," "glorious," or from its root, the Greek word κλειτός, of the same meaning.

[64] Generally called Edwy.

[65] The reading in the text is Blandimum; it should be Blandinium. The monastery of Blandigny, or St. Peter, was in the city of Ghent.

[66] In Northamptonshire.

[67] "Sub propriâ uxore." It is not universally agreed that king Edwy was married. Bridferth, one of the early writers, says that Edwy was intimate with two women, mother and daughter.

prophecy, was removed from human affairs, and carried by the hands of angels into Paradise. He was succeeded by Elfsin, bishop of Winchester, and in his place Brihtelm was ordained to the see of Winchester.

In the year 959, Elfsin, archbishop of Canterbury, while proceeding to Rome to obtain his pall, perished, frozen with ice and snow, upon the Alpine mountains. Edwy also, king of the West Saxons, after having reigned four years, departed this life at Winchester, and was buried in the new monastery there; on which he was succeeded in the kingdom by his brother, Edgar, king of Mercia, who was elected king by the people of all England, and united the kingdom, before divided, into one. This took place in the sixteenth year of his age, five hundred and ten years after the arrival of the Angles in Britain, and in the three hundred and sixty-third year after Saint Augustine and his companions had come to England.

Brihtelm, bishop of the people of Dorset,[66] was elected to the primacy of the see of Canterbury, but as he was not suited for an office of such importance, by command of the king he left Canterbury, and returned to the church which he had lately left. Upon this, by the Divine will, and the counsel of the wise, Saint Dunstan, the bishop of Worcester, was appointed primate and patriarch of the mother church of the English; by whom and other prudent men, Edgar, the king of the English, being becomingly instructed, he everywhere checked the wicked, reduced the rebellious under the yoke of correction, cherished the virtuous and modest, restored and enriched the churches of God that had been laid waste, and having removed all corruptions[68*] from the monasteries of the secular[69] clergy, gathered together multitudes of monks and nuns for the praise of the mighty Creator, and ordered more than forty monasteries to be erected for them. All these he honored as brethren, and cherished as most beloved sons, admonishing by his example the pastors whom he had set over them, to exhort them to live regularly and without reproach, to the end that they might please Christ and his saints in all things.

[66] Meaning bishop of Winchester, and not bishop of Dorchester, in Oxfordshire, of which Leowin was at this time bishop.

[68*] The word in the text is " venenis," perhaps too strong a word to be the correct one.

[69] In the original, " scholarium ;" probably a mistake for "secularium."

In the year 960, Saint Dunstan went to the city of Rome, in the third year of the indiction, and received the pall from pope John, and then returned to his country in the paths of peace.   In the lapse of a few months after this, he repaired to the royal threshold, and, knocking at the gate of the palace, with suggestions for the exercise of the royal piety and with most humble prayers, he entreated the king that he would promote to the honor of the bishopric of Worcester the blessed Oswald, the cousin of his own predecessor Odo, a monk noted for his piety, meekness, and humility, and who, by real experience, he had proved to wax strong in the Divine fear and in the holy exercise of virtue.   King Edgar assented to the requests of Saint Dunstan, and the blessed Oswald was installed by himself in the high priesthood.

In the year 963, on the death of Brihtelm, Saint Ethelwald, the venerable abbat,[70] who had been educated by the blessed Dunstan, received the bishopric of Winchester, and in the same year, by the king's command, the clergy[71] having been expelled, filled the old monastery with monks ; for he had especially persuaded the king, whose chief adviser he was, to expel the clergy from the monasteries, and to place in them monks and nuns.

In the year 964, Edgar the Peaceful, king of the English, took to wife Elfthritha,[72] the daughter of Ordgar, duke of Devonshire, after the death of her husband, Elfwold, the glorious duke of the East Angles; by whom he had two sons, Edmund and Egelred; he had also before this, by Egelfleda[73] the Fair, the daughter of duke Ordmar, Edward, afterwards king and martyr ; and by Saint Elfthritha,[74] he had a daughter, Editha, a virgin most strictly consecrated to God.

In the same year, the same king placed monks in the new monastery[75] and in that at Middleton, and over the former he appointed Ethelgar, over the latter, Kineward, abbats.

In the year 967, Edgar the Peaceful, king of the English,

[70] Of Abingdon.   [71] The secular clergy.

[72] More generally called Elfrida.   [73] More generally called Elfleda.

[74] She is called Wulfreda by Roger of Wendover and William of Malmesbury.   By the term, " sancta," our author would seem to imply that she was a nun ; but William of Malmesbury says, " it is certain that she was not a nun at that time. but being a lay virgin, had assumed the veil through fear of the king, though she was immediately afterwards forced to the royal bed."   Roger of Wendover gives the same account.   [75] At Winchester.

placed nuns in the monastery of Rameseie,[76] which his grand-father, king Edward the Elder, had built, and appointed Saint Merwinna abbess over them.

In the year 968, bishop Aldred died at St. Cuthbert's, in Cuneceastre,[77] and was succeeded in the bishopric by Elfsin.

In the year 969, Edgar the Peaceful, king of the English, commanded Saint Dunstan, archbishop of Canterbury, and the blessed Oswald, bishop of Worcester, and Saint Ethelwald, bishop of Winchester, to expel the secular clergy in the larger monasteries, that were built throughout Mercia, and to place monks in them. In consequence of this, Saint Oswald, having gained his wish, expelled from the monastery the clergy of the church of Worcester, who refused to assume the monastic habit; but those who consented to do so, the bishop himself ordained as monks, and appointed over them as prior,[78] Winsin, a man of great piety.

In the year 970, one hundred and ten years after his burial, in the fourteenth year of the indiction, on the ides of July, being the sixth day of the week, the relics of the holy and venerable bishop Swithin were removed from the place of their sepulture by Saint Ethelwald, the venerable bishop, Elstan, the abbat of Glastonbury, and Ethelgar, the abbat of the new monastery,[79] and were interred in the church of the apostles Saint Peter and Saint Paul.

In the year 971, the Clito Edmund, son of king Edgar, died, and was honorably interred in the monastery of Rameseie. Shortly after this, Ordgar, duke of Devonshire, the father-in-law of king Edgar, departed this life, and was buried at Exancestre.[81]

In the year 972, Edgar the Peaceful, king of the English, having completed the church of the new monastery, which had been begun by his father, king Edmund, caused it to be dedicated with all honor. Oskitel, the archbishop of York, having departed this life, his kinsman, Saint Oswald, the bishop of Worcester, was chosen archbishop in his room.

In the year 973, in the thirtieth year of his age, being the fifth year of the indiction, on the fifth day before the ides of May, being the day of Pentecost, Edgar the Peaceful, king of

[76] Ramsey.   [77] Chester-le-street.
[78] "Decanum," properly, "dean;" an older term, meaning the same as prior.   [79] At Winchester.   [81] Exeter.

the English, received the blessing from Saints Dunstan and Oswald, the archbishops, and from the other bishops of the whole of England, as the city of Accamann,[62] and was consecrated with very great pomp and glory, and anointed king.

In the lapse of a short time after this, sailing round the north of Britain with a large fleet, he came to the city of the Legions,[63] where, according to his command, his eight tributary kings met him, namely, Rinath, king of the Scots; Malcolm, king of the Cumbrians; Maccus, king of numerous islands; and five others—Dusnal, Sifreth, Huwald, James, and Inchil;[64] and there they swore that they would be faithful to him, and would be ready to assist him both by land and by sea.

On a certain day he embarked with them in a vessel, and they taking their places at the oars, he himself took the helm, and steered it skilfully according to the course of the river; and amid all the multitude of his chieftains and nobles who attended in similar vessels, he sailed from the palace to the monastery of Saint John the Baptist, where prayers having been offered up, he returned in the same state to the palace; on entering which, he is reported to have said to his nobles, that now at last each of his successors would be able to boast that he was king of the English, after he had enjoyed the display of such honors, so many kings paying obedience to him. In this year Saint Oswald received the pall from Stephen, the hundred and thirty-fourth pope.

In the year 974, there was a great earthquake throughout the whole of England.

In the year 975, king Edgar the Peaceful, the monarch of the English land, the flower and grace of the kings his predecessors, departed this life; not less worthy of remembrance among the English than Romulus among the Romans, Cyrus among the Persians, Alexander among the Macedonians, Arsaces among the Parthians, Charles the Great among the French, Arthur among the Britons. After having accomplished all things in a royal manner, he departed this life in the thirty-

[62] Bath: which by the Saxons was called Akemancester.

[63] Chester.

[64] These five subreguli, with their territories, are thus mentioned by Roger of Wendover—"Dusnal, king of Demetia (South Wales); Siferth and Huwall, kings of Wales; James, king of Galwallia; and Inkil, king of Westmoreland."

second year of his age, the nineteenth of his reign over Mercia and Northumbria, the sixteenth of his rule over all England, in the third year of the indiction, and on the eighth day before the ides of July, it being the fifth day of the week, leaving his son Edward heir to his kingdom and his virtues. His body was carried to Glastonbury, and there interred with royal honors.

He, during his lifetime, had collected together three thousand six hundred ships; and it was his custom every year, after the solemnities of Easter were concluded, to collect twelve hundred of these on the eastern, twelve hundred on the western, and twelve hundred on the southern coast of the island, and to row to the western side with the eastern fleet, and then sending that back, to row to the north with the western one; and again sending that back, to row to the east with the northern one; and in this manner it had been his usage every summer to sail around the whole island, manfully acting thus for the defence of his kingdom against foreigners, and for the exercise of himself and his people in military affairs.

But in the winter and spring it was his practice to pass along the interior of his kingdom throughout all the provinces of the English, and to see how his legal enactments, and his decrees and statutes, had been observed by the men in power. He was also accustomed to use every possible precaution that the poor might not receive detriment by oppression from the rich. Thus, in one respect, his object was military strength, in the other, justice; and in both he consulted the welfare of the people and of the realm. By reason of this he was held in fear by his enemies on every side, while he was endeared to those who were subjected to him; at his departure the whole kingdom was in a state of perturbation, and after a period of gladness, because the country flourished in peace in his days, tribulation began to arise in every quarter.

For Elpher, the duke of the Mercians, and many chief men in the kingdom, blinded by great bribes, expelled the abbats and monks from the monasteries in which king Edgar the Peaceful had placed them, and introduced there secular clergy with their wives; but the madness of this rash man was resisted by Ethelwin, the duke of East Anglia, a friend of God, and his brother Elfwold, and earl Britnoth, who holding a synod, declared that they could never allow the monks to be expelled from the kingdom, inasmuch as it was they who kept all religion within the realm ; after which, collecting an army, they defended the monasteries of East Anglia with the greatest determination.

While this was going on, a dissension about the election of a king arose among the nobles of the realm, as some favoured Edward, the son of the deceased king, and others his brother Egelred. For which reason the archbishops Dunstan and Oswald convened the bishops, abbats, and a great number of the nobles, and, having elected Edward, as his father had commanded, consecrated him, and anointed him king. In the autumn of this year a comet was seen.

In the year 977, a very great synod was held in East Anglia, at a town which is called Kirding.⁸⁵ After this, while another synod was being held at Calne, a royal town, the elders of all England, who were there assembled, fell from an upper chamber, with the exception of Saint Dunstan ; some of them were killed, while some with difficulty escaped death. In the year from the incarnation of our Lord 978, Edward, king of the Angles, was unrighteously slain by his people, by the command of his stepmother, Elfritha, at a place which is called Corvesgate,⁸⁶ and was buried without royal pomp at Wereham.⁸⁷ His brother, Egelred,⁸⁸ succeeded him, a distinguished prince, of elegant manners, beauteous countenance, and graceful aspect. He was consecrated king, at Kingestun, by the holy archbishops Dunstan and Oswald, and ten bishops, in the sixth year of the indiction, on the eighth day before the calends of May, being the Lord's day after the festival of Easter. Saint Dunstan, being filled with the spirit of prophecy, foretold to him that in his reign he would suffer much tribulation, in these words : " Because thou hast aspired to the kingdom through the death of thy brother, whom thy mother hath slain, hear, therefore, the word of the Lord ; thus saith the Lord, ' The sword shall not depart from thy house, but shall rage against thee all the days of thy life, and shall slay thy seed, until thy kingdom shall be transferred unto another

⁸⁵ A misprint for Kirtling, now Kirtlington, in Cambridgeshire. The subject discussed by the synod was the marriage of the priesthood.
⁸⁶ Corfe Castle, in Dorsetshire. ⁸⁷ Wareham.
⁸⁸ V. r. Etheired, by which name he is generally known.

kingdom, whose manners and whose language the people whom thou dost govern knoweth not; nor shall thy sin be expiated but by a prolonged vengeance, the sin of thyself, and the sin of thy mother, and the sin of the men who have shared in her unrighteous counsels.' " Therefore, after this, a cloud appeared at midnight throughout all England, at one time of a bloody, at another of a fiery, appearance, which afterwards changed to various hues and colours; it disappeared towards dawn.

In the year 979, Elpher, duke of the Mercians, came to Werham[89] with a multitude of people, and ordered the holy body of Edward, the precious king and martyr, to be taken up from the tomb, where many miracles had taken place. When it was stripped, it was found to be whole and entirely free from all corruption and contagion; it was then washed and arrayed in new vestments, and conveyed to Scaftesbirig,[90] and honorably buried there.

In the year 980, Southampton was ravaged by the Danish pirates, and almost all of its citizens either killed or carried away captives. Shortly after this, the same army devastated the isle of Tenedland.[91] In this year, also, the province of the city of the Legions[92] was laid waste by the Norwegian pirates.

In the year 981, the monastery of Saint Petroc[93] the confessor, in Cornwall, was ravaged by the pirates, who, the year before, had laid waste Southampton, and were then committing frequent ravages in Devonshire, and in Cornwall near the sea-shore.

In the year 982, three ships touched on the coast of the province of Dorset, and laid waste Portland. In this year the city of London was burned with fire.

In the year 983, Alpher, duke of the Mercians, a kinsman of Edgar, king of the English, departed this life, on which his son Alfric succeeded to the dukedom

In the year 984, Saint Ethelwold, bishop of Winchester, departed from this world to the Lord, in the second year of the indiction, on the calends of August; and was succeeded by Elphege,[94] abbat of Bath. He had assumed the religious habit at the monastery which is called Dehorhirst.[94*]

[89] Wareham.   [90] Shaftesbury.   [91] The isle of Thanet.
[92] Chester.   [93] Padstow.   [94] The second bishop of that name.
[94*] Deerhurst, near Gloucester.

In the year 986, by reason of certain dissensions, Egelred, king of the English, laid siege to the city of Rochester, but perceiving the difficulty of taking it, departed in anger, and laid waste the lands[95] of Saint Andrew the Apostle. Alfric, the duke of the Mercians, son of duke Alfer, was this year banished from England.

In the year 987, there occurred two plagues, unknown to the English nation in preceding ages, namely, a fever affecting the people, and a murrain among animals, which, in the English language, is called "Scitha," being a flux of the bowels; these greatly ravaged the whole of England, and affected both men and animals with great devastation, and, consuming the inner parts of the body, raged in an indescribable manner throughout all the territories of England.

In the year 988, Wesedport[96] was ravaged by the Danish pirates, by whom, also, Goda, earl of Devon, and Stremewold, a very brave warrior, were slain; but a considerable number of the enemy having been killed, the English became masters of the place.[97]

In the first year of the indiction, on the fourteenth day before the calends of June, it being the Sabbath, Saint Dunstan the archbishop departed this life, and attained a heavenly kingdom; in his stead Ethelgar, bishop of Selsey,[98] received the archbishopric, and held it one year and three months.

In the year 989, archbishop Aldred[99] died, and was succeeded by Aldune.

In the year 991, Gippeswic[1] was ravaged by the Danes. Their leaders were Justin, and Guthmund, the son of Steitan; with them, not long after this, Brithnoth, the brave duke of the East Saxons, engaged in battle near Meldun;[2] but, after a multitude on both sides had fallen, the duke himself was slain, and the Danish fortunes prevailed. Moreover, in this year, by the advice of Siric, the archbishop of Canterbury, and the dukes Ethelward and Alfric, a tribute, which consisted of ten

[95] Belonging to the bishopric of Rochester.
[96] Probably Watchet, in Somersetshire.
[97] "Loco fluminis" in the original; "fluminis" being probably an error for some other word.
[98] In Sussex.
[99] The same who just before is called Ethelgar.
[1] Ipswich.   [2] Maldon.

pounds,[3] was for the first time paid to the Danes, in order
that they might desist from the continued pillage, conflagrations, and slaughters of the people, of which they were repeatedly guilty near the sea-shore, and might observe a
lasting peace with them.

Saint Oswald the archbishop, on the sixth day before the
ides of November, being the third day of the week, consecrated the monastery of Rawele, which he and Ethelwin,
the duke of East Anglia, a friend of God, aided and comforted
by the Divine counsel and assistance, had erected.

In the year 992, being the fifth year of the indiction, on the
day before the calends of March, being the second day of the
week, Saint Oswald the archbishop departed this life before
the feet of the poor, where, according to his usual custom, he
was performing the Divine command,[4] in the manner he had
previously predicted, and attained the joys of the kingdom of
heaven ; he was buried in the church of Saint Mary, at Worcester, which he himself had erected from the very foundation.
He was succeeded by Adulph, the venerable abbat of Medeshampstead ;[5] and not long after the death of the blessed father
Oswald, duke Ethelwin, of illustrious memory, the friend
of God, departed this life, and was honorably buried at
Ramesege.[6]

In the year 993, the above-mentioned army of the Danes
took Bebbanburgh,[7] and carried off all they could find in it.
After this, they directed their course to the mouth of the river
Humber, and, having burned many towns and slain many persons in Lindesey and Northumbria, took considerable booty.
Against them a great number of the people of the district
collected with all haste; but when they were about to engage,
the leaders of the army, whose names were Frana, Frithe-
gist, and Godewin, because, on the fathers' side, they were of
Danish origin, betrayed their followers, and were the first to
set the example of flight. .

In the year 994, Anluf, the king of the Norwegians, and
Sweyn, the king of the Danes, arrived at London, on the day
of the nativity of Saint Mary, with ninety-four galleys, and

---

[3] The Anglo-Saxon Chronicle and Roger of Wendover say that it was
ten thousand pounds, which no doubt is the correct statement.
  [4] In washing the feet of the poor.
  [5] Peterborough.   [6] Ramsey.   [7] Bamborough.

immediately attempted to force an entrance and burn it : but by the aid of God and of His Mother, they were repulsed by the citizens, with no small loss to their army. Thereupon, being exasperated with rage and sorrow, on the same day they betook themselves thence, and first in Essex and in Kent, and near the sea-shore, and afterwards in Sussex and in the province of Southampton, they burned houses, laid waste the fields, and without respect to sex or age destroyed a very great number of people with fire and sword, and carried off a large amount of spoil ; at last, having obtained horses for themselves, furiously raging, they traversed many provinces to and fro, and spared neither the female sex nor yet the innocent age of infants, but, with the ferocity of wild beasts, consigned all to death.

Upon this, king Egelred, by the advice of his nobles, sent ambassadors to them, promising that he would give them tribute and provisions, on condition that they should entirely put an end to their cruelty. Assenting to this request of the king, they returned to their ships, and then the whole of the army assembled together at Southampton and passed the winter there. The provisions were provided for them by the whole of Wessex ; and by the whole of England the tribute, which amounted to sixteen pounds, was paid. In the meantime, by the command of king Egelred, Elphege, the bishop of Winchester, and the noble duke Ethelwald, proceeded to king Alaf, and, having given hostages, brought him with great honor to the royal town of Andeafaran,[8] where the king was staying.

He was honorably received by the king, who caused him to be confirmed by the bishop, and, adopting him as his son, presented him with royal gifts, on which he promised king Egelred that he would no more come with an army to England ; and, after this, he returned to the ships, and at the approach of summer returned to his own country, and carefully adhered to his promise.

In the year 995, Aldune, the bishop, removed the body of Saint Cuthbert from Cestre[9] to Dunholm.[10]

In the year 996, Elfric was consecrated archbishop of Canterbury.

In the year 997, the army of the Danes, which had remained

[8] Andover.   [9] Chester-le-Street.   [10] Durham.

in England, having sailed round Wessex, entered the mouth
of the river Severn, and at one time laid waste South Britain ;[11]
at another, Cornwall ; at another, Wesedport, in Devonshire ;
and, burning a vast number of towns, put multitudes of people
to the sword ; and after this, again going round Penwithsteort[12] up to the mouth of the river Tamar, their ships
having coasted along Devonshire and Cornwall, they disembarked from their ships, leaving them behind, and, there being
no one to prevent them, continued their conflagrations and
slaughter as far as Lideford.[13] In addition to this, they
burned the monastery of the primate, Ordulf, which is called
Taustoke,[14] and, laden with great booty, made their way back
to their ships, and wintered at that place.

In the year 998, the above-named army of the pagans, leaving the mouth of the river which is called Frome, repaired
again to Dorsetshire, and, after their usual manner, betook themselves to plundering ; and, as often as they took
up their quarters in the Isle of Wight,[15] levied supplies upon
Sussex and the province of Southampton.   Against such
an outburst as this, forces were often gathered together ; but,
as often as the English were about to engage in battle, either
through treachery or some misfortune, they turned their backs
and left the victory in the hands of the enemy.

In the year 999, the army of the pagans so often mentioned,
entering the mouth of the river Thames, passed up the river
Meodewege,[16] as far as Rochester, and for a few days laid strict
siege to it, upon which, the people of Kent, uniting together
to repel them, had a severe engagement with them ; but, after
many had been slain on both sides, the Danes remained masters
of the river.   After this, taking horse, the Danes laid waste
almost the whole of the western coast of Kent.   On hearing
of this, Egelred, the king of the English, by the advice of his

[11] South Wales.
[12] Of this place Lambarde says : " The country that lieth next the
point of Cornwall is to this day called Penwith ; and, therefore, the Saxons
adding ' steort,' which signifyeth a last of a region or promontory that
runneth narrow into the sea, called that cape Penwithsteort."
[13] A town in Devonshire, on the river Tamar.   [14] Tavistock.
[15] As a sample of the state of the text, this passage is thus printed :
" Et quotiescunque invecta jacuit de Suthsaxonia, et Suthamtunensi pro-
vinciâ sibi victum accepit."
[16] Medway.

principal men, collected together both a fleet and a land force. But, in the end, neither the land nor the naval force effected anything for the public good, beyond harassing the people, wasting money, and arousing the vengeance of the enemy.

In the year 1000, the above-mentioned fleet of the Danes invaded Normandy. Egelred, king of the English, laid waste the lands of the Cumbrians. He gave orders to his fleet, that, sailing round the north of Britain, it should meet him at a place named; but, being prevented by the violence of the winds, it was unable to do so. However, it laid waste the island which is called Monege.[17]

In the year 1001, the above-mentioned army of the pagans, returning from Normandy into England, entered the mouth of the river Exe, and shortly after commenced the siege of the city of Exancester; but, while attempting to destroy the walls, they were repulsed by the citizens, who manfully defended the city. Upon this, being greatly incensed, after their usual manner, they wandered through Devonshire, burning towns, ravaging the fields, and slaughtering the people; and, in consequence, the men of Devonshire and Somerset uniting together, gave them battle at a place which is called Penhou.[18] But the English, by reason of the small number of their soldiers, were not able to cope with the multitude of the Danes, and took to flight; whereon, the enemy having made a great slaughter, gained the day. After this, taking horse, throughout almost the whole of Devonshire they committed worse excesses than before, and, having collected much booty, returned to their ships. After this, they turned their course to the Isle of Wight; and, for a long time, there being no one to resist them, occupied themselves in plundering as usual, and raged to such a degree against the people with the sword, and against the houses with fire, that no fleet would dare to engage with them at sea, and no army by land. In consequence, the sadness of the king was far from slight, while the people were afflicted with incredible sorrow.

In the year 1002, Egelred, king of the English, having held a council with his chief men, thought proper to make peace with the Danes, and to give them provisions and tribute to appease them, in order that they might cease from their

[17] Mona, or Man.

[18] Penhoe; a place either in Somersetshire or Dorsetshire.

evil-doings.   For this purpose duke Leofsy was sent to
them, who, on coming, asked them to receive the supplies and
the tribute; whereupon they willingly received his embassy,
and acceding to his request, fixed the amount of tribute
that should be paid them for keeping the peace.   And, not
long after this, the sum of twenty-four pounds was paid them.

In the meantime, the same duke Leofsy slew Easig, a nobleman, the king's high steward, for which reason, the king,
being inflamed with anger, banished him from the country.
In the same year king Egelred took to wife Emma, called in
Saxon Elgiva, the daughter of Richard, the first duke of the
Normans.   In this, the twenty-fifth year of the reign of king
Egelred, and the fifteenth of the indiction, on the seventeenth day before the calends of May, being the fourth day of
the week, Ardulph, archbishop of York, the abbats, priests,
monks, and religious men being there assembled, raised the
bones of Saint Oswald, the archbishop, from the tomb, and
placed them, with due honor, in a shrine which he had prepared; and not long after this, that is to say, on the day
before the nones of May, he himself died, and was buried in
the church of Saint Mary, at Worcester, being succeeded by
the abbat Wulstan.

In this year, also, king Egelred ordered all the Danes who
lived in England, both great and small, and of either sex, to
be slain, because they had endeavoured to deprive him and
his chief men of kingdom and life, and to reduce the whole of
England under their dominion.

In the year 1003, by reason of the carelessness and treachery
of Hugh, the Norman earl, whom queen Emma had appointed
over Devonshire, Sweyn, king of the Danes, entered the city
of Exeter by storm and sacked it, destroying the walls from
the eastern as far as the western gate, and filling[19] his ships
with much spoil.   After this, while he was laying waste the
province of Wiltshire, a stout army manfully assembled from
the provinces of Southampton and Wiltshire, and went up
with fixed determination to fight against the enemy; but
when the armies were so near that the one could see the other,
Alfric, the above-named earl, who was at the time in command of the English, forthwith had recourse to his old

_____

[19] " Reperiit" is evidently a mistake for " replevit."

devices,[20] and, pretending illness, began to vomit, saying that a severe fit of illness had come upon him, and that in consequence he was unable to fight with the enemy.

When the army saw his inertness and timidity, in sorrow they turned away from the enemy without fighting, making good the ancient adage—"When the leader trembles in battle, all the other soldiers become still more fearful." Sweyn, on observing the irresoluteness of the English, led his army to Wilton, and spoiled and burned it; in like manner, he also ravaged Salisbury, and then returned to his ships.

In the year 1004, Sweyn, king of the Danes, coming with his fleet to Norwich, laid it waste and burned it. Upon this, Ulfketel, duke of East Anglia, a man of great activity, as Sweyn had come unawares, and he had had no time for collecting an army against him, after taking counsel with the chief men of East Anglia, made peace with him; but he, breaking the treaty the third week after, secretly stole forth from the ships with his forces, and attacking Theodford,[21] laid it waste, and after staying in it one night, burned it at daybreak. On learning this, duke Ulfketel gave orders to some men of the province to break up the ships of the enemy; but they were either afraid to do so, or neglected to obey his commands. He himself, however, as soon as he possibly could, having secretly collected an army together, boldly advanced against the enemy; and, on their return to the ships with an unequal number of soldiers, he met them, and had a most severe engagement with them; and many on both sides being slain, the most noble men of East Anglia fell, and the Danes escaped with difficulty. But if the full forces of the East Anglians had been present, the Danes could have never regained their ships; as, indeed, they themselves bore witness that they had never experienced in England a more severe and hard-fought battle than that in which duke Ulfketel had engaged with them.

In the year 1005, a severe and dreadful famine afflicted England. For this reason Sweyn, king of the Danes, returned to Denmark, with the intention of returning before long.

In the year 1006, Alfric, archbishop of Canterbury, departed this life, and was succeeded by Elphege, bishop of Winchester, who was succeeded in his bishopric by Kenulph. In the

[20] "Arces," a mistake for "artes."   [21] Thetford.

month of July an innumerable fleet of Danes arrived in England, and entered the port of Sandwich, and ravaging all places with fire and sword, first in Kent and then in Sussex, collected a very large quantity of spoil. On this, king Egelred assembled an army in Mercia and Wessex, and resolved to fight manfully with them ; but they would under no circumstances engage with him openly, but frequently committed their ravages, now in one place, and now in another, immediately, after their usual manner, retreating to their ships ; and in this way, throughout the autumn, they harassed the army of the English.

At length, on the approach of winter, as they were returning homeward with enormous booty, they repaired to the Isle of Wight, and remained there until the Nativity of our Lord ;[22] on the approach of which, as the king was at that period staying in the province of Shrewsbury, they made way through the province of Southampton to Berkshire, and burned Reading, and Wallingford, and Ceolesy,[23] with a great number of men. Moving thence, they passed Easterdune[24] and came to Cwichelmelow ;[25] returning from there by another road, the pirates provoked the natives of the place to battle, and at once engaging with them, put them to flight, and then retreated to the ships with the booty they had taken.

In the year 1007, by the advice of his chief men, Egelred, king of the English, sent ambassadors to the Danes, and told them that he was willing to give them sustenance and tribute, on condition that they should desist from their ravages, and keep a lasting peace with him ; to this request they consented, and from that time, provisions, and a tribute of thirty-six thousand pounds, were given to them from the whole of England. In this year, also, king Egelred made a certain Edric, whose surname was Streone, duke of the Mercians ; who, although he had Edgitha the king's daughter in marriage, was still frequently found, by his shifting craftiness, to be a perfidious traitor to his country, and a public enemy, as will appear in the sequel ; at last, in the reign of king Canute, he received a worthy reward for his treachery.

In the year 1008, Egelred, king of the English, ordered for

[22] Christmas Day.   [23] Cholsey.
[24] Ashdown, in the Anglo-Saxon Chronicle.
[25] The same place that is also called Ceolesy ; it is four miles from Wallingford, in Berkshire.

every one hundred and ten hides of land, one galley to be built, and for every nine,[26] a coat of mail and a helmet to be provided, and gave directions that ships should be built with all speed throughout the whole of England. These being prepared, he put on board of them picked soldiers, with provisions, and that they might protect the extremities of his kingdom from the incursions of the foreigners, collected them at the port of Sandwich. At this period, Brithric, the brother of the perfidious duke Edric Streone, a slippery, ambitious, and haughty man, unjustly accused before the king, Wulnoth,[27] a thane of the South Saxons, who shortly after took to flight to avoid being seized, and having obtained nine vessels, committed numerous ravages near the sea-shore.

But when word was brought to the royal fleet, that if any one wished, he might easily take him; Brithric, having collected eighty galleys, set out to give him chase; however, after he had sailed for some time with a fair wind, on a sudden a most violent tempest arose, and wrecked and shattered his ships, and threw them ashore, where they were shortly after burnt by Wulnoth. On this being known, the king with his chieftains and nobles returned home. But by his orders the fleet repaired to London, and thus this mighty labour of the people was wasted.

In the year 1009, the Danish earl Turkill came with his fleet to England, and afterwards, in the month of August, another innumerable fleet of the Danes, the chiefs of which were Hemming and Ailaf, came to the Isle of Tenedland,[28] and without delay united with the aforesaid fleet, after which both of them entered the harbour of Sandwich, and the men disembarking, hastily attacked the city of Canterbury, and began to storm it; but shortly after, the citizens of Canterbury, with the people of East Kent, suing for peace, obtained their request, and gave them, in consideration of a treaty of peace, three thousand pounds.

Upon this they returned to their ships, and steered their course to the Isle of Wight, and after that, according to their usual practice, frequently collected spoil in Sussex and in the

[26] Roger of Wendover and the Anglo-Saxon Chronicle say, "for every eight."
[27] The father of Earl Godwin. He was accused of treason.
[28] Thanet.

province of Southampton, in the neighbourhood of the sea-shore, and burned a great number of towns. On this, king Egelred collected an army throughout all England, and stationed it in the provinces adjoining the sea, as a protection against their incursions; but for all this, the enemy did not cease committing ravages in all quarters, according to the situation of the places. But upon one occasion, when they had made a descent for plunder at a greater distance than usual from the sea, and were returning laden with spoil, the king, attended by many thousands of armed men, got before them, prepared, as was all his army, to conquer or die.

But the perfidious duke Edric Streona, his son-in-law, used his endeavours in every way, both by treachery and ambiguous speeches, that they might not engage, but for that time let the enemy escape. To this he persuaded the king, and prevailed, and, like a traitor to his country, rescued the Danes from the hands of the English, and allowed them to escape; on which, taking a different direction, with great joy they returned to their ships. After the feast of Saint Martin, they arrived in Kent, and chose their winter quarters on the river Thames, and collected provisions in Essex and other provinces that were adjoining either bank of the river. They also frequently attacked the city of London, and endeavoured to take it, but were repulsed by the citizens, not without some little loss to themselves.

In the year 1010, the above-mentioned army of the Danes, in the month of January, disembarking from their ships, came through the forest which is called Cyltern,[29] into Herefordshire, and after laying it waste ravaged it with flames, and on their return collected booty on both banks of the river Thames. When they had been informed that an army was collected against them at London, and was about to engage with them, a part of the army passed over to the southern side of the river, at a place which is called Stane,[30] and having united and enriched themselves with abundance of spoil, proceeded through Surrey, and then returned to their ships, which during the season of Lent, while they were staying in Kent, they refitted.

After Easter, they came to East Anglia, and having disembarked near Gipeswic,[31] marched to a place which is called Rigmere, where they had learned that duke Ulfketel was en-

[29] Chiltern.   [30] Staines.   [31] Ipswich.

camped with his army, and fought a severe battle with him on
the third day before the nones of May. But while the battle
was being hotly contested, the East Angles turned their backs,
a certain thane of the king, a man of Danish origin, Turketel,
surnamed Merenheauod, being the first to begin the flight; but
the men of Cambridgeshire, manfully fighting, made a stout resistance, till at last, being overpowered, they took to flight.

In this battle fell Ethelstan, the king's son-in-law, Oswy, a
noble thane, together with his son, Wulfric the son of Leofwin,
Edwy, the son of Effuic, and many other noble thanes, and an
innumerable multitude. The Danes being masters of the field
of slaughter, gained possession of East Anglia; and taking to
horse, did not cease for three months ravaging the whole province, collecting booty, burning towns, and slaughtering men
and animals; after which they laid waste Thetford and
Grantebrige,[32] and burned them; having accomplished which,
the foot on board ship, and the cavalry on horseback, returned
again to the river Thames. After the lapse of a few days,
they again sallied forth to plunder, and made straight for the
province of Oxfordshire, and first ravaged it, and then the districts of Buckinghamshire and Bedfordshire, burning the
towns, and slaughtering the men and cattle, after which they
returned to their ships with vast booty.

After this, about the time of the festival of Saint Andrew
the Apostle, they committed to the flames Northampton and
its vicinity, as far as they pleased, and then crossed the river
Thames and entered Wessex, where, having consigned to the
flames Caning's-marsh,[33] and the greater part of the province
of Wiltshire, after their usual manner, they returned with great
booty to their ships about the Nativity of our Lord.

In the year 1011, on the northern side of the Thames, the
provinces of East Anglia, Essex, Middlesex, Herefordshire,
Buckinghamshire, Oxfordshire, Bedfordshire, Grantebrige-
shire,[34] the middle parts of Huntingdonshire, and the villages
of a great part of Northamptonshire, were ravaged; and on
the southern side of the river Thames, the provinces of Kent,
Surrey, Sussex, Southampton, Wiltshire, and Berkshire were
laid waste by the above-mentioned army of the Danes, with fire
and sword; upon which Egelred, king of the English, and the

[32] Cambridge.   [33] A large tract of land in Wiltshire.
[34] Cambridgeshire.

chief men of his kingdom, sent ambassadors to them to sue for peace, and request them to cease from their ravages, promising them provisions and tribute; on hearing which, not without treachery and dissimulation, as the event proved, they consented to his offer.

For, although food was provided for them in abundance, and tribute paid as much as they pleased, still, they did not desist from making incursions in straggling bodies throughout the provinces wherever they chose, laying waste towns, spoiling some wretched people of their property and slaying others.

In the same year, after having ravaged a great part of England, an army of the Danes, between the Nativity of Saint Mary and the feast of Saint Michael, drawing their lines around it, laid siege to the city of Canterbury. On the twentieth day of the siege, through the treachery of the archdeacon Elmer, whom Saint Elphege had before rescued from being condemned to death, a part of the city was burnt, and, the army effecting an entrance, the city was taken. Some were slaughtered with the sword, some destroyed by the flames. Many were also thrown from the walls, while some were put to death by being hung up by their secret parts. The women were dragged by their hair through the streets of the city, and then, being thrown into the flames, were thus put to death; infants were torn from their mother's breasts, and were either caught on the points of spears, or ground to pieces under the wheels of vehicles.

In the meantime archbishop Elphege was taken, bound in fetters, kept in confinement, and put to various torments. Ailmar, abbat of the monastery of Saint Augustine, was allowed to depart. Godwin, the bishop of Rochester, was also taken, and Leoufruna, abbess of the monastery of Saint Mildred, Elfrige, the king's steward, the monks also and secular clergy, and an innumerable multitude of either sex. After this, Christ's Church was sacked and burnt; a multitude of monks, and a crowd, consisting not only of men, but even women and children as well, were decimated, and nine were put to death, while the tenth was reserved alive: the amount of the decimated thus saved was four monks and eight hundred men. After the people had been slaughtered and the whole of the city burnt, archbishop Elphege was dragged forth in fetters, hurried along with violence, grievously wounded, and afterwards led away to the fleet and thrust into prison, where he was tortured for seven months.

In the meantime the wrath of God, waxing fierce against this murderous race, put an end to two thousand of them by a tormenting pain in the intestines. The others being attacked in a similar manner, were appealed to by the faithful, to make reparation to the archbishop, but refused to do so. In the meantime, the mortality increased, and at one time would put an end to ten, at another twenty, and at another a still greater number at the same instant.

In the year 1012, the perfidious duke Edric Streona, and all the chief men of England, assembled at London before Easter, and remained there until the tribute promised to the Danes, which consisted of forty-eight pounds,[35] was paid. In the meantime, on the holy Sabbath of the rest of our Lord, a proposal was made to archbishop Elphege by the Danes, that if he wished to preserve his life and liberty, he should pay three thousand pounds. Upon his refusal, they deferred his death until the next Sabbath, on the approach of which they were inflamed against him with great anger, both because they were intoxicated with excess of wine, and because he had forbidden that any thing should be given for his liberation. After this, he was brought forth from prison, and dragged before their council. On seeing him, they instantly sprang from their seats, struck him down with the butt ends of their axes, and overwhelmed him with stones, bones, and the skulls of oxen.

At length, a certain person, whose name was Thrum, and whom he had confirmed the day before, moved with pity at this wickedness,[36] struck him on the head with an axe, upon which he immediately fell asleep in the Lord, on the thirteenth day before the calends of May, and sent his soul exulting in the triumph of martyrdom to heaven. On the following day his body was carried to London, and being received with due honor by the citizens, was buried by the bishops Ednoth of Lincoln, and Alphune of London, in the church of Saint Paul.

After this, when the tribute had been paid and peace established with the Danes on oath, the Danish fleet which had been collected, dispersed far and wide; but five-and-forty ships remained with the king, and swore fealty to him, and

[35] Evidently a mistake for forty-eight thousand pounds, mentioned by Roger of Wendover and the Anglo-Saxon Chronicle.

[36] " Impiâ motus pietate," can hardly be a correct reading here.

promised that they would defend England, on condition of his giving them food and clothing.

In the year 1013, Living was appointed to the archbishopric of Canterbury. In the month of July, Sweyn, king of the Danes, arrived at the port of Sandwich with a strong fleet, and after remaining there a few days, took his departure, and sailing round East Anglia, entered the mouth of the river Humber, from which, entering the river Trent, he sailed up to Gainesburg,[37] where he pitched his camp. Without delay there made submission to him, first, earl Ucthred and the people of Northumbria and Lindesey, and after them the people of the Five Boroughs,[38] next all the people living in the district north of Watlingastrete, the road which the sons of king Wethle made through England, from the Eastern Sea to the Western; all these made submission, and having entered into a treaty of peace with him and given hostages, swore fealty to him, and were ordered to provide horses and food for his army.

These things being done, and the fleet with the hostages entrusted to his son Canute, he took chosen men as auxiliaries from those who had been surrendered, and made an expedition against the South Mercians. Having passed over Watlingastrete, he issued an edict to his followers that they should lay waste the fields, burn the towns, spoil the churches, slay without regard or mercy all those of the male sex who should fall in their hands, and reserve the females to satisfy their lust, doing all the mischief they possibly could.

They acting in this manner, and raving with the rabidness of wild beasts, he came to Oxford, and took it more speedily than he had previously expected; having received hostages, he passed on in haste to Winchester, and arriving there, the citizens, being alarmed, made peace with him without delay, and gave him hostages, such and as many as he demanded. Having received these, he moved on his army towards London; and great numbers of them being drowned in the river Thames, perished there, having never attempted to find either a bridge or a ford. On arriving at London, he endeavoured in many ways to capture it either by stratagem or by force.

[37] Gainsborough.
[38] These were Lincoln, Nottingham, Leicester, Stamford and Derby.

But Egelred, king of the English, with the citizens and the aid of the Danish earl, Turkill, so often mentioned, who was with him at the time, manfully defended the walls of the city, and held out against him. Being repulsed, he repaired first to Wallingford, then to Bath, ravaging and laying waste everything in his progress, according to his usual practice, and there he sat down with his forces to refresh them. Then came to him Athelmar, the earl of Devon, and with him the thanes of the west, and having made peace with him, gave him hostages. All these things being thus accomplished to his wish, on returning to his fleet, he was by all the people styled and considered king, although he acted in most respects in a tyrannical manner.

The citizens of London, also, sent hostages to him, and made peace with him; for they were afraid that his fury would be so inflamed against them, that, taking away all their possessions, he would either order their eyes to be put out, or their hands or feet to be cut off. When king Egelred saw this, he sent queen Emma by sea to Normandy, to her brother Richard, the second duke of Normandy, and her sons Edward and Elfred, together with their tutor, Elphune, bishop of London, and Elfsy, abbat of Medeshampstead.[39] But he himself remained for some time with the Danish[40] fleet, which lay in the Thames at a place called Grenwic;[41] and afterwards proceeding to the Isle of Wight, there celebrated the Nativity of our Lord; after which, he passed over to Normandy, and was honorably entertained by duke Richard.

In the mean time, the tyrant Sweyn ordered provisions to be prepared in abundance for his fleet, and an amount of tribute to be paid that could hardly be endured. In like manner, in all respects, earl Turkill ordered payment to be made to the fleet which lay at Grenwic. In addition to all this, each of them, as often as they thought proper, collected spoil, and did much mischief.

In the year 1014, the tyrant Sweyn, after innumerable and cruel misdeeds, which he had been guilty of either in England or in other countries, to complete his own damnation, dared to exact a heavy tribute from the town where lies interred the uncorrupted body of the royal martyr, Edmund; a thing that no one had dared to do before, from the time when that town[42]

---

[39] Peterborough.   [40] Qy. English?   [41] Greenwich.
[42] Bury St. Edmunds.

had been given to the church of the above-named saint; he repeatedly threatened, also, that if it was not quickly paid, beyond a doubt he would burn the town, together with the townsmen, utterly destroy the church of the martyr himself, and torment the clergy with various tortures. In addition to this, he even dared frequently to speak slightingly of the martyr himself, and to say that he was no saint at all. But, inasmuch as he was unwilling to put an end to his misdeeds, the Divine vengeance did not permit this blasphemer to live any longer.

At length, towards the evening of the day on which, in a general council which he had held at a place which is called Geagnesburt,[43] he had again repeated these threats, while surrounded with most numerous crowds of Danes, he alone beheld Saint Edmund coming armed towards him; on seeing whom, he was terrified, and began to cry out with loud shrieks, exclaiming, " Fellow-soldiers, to the rescue, to the rescue! behold Saint Edmund has come to slay me;" after saying which, being pierced by the Saint with a spear, he fell from the throne[44] upon which he was sitting, and, suffering great torments until nightfall, on the third day before the nones of February, terminated his life by a shocking death.

After his death, the fleet of the Danes elected his son, Canute, king. But the elders of the whole of England, with one consent, in all haste sent messengers to king Egelred, declaring that they loved no one, and would love no one, more than their own natural lord, if he would either rule them more becomingly, or treat them with more mildness than he had previously done. On hearing this, he sent his son, Edward, to them, with his deputies, and in a friendly way greeted his people, both great and small, promising that he would be to them a loving and affectionate lord, and would consult their wishes in all things, would listen to their advice, and with a forgiving temper pardon whatever had been said in abuse, or done in contradiction by them to himself or his family; if, on the other hand, they would be ready to restore him with unanimity and without guile, to his kingdom. To this they all made answer in kindly terms, and full friendship was

---

[43] Probably Gainsborough.

[44] "Emissario" is the word in the text, probably a mistake for some other word. "Missarius" means one that strikes or wounds; but if it is to be retained here, some other word is omitted.

established on either side, both by words and by pledge.   In
addition to this, the nobles unanimously made promise that they
would no more admit a Danish king into England.

On these things being concluded, a deputation was sent by
the English to Normandy, and the king was brought back in
all haste during the season of Lent, and received with due
honor by all.   In the meantime it was arranged by Canute
and the men of Lindesey,[45] that, procuring horses for the
army, they should make a descent for the purpose of plunder.   But, before they were prepared, king Egelred came
thither with a strong army, and, Canute with his fleet
being put to flight, laid waste the whole of Lindesey, and
ravaged it with fire, slaughtering all the inhabitants he could.
But Canute, at once taking safety in flight, directed his course
towards the south of England, and in a short time came to the
port of Sandwich, where he put on shore the hostages that had
been given to his father by the whole of England, and, having
cut off their hands, ears, and nostrils, allowed them to depart, and then set sail for Denmark, to return in the ensuing
year.   In addition to all these evils, king Edward ordered to
be paid to the fleet, which lay at Grenwic, a tribute which
amounted to thirty thousand pounds.

On the third day before the calends of October, the sea
overflowed its shores, and drowned a great number of towns
in England and numberless multitudes of people.

In the year 1015, while a great council was being held in
secret at Oxford, the perfidious duke Edric Streona, by stratagem enticed Sigeferth and Morcar, the sons of Earngrim, the
very worthy and influential thanes of the Seven Boroughs,
into his chamber, and there ordered them to be put to death.
King Egelred thereupon took possession of their property, and
ordered Aldgitha, the relict of Sigeferth, to be taken to the city
of Maidulph.[46]   While she was being kept in confinement there,
Edmund, the king's son, surnamed Ironside, came thither, and,
against the will of his father,[47] took her to wife, and, between
the feasts of the Assumption and the Nativity of Saint Mary,
set out for the Five Boroughs, and invading the territories of
Sigeferth and Morcar, subjected their people to himself.

[45] Roger of Wendover says that he had gained them over to his cause.
[46] Malmesbury.
[47] Roger of Wendover says, without his father's knowledge.

At the same time, Canute, king of the Danes, came with a great fleet to the port of Sandwich; and then, sailing round Kent, entered the mouth of the river Frome, and collected great booty in Dorsetshire, Somersetshire, and the province of Winchester.[48] At this period, because king Egelred lay sick at Corsham, the Clito Edmund, his son, acted in his behalf, and, with the duke Edric Streona, who was full of guile and treachery, collected a large army: but, when they had met together, duke Edric in every possible way laid snares for the Clito Edmund, and tried by treachery to cut him off. On Edmund learning this, they soon separated from each other, and left the place to the enemy. Not long after this, the same duke enticed away forty ships of the royal fleet, manned with Danish soldiers, and, going over to Canute, made submission to him. The men of Wessex did the same, and gave hostages, and afterwards provided horses for his army.

In the year 1016, Canute, king of the Danes, and the perfidious duke Edric Streona, with a large retinue,[49] crossed the river Thames at a place which is called Cricklade; and, on the approach of the Epiphany of our Lord, made a hostile irruption into Mercia, and laying waste many towns in the province of Warwick, burned them, and slew all the persons they could find. When the Clito Edmund, surnamed Ironside, heard of this, in all haste he collected an army; but, after it was brought together, the men of Mercia were unwilling to engage with the men of Wessex and the Danes, unless king Egelred and the citizens of London were with them. In consequence of this, the expedition was given up, and each one returned home.

After the festival was concluded, the Clito Edmund again formed a still greater army; after which, he sent messengers to London, to beg his father to meet him as soon as possible, with all the men he could find. But, after an army had been collected together, intimation was given to the king, that, if he did not take due precaution, some of his allies were about to betray him. The army was soon broken up in consequence, on which he returned to London; but the Clito proceeded to Northumbria. For which reason some thought that he still intended to form a greater army against Canute; but in the

[48] It ought to be " Wiltonensi," Wiltshire.
[49] V. r. " Equitatu," body of cavalry.

same way that Canute and Edric did on their part, so did he and Ucthred, the earl of Northumbria, lay waste some of the provinces. For first they ravaged Staffordshire, and next the provinces of Shrewsbury and Leicester, because they had refused to go out to fight against the army of the Danes.

In the meantime, Canute and Edric Streona laid waste, first the provinces of Buckinghamshire, Bedfordshire, Huntingdonshire, Northamptonshire, Somersetshire, and Nottinghamshire, and, afterwards, Northumbria. On hearing this, the Clito Edmund Ironside, pausing in his ravages, hastened to London to his father; while, on the other hand, earl Ucthred returned home with all speed, and, compelled by necessity, betook himself, with all the Northumbrians, to Canute, and gave him hostages; yet, for all that, either by his command or with his sanction, he was slain by Turebrand, a noble Dane, together with Turketel, the son of Navena. After his death, Canute appointed Eiric earl in place of Ucthred; and after that, returning in all haste to the south,[50] before the festival of Easter, with the whole of his army retreated to his ships.

At this period, in the fourth year of the indiction, on the ninth day before the calends of May, being the second day of the week, Egelred, king of the English, departed this life at London, after having in his life experienced great troubles and many tribulations, which Saint Dunstan had prophesied to him should come upon him for the death of his brother Edward, as I have mentioned under the first year of his reign. His body was becomingly buried in the church of Saint Paul.

After his death, the bishops, abbats, and most noble men of England met together and with one consent elected Canute their lord and king, and coming to him at Southampton, repudiated and rejected in his presence all the family of king Egelred, and made peace with him, and took the oaths of fealty to him; on which he swore to them that before God and men he would be a faithful master to them.

But the citizens of London, and a part of the nobles who were at that time staying there, with unanimous consent elected the Clito Edmund king, who, being thus elevated to the royal throne, fearlessly entered Wessex, and being received by all the people with great congratulations, reduced it very

[50] A various reading has here, "Edmund Ironside returning in all haste to the south by another road."

speedily to subjection; on hearing which, many of the people of England with alacrity voluntarily submitted to him. But Canute, in the meanwhile, about the time of the Rogation days, came up with all his fleet to London; and on arriving there, the Danes dug a great ditch[51] on the southern side of the Thames, and towed their ships along to the western side, after which, surrounding the city with a wide and deep trench, in strict siege they shut out all from either ingress or egress.   They also made frequent attempts to take it by storm; but, the citizens making a stout resistance against them, they were repulsed from the walls,; in consequence whereof, the siege being put off for a time, and a part of the army left to guard the ships, they hastened with all speed to Wessex, and gave king Edmund Ironside no time for collecting a large army.

However, with the army which in such a short period he had collected, relying on the aid of God, he boldly met them in Dorsetshire, and attacking them at a place which is called Penn,[52] near Gillingham, fought with them, and conquered, and put them to flight.   After this, midsummer being past, he again collected a still larger army than before, and resolved to engage boldly with Canute; this took place in Worcestershire, at a place which is called Eearstain,[53] where he drew up his army as the situation and his own strength would allow him, and placing all his best men in the front rank, the rest of the army he set in reserve; and then appealed to them, calling each by name, and exhorting and entreating them that they would bear in mind that they were fighting for their country, their children, their wives, and their homes; and, in the most encouraging language having kindled the spirits of the soldiers, he then ordered the trumpets to sound, and his troops to advance at a gentle pace.   The army of the enemy did the same.   When they had come to the spot where the battle was able to be commenced, with immense clamour they rushed on with hostile standards, and the combat was waged with lances

---

[51] This is supposed to have been commenced on the eastern side of London Bridge, at either Deptford or Rotherhithe, and running through the present St. George's Fields, to have entered the river at Vauxhall.

[52] It is wrongly called in the text " Peomum."

[53] Properly Sherston.   According to Hardy, this is supposed to have been a stone which divided the four counties of Oxford, Gloucester, Worcester, and Warwick.

and swords, and the engagement carried on with the greatest vigour. In the meantime, king Edmund Ironside fought bravely in the front rank, hand to hand, while giving all requisite orders. He himself fought most valiantly, and struck down many an enemy, at the same moment performing the duties of a valiant soldier and of a good general; but, inasmuch as his brother-in-law Edric Streona, that most perfidious duke, and Almar the beloved, and Algar, the son of Mehu, who ought to have been aiding him, together with the men of the provinces of Southampton and Wiltshire, and an innumerable multitude of people, were on the side of the Danes, his army had to struggle hard for victory.

However, on the first day of the week, Monday to wit, so severe and so bloody a battle was fought, that either army, from exhaustion being no longer able to fight, at sunset ceased of its own accord. Still, on the following day, king Edmund would have crushed all the Danes, if it had not been for the treachery of the perfidious duke Edric Streona. For, when the battle was at its height, and he saw that the English were prevailing, having cut off the head of a man, Osmer by name, who very strongly resembled king Edward in features and hair, raising it aloft, he exclaimed: "Englishmen! it is in vain you fight!" adding, "You men of Dorset, Devon, and Wiltshire, your chieftain is slain, — take to flight with all speed.⁵⁴ Behold the head of Edmund, your king! I hold it in my hand; give way, then, instantly!"

When the English heard this, they were more shocked at the atrocity of the deed than alarmed through belief in him who announced it. Hence it came to pass that the more unsteady ones were nearly taking to flight, but instantly, on it being found that the king was alive, they recovered their courage, and boldly rushing upon the Danes, slaughtered many of them, fighting with all their might until twilight, on the approach of which, as on the preceding day, they separated of their own accord. But when the greater part of the night had passed, Canute commanded his men to decamp in silence, and taking the road towards London, returned to the ships, and shortly after again laid siege to it.

On the next day, when king Edmund Ironside found that the Danes had fled, he returned into Wessex to collect a

⁵⁴ " Præcipites" seems a better reading here than " principes."

larger army. His brother-in-law, the perfidious duke Edric, seeing his valour, sought him again as his natural lord, and making peace with him, swore that he would continue faithful to him; upon which, with an army collected together for the third time, the king liberated the citizens of London from the siege, and drove the Danes to their ships. Two days after this, he passed over the Thames at a place which is called Brentford, to engage with the Danes for the third time; there he joined battle with them, and having put them to flight, gained the victory. On this occasion many men on the side of the English, while crossing the river without due precautions, were drowned. After this, the king hastened to Wessex, for the purpose of collecting a more numerous army; on which, the Danes again repaired to London, laid siege to it, and stormed it on every side; but, by the aid of God, they were unsuccessful.

Upon this, they returned thence with their fleet, and entered the river which is called Arewe,[55] and, landing from their ships, proceeded into Mercia for the purpose of plunder, after their usual manner slaughtering all they met, burning towns, and carrying off the spoil: after which, they returned to their ships, and the land forces were conveyed by sea to the river which is called Meodewege,[56] while the cavalry endeavoured to drive the live-stock, which formed part of their booty, by land.

In the meantime, king Edmund Ironside for the fourth time collected a valiant army throughout the whole of England, and passing over the Thames at the place[57] where he had done so previously, quickly entered Kent, and fought a battle with the Danes near Ottaford; on which, being unable to resist his attack, they turned their backs and fled with their horses to Scepege.[58] However, he slew all he could overtake, and had not the perfidious duke Edric Streona, with his treachery, withheld him at Eagleford,[59] from pursuing the enemy, he would that day have gained a complete victory. After returning into Wessex, Canute crossed over with his forces into Essex, and proceeded again to Mercia, for the sake of plunder, giving orders to his army to commit still greater excesses than before.

---

[55] The Orwell, in Suffolk.   [56] The Medway.
[57] Brentford.   [58] The Isle of Sheppey.   [59] Aylesford, in Kent.

On this, with the greatest alacrity, they obeyed his commands, and having slaughtered all who fell into their hands,
and burned a very great number of towns, and laid waste
the fields, greatly enriched, they repaired with all haste to
their ships.   Edmund Ironside, king of the English, pursuing them with an army which he had levied from the
whole of England, came up with them, as they were retreating, at a hill which is called Assendun,[60] that is to say, "the hill
of the ass."   There, with all expedition, he drew up his troops
in three divisions, and then going round each troop, exhorted
and entreated them, bearing in mind their ancient valour and
victories, to defend him and his kingdom from the avarice of
the Danes, and reminded them that they were about to engage
with those whom they had conquered already.

In the meantime, Canute slowly led his forces to a level
spot; while, on the other hand, king Edmund quickly moved
his line in the order in which he had drawn it up, and suddenly giving the signal, fell upon the Danes; on both sides
they fought with the greatest valour, and in every quarter
multitudes fell.   But that most perfidious and most wicked
duke, Edric Streona, seeing the line of the Danes wavering, and
the English likely to gain the victory, just as he had previously
arranged with Canute, took to flight with the people of Maiseveth[61] and the part of the army which he commanded, and
by treachery betrayed his lord, king Edmund, and the army
of the English.   There were slain in that battle duke Alfric,
duke Godwin, Ulfketel duke of East Anglia, duke Ethelward,
son of Ethelwin, the friend of God, duke of East Anglia, and
almost the entire mass of the nobility of England, which in
no battle ever sustained a greater wound than it did there.
Eadnoth, also, the bishop of Lincoln, and the abbat Wulsy,
who had come for the purpose of invoking the Lord on behalf
of the soldiers while waging the battle, were slain.

A few days having intervened after this, king Edmund
Ironside being still desirous to come up with Canute, while
the most iniquitous and treacherous Edric and some others
did not wish that to take place, they gave him advice to make
peace with Canute and divide the kingdom between them.
At length, though with some reluctance, he yielded to their
suggestions, and messengers going from one to the other, and

[60] Ashendon, in Essex.   [61] Radnorshire.

hostages being given on either side, the two kings met at a place which is called Deerhurst; Edmund pitched his camp with his men on the western bank of the Severn, while Canute encamped with his on the eastern side.

Upon this, the two kings were conveyed in boats[63] to the island called Olanege,[64] which is situate in the middle of the river; where[65] peace, friendship, and brotherhood having been established by pledge and by oath, the kingdom was divided. Then, after having exchanged arms and clothes, the tribute being agreed upon which should be paid to the fleet, they separated from each other. The Danes, however, returned to their ships with the spoil which they had collected, and the citizens of London made peace with them, paying a price for it, and allowing them to winter there.

After these things, in the fifteenth year of the indiction, about the time of the feast of Saint Andrew the Apostle, king Edmund Ironside died at London,[66] but was buried at Glastonbury, with his grandfather, king Edgar the Peaceful. After his death, king Canute ordered all the bishops and chieftains, and all the nobles and principal men of the English nation, to be assembled at London. When these had come before him, as though he did not know it, he cunningly asked those who had acted as witnesses between him and king Edmund when they made the treaty of friendship and partition of the kingdom between them, to what effect he and king Edmund had expressed themselves about the brothers and sons of the latter, as to whether it should be allowed the same to reign over the kingdom of Wessex after their father, in case Edmund should die while he was still living : on which they began to say that, beyond a doubt, they were quite certain that king Edmund neither living nor dying had bespoken any portion of the kingdom for his brothers. But, as to his sons, they said that they knew this, that king Edmund wished Canute to be their guardian and protector, until they should be of fit age to reign.

[63] "Trabariæ," the word used in the text, were boats like canoes, made out of a single piece of wood.   [64] Olney.

[65] According to Roger of Wendover and other historians, Edmund Ironside and Canute first engaged there in single combat.

[66] Roger of Wendover says at Oxford, where he was barbarously murdered by the son of Edric Streona.

But they, God testifying thereto, gave false testimony and treacherously lied, thinking both that Canute would prove more kind to them by reason of their falsehoods, and that they should gain great rewards from him; whereas, not long after, some of these false witnesses were slain by the same king. After having put the above question, king Canute received the oaths of fealty from the nobles above-mentioned; on which they swore to him that they willingly chose him for their king, and would readily obey him, and pay tribute to his army; and having received pledges from his bare hand, together with the oaths of the principal men among the Danes, they utterly disregarded the brothers and sons of king Edmund, and declared that they should not be their kings.

Now, one of the above-mentioned Clito's was Edwin the Excellent, a most revered brother of king Edmund, whom on that occasion, with most wicked counsels, they pronounced deserving of banishment. When, therefore, Canute had listened to the adulation of the persons above-mentioned, and the contempt in which they held Edwin, rejoicing, he entered his chamber, and calling to him the perfidious duke Edric, inquired of him in what way he might be able to beguile Edwin to the risk of his life; on which Edric made answer, that he knew a certain man named Athelward, who could very easily put him to death, with whom he should be able to have some conversation, and to whom he would offer a very considerable reward.

However, on learning the name of the man, the king cunningly sent for him, and said: "Thus and thus has duke Edric informed me, saying that you are able to beguile the Clito Edwin, so that he may be slain; do you only assent to my proposal, and obtain for me his head, and you shall enjoy all the honors and dignities of your forefathers, and shall be dearer to me than my own born brother." On this, he made answer that he was willing to seek for him in order that he might be slain, if in any way he could effect it: but, in reality, he did not wish to kill him at present, but, by way of excuse, made this promise: he was a person sprung from a most noble English family.

In this year king Canute obtained the rule of the whole of England, and divided it into four parts; Wessex he took for himself, East Anglia he gave to earl Turkill, Mercia to the perfidious duke Edric, and Northumbria to earl Eiric. He also made a treaty with the nobles and all the people, and they established by oath a firm friendship between them, and, laying them aside, set at rest all ancient enmities. Then, by the counsel of the perfidious duke Edric, king Canute banished the Clito Edwin, the brother of king Edmund, and Edwin,[67] who was styled " the King of the Churls;" but this Edwin was reconciled to the king. The Clito Edwin, however, being deceived by the treachery of those whom he had hitherto deemed to be most friendly disposed to him, at the request and entreaty of king Canute, was, the same year, without guilt on his part, put to death.

Edric also gave him this advice, that he should put to death the younger Clito's, Edward and Edmund, the sons of king Edmund ; but as it seemed to him a great disgrace for them to be put to death in England, after the lapse of a short time he sent them to the king of Sweden to be slain; he however, although there was a treaty between them, would by no means assent to his request, but sent them, for the preservation of their lives, to Salomon, king of the Hungarians, to be brought up; and one of them, namely, Edmund, in process of time, ended his life there. But Edward received in marriage Agatha, the daughter of the emperor, by whom he had Margaret, afterwards queen of the Scots, Christina, a virgin, who became a nun, and the Clito Edgar.

In the month of July, king Canute took to wife queen Emma, the widow of king Egelred, by whom he had a son, named Hardicanute, afterwards king, and a daughter, named Gunhilda, who was afterwards married to Henry, the emperor of the Romans.

In the year 1018, at the Feast of the Nativity of our Lord, while Canute was in London, he ordered the perfidious duke Edric Streona to be slain in his palace, because he feared lest he should be on some occasion betrayed by his treachery, just as his former masters Egelred and Edmund had been frequently betrayed. He also ordered his body to be thrown over the walls of the city, and to be cast out without burial ; together with him duke Norman, the son of duke Leofwin, and brother of earl Leofric, Ethelward, the son of duke Engelmar, and Brithric, the son of Elphege, earl of Devonshire, were slain without any guilt on their parts. In this year, by the whole of England, seventy-two pounds, and by London, four hundred and ten pounds,[68] were paid to the army of the Danes. Aldun,

[67] Properly Edwy.

[68] These numbers are manifestly wrong; the Anglo-Saxon Chronicle

bishop of Durham, departed this life, and a great battle was fought between the English and the Scots at Carre.[69] The English and the Danes came to an understanding at Oxford as to the observance of the laws of king Edgar.

In the year 1019, Canute, king of the English and of the Danes, crossed to Denmark, and remained there throughout the whole of the winter.

In the year 1020, king Canute returned to England, and at the festival of Easter held a great council at Cirencester. Edmund was appointed to the see of Durham, and Living, archbishop of Canterbury, departing this life, was succeeded by Agelnoth, who was called the Good, the son of Agelmar, a nobleman.   In the same year, the church which king Canute and earl Turketel had built on the hill which is called Assendun,[70] was dedicated in their presence with great honor and pomp by Wulstan, the archbishop of York, and many other bishops.

In the year 1021, Canute, king of the English and of the Danes, before the feast of Saint Martin, expelled the earl Turkill so often mentioned, together with his wife, Egitha, from England.   Algar, the bishop of East Anglia, departed this life, and was succeeded by Alfwin.

In the year 1022, Agelnoth, the archbishop of Canterbury, went to Rome, and being received by pope Benedict with great honor, the pall was given to him.

In the year 1023, the body of Saint Elphege the Martyr was transferred from London to Canterbury.   Wulstan, the archbishop of York, departed this life at York, on the day before the calends of July, being the third day of the week, but his body was carried to Ely, and there buried.   He was succeeded by Alfric, the prior of Winchester.

In the year 1026, Alfric, the archbishop of York, went to Rome, and received the pall from pope John.   Richard, the second duke of Normandy, departed this life; and was succeeded by Richard the Third, who died in the same year, being succeeded by his brother Robert.

In the year 1027, it having been intimated to the king of the English and of the Danes that the people of Norway greatly despised their king, Olaf, for his simplicity, mildness, justice

states the amount paid by the whole of England as 72,000 pounds, and that paid by the city of London, 10,500.

[69] Probably Carron.   [70] Ashendon, in Essex.

and piety, he sent to certain of them a great quantity of gold and silver, begging them, with many intreaties, that, having deposed and expelled him, they would become subject to him, and permit him to reign over them. Receiving, with great avidity, what he sent them, they ordered word to be sent him, that they were ready to receive him whenever he chose to come.

In the year 1028, Canute, king of the English and of the Danes, crossing over to Norway with fifty large ships, expelled king Olaf, and rendered it subject to himself.

In the year 1029, Canute, king of the English, of the Danes, and of the Norwegians, returned to England; and shortly after sent into exile Hacun, a Danish earl, on the pretext that he was sending him on an embassy, as he feared lest he should be deprived of his life by him. He was married to a noble woman, Gunhilda, the daughter of his own sister and of Wertgeorn, king of the Windi.

In the year 1030, the above-named earl Hacun perished at sea; some say that he was slain at this period in the island of Orkney. Saint Olaf, the king and martyr, son of Harold, king of Norway, whom king Canute had expelled, returning to Norway, was unrighteously slain by the Norwegians.

In the year 1031, Canute, king of the English, of the Danes, and of the Norwegians, set out with great state from Denmark for Rome, and presented to Saint Peter, the chief of the Apostles, vast gifts of gold and silver and other precious things, and obtained, at his request, from pope John, that the school of the English at Rome should be exempt from all tax and tribute; also, in going and returning he bestowed bounteous alms on the poor, and put an end to many barriers on the road where toll was exacted from strangers, by payment of a large sum of money; before the tomb of the Apostles he also made a vow to amend his life and manners.

In the year 1032, the church of Saint Edmund, the king and martyr, was dedicated. Conflagrations, almost unextinguishable, ravaged many places throughout England. Elphege, the bishop of Winchester, departed this life, and was succeeded by Elfwyn, the king's priest.

In the year 1033, died Leolf, bishop of the Wiccii,[72] a man of great piety and modesty, at the episcopal town of

[72] Worcester.

Kemeys.[73] He died on the fourth day before the calends of
September, being the third day of the week, and, as we have
reason to believe, departed to the kingdom of heaven; his body
was buried with due honor in the church of Saint Mary, at
Worcester.   To his see was elected Brithege, abbat of Pershore, son of the sister of Wulstan, the archbishop of York.

In the year 1034, Malcolm,[74] the king of the Scots, departed
this life, and was succeeded by Machetad.

In the year 1035, Canute, king of the English, just before
his death appointed his son, Sweyn, king of the Norwegians;
and of the Danes Hardicanute, his son by queen Emma; his
son Harold, whom he had by Elfgiva of Southampton, he appointed king of England; and shortly after, in the same
year, on the second day before the ides of November, being
the fourth day of the week, he departed this life at Shaftesbury, but was buried at Winchester, with all due honors,
in the old monastery there.   After his burial, queen Elfgiva,[75]
who was also called Emma, took refuge [76] at that place.

But Harold, on obtaining the royal dignity, sent his followers with all haste to Winchester, and took away from her, in a
tyrannical manner, the largest and best portion of the treasures
which king Canute had left her ; and after having spoiled her,
dismissed her, to take her seat there as she had previously done.
With the consent, also, of the greater part of the elders of
England he began to reign, as being the lawful heir; but
yet not with such power as did Canute, because [by some]
Hardicanute was looked for as being the more lawful heir.
For which reason, shortly afterwards, the kingdom of England
was divided by lot, and the northern part fell to Harold, the
southern to Hardicanute.   Robert, duke of the Normans, died,
and was succeeded by his son, William the Bastard, at a very
youthful age.

In the year 1036, the innocent Clito's Alfred and Edward,
the sons of Egelred, the former king of the English, crossed
over to England with a few ships from Normandy, where they
had remained for a long time with their uncle Richard, and,

[73] In Pembrokeshire.   [74] The Second.
[75] A suspicion is mentioned by some of the chroniclers that this woman
palmed off the children of a priest and a cobbler on Canute as his own.
She herself was the daughter of earl Elfelm.
[76] This was for protection from the violence of Harold.

attended by a great number of Norman soldiers, came to Winchester, to have an interview with their mother, who was staying at that place. This some of the men in power took amiss, and were indignant at it; because, although unjustly so, they were much more devoted to king Harold than to them, and especially, as it is said, the earl Godwin.

He, after having hurried on Alfred towards London for the purpose of an interview with king Harold, in obedience to his commands, detained him and placed him in close custody. Some of his attendants he dispersed, some he placed in chains, and afterwards put out their eyes; some he scalped and tortured, and deprived of their hands and feet, by cutting them off. Many, also, he caused to be sold, and by various and shocking deaths he put to death six hundred men at Guilford. But their souls, we believe, are now rejoicing in Paradise with the Saints, whose bodies, without cause, were so cruelly consigned to death on earth.

On hearing this, queen Emma in great haste sent back her son Edward, who had remained with her, into Normandy; whereupon, by the command of Godwin and certain others, the Clito Alfred was led in the most strict bonds to the isle of Ely; but as soon as the ship came to shore, on board of it, they instantly in the most cruel manner put out his eyes, and then, being led to the monastery by the monks, he was delivered into their charge; here, shortly afterwards, he departed this life, and his body was buried with due honor in the south porch on the western side of the church, while his soul enjoys the delights of Paradise.

In the year 1037, Harold king of the Mercians and Northumbrians, was chosen king by the nobles and the people, to reign over all England. But Hardicanute, because he stayed too long in Denmark and delayed coming to England as he had been requested, was entirely set aside, and his mother Elfgiva, who was also called Emma, the former queen of the English, at the beginning of the winter, was expelled from England without mercy, and shortly afterwards, passing over in a ship to Flanders, was received with honor by earl Baldwin. He, in the way that became such a man, as long as her need demanded it, willingly took care that all necessaries were provided her. In the same year, a short time before this, Avic, the prior of Evesham, a man of great piety, died.

In the year 1038, Egelnoth, archbishop of Canterbury, departed this life, on the fourth day before the calends of November, on the seventh day after whose death, Egelred, bishop of Sussex,[77] died: for he had asked of God, that he might not live long in this world after the death of his most beloved father Egelnoth. Grimketel succeeded Egelred in the bishopric, and Eadsy, the king's chaplain, succeeded Egelnoth as archbishop. In the same year also, died Brithege, the bishop of Worcester, on the fourteenth day before the calends of January, being the fourth day of the week, and was succeeded by Living.

In the year 1039, there was a very severe storm. Brithmar, bishop of Lichfield, died, and was succeeded by Wulsy. Hardicanute, king of the Danes, crossed over to Flanders, and visited his mother Emma.

[In the year 1040], Harold, the king of the English, died at London, and was buried at Westminster; after his burial, the nobles of almost the whole of England sent ambassadors to Hardicanute at Bruges, where he was staying with his mother, and thinking that they were acting rightly, entreated him to come to England, and receive the sceptre of the kingdom. Having prepared forty ships, and equipped them with Danish soldiers, before midsummer he arrived in England, and was joyfully received by all, and shortly after elevated to the throne of the kingdom. But, during the period of his reign, he did nothing worthy of the royal dignity. For as soon as he began to reign, not forgetting the injuries which his predecessor Harold, (who was supposed to be his brother), had done either to him or to his mother, he sent Elfric, archbishop of York, earl Godwin, Stir, master of the household, Edric, his keeper of the purse, Thrond, his executioner, and other men of high rank to London, and ordered them to dig up the body of Harold, and cast it into a swampy place. After it had been thrown up on shore there, he ordered it to be dragged out, and to be cast into the river Thames. But a short time after, it was taken up by a certain fisherman, and carried off in haste by the Danes, and honorably buried by them in the burying ground which they had at London.

These things being done, king Hardicanute ordered eight marks to be paid by the whole of England to each rower, and twelve to each pilot of his fleet, a tribute so heavy, that

[77] Bishop of Selsey.

hardly any person was able to pay it.   In consequence of this,
to all who, before his arrival, greatly wished for it, he became exceedingly odious.   Added to this, he was extremely exasperated against earl Godwin, and Living, the bishop of Worcester, for the death of his brother Alfred, Alfric, the archbishop
of York, and certain others being their accusers.   He therefore
took away the bishopric of Worcester from Living, and gave it
to Alfric ; but in the following year he took it from Alfric, and
restored it, with marks of kindness, to Living, with whom he
had become reconciled.

But Godwin, to make his peace, presented to the king a galley
or ship, of exquisite workmanship, having a gilded beak, provided with the choicest equipments, and fitted out with splendid
arms and eight hundred[78] picked soldiers.   Each one of these
had on his arms bracelets of gold, weighing sixteen ounces, a
triple coat of mail, a helmet on his head partly gilded, a
sword girt to his loins with a gilded hilt, a Danish battle-axe
ornamented with gold hanging from the left shoulder, in his
left hand a shield, the boss and studs of which were gilded,
and in his right a lance, which in the English language is
called " Ategar."

In addition to this, he made oath before the king, and almost
all the nobles and most dignified thanes of England, that it
was neither by his advice or concurrence that his brother had
been deprived of his sight, but that his lord, king Harold, had
ordered him to do what he did do.

In the year 1041, Hardicanute, king of the English, sent the
servants of his household throughout all the provinces of the
kingdom, to collect the tribute which he had ordered.   A
sedition arising in consequence, two of them, Feader and Tur-
stan by name, were slain by the people of the province of Worcester and the citizens, in the upper room of a tower in the
monastery of Worcester, whither they had fled for the purpose
of concealment; this took place on the fourth day before the
nones of May, being the second day of the week.   In consequence of this, the king, being aroused to anger, for the purpose
of avenging their death, despatched thither, Thuri, earl of Mid-
Anglia, Leofric, earl of Mercia, Godwin, earl of Wessex, Si-

---

[78] " Octingesimo " in the text.   Eighty, spite of the eight hundred of
Roger of Wendover, is much more probable.

ward, earl of Northumbria, Rome, earl of Maiseveth,[79] and the earls of the whole of England, and nearly all his own household servants, with a great army, Alfric then being bishop of Worcester; these he sent thither, with orders to slay all they could, and, after plundering the city, to set it on fire and lay waste the whole province.

A short time after the feast of All Saints, they began to lay waste the city and the province, and ceased not to do so for four days; however, they took and slew but few of the citizens or provincials, because, their approach being known beforehand, the provincials had taken to flight in various directions; but a multitude of the citizens had fled for refuge to a certain little island, situate in the middle of the river Severn, which is called Beverege, and, having thrown up fortifications there, stoutly defended themselves against their enemies, until peace was restored and they had free liberty to return home. On the fifth day, therefore, after the burning of the city, every man returned home laden with considerable spoil, and the king's anger was immediately appeased. Not long after this, Edward, the son of Egelred the former king of the English, came to England from Normandy, where he had been in exile many years, and being honorably entertained by his brother, king Hardicanute, took up his residence at his court.

In the year 1042, Hardicanute, king of the English, was present at a banquet, at which Osgod Clapa, a man of high rank, was marrying his daughter Gyta, to Tuvy, a Dane, and a very influential man, at a place which is called Lamtithe;[80] while in merry mood, and in perfect health and good spirits, he was enjoying the hilarity of the nuptials by the side of the bride, and standing up, was drinking to certain men, he suddenly fell to the earth with a dreadful shock, and remaining speechless, expired on the sixth day before the ides of July, being the third day of the week, and being carried to Winchester, was buried near king Canute, his father.

Upon this, his brother Edward, by the especial aid of earl Godwin and Living, the bishop of Worcester, was elevated to the dignity of king, at London; his father was Egelred, whose

---

[79] Radnorshire.
[80] Lambeth, in Surrey. This event took place at Clapham, which was formerly in the parish of Lambeth.

father was Edgar, whose father was Edmund, whose father was Edward the Elder, whose father was Alfred.

In the year from the incarnation of our Lord 1043, on the first day of Easter, being the nones of April, Edward was anointed king at Winchester, by Eadsy, archbishop of Canterbury, and Alfric, archbishop of York, and nearly all the other bishops of England.

In the same year, after the feast of Saint Martin, the king, with Leofric, Godwin, and Siward attending him, suddenly proceeded from the city of Gloucester to Worcester, and following the advice which they had given him, took away from his mother all the valuables she had, consisting of gold, silver, jewels, precious stones, and other things; either because before he had been made king, or since then, she had given him less than he required, and had been extremely harsh towards him.

Edmund, bishop of Durham, having departed this life, he was succeeded by Egelric, Siward being at that time earl of Northumbria.

In the year 1044, Alword, bishop of London, who, both before he was bishop, and in the time of his episcopate, was abbat of the monastery of Evesham, being unable to perform the duties of the see by reason of his infirmities, wished to reside at Evesham, but the brethren of that place would by no means consent thereto. Consequently, taking away most of the books and ornaments that he had given to that place, and as some say, some things that other persons had given, he retired to the monastery of Ramsege,[81] and gave to Saint Benedict all that he brought; there he took up his abode, and dying there in the same year, on the eighth day before the calends of August, being the fourth day of the week, he was buried at that place.

At a general synod, which at this time was held at London, a religious monk of Evesham, who had also been a monk in the Isle of Man,[82] was chosen abbat of Evesham, and was ordained on the fourth day before the ides of August, being the sixth day of the week. In the same year, the noble matron Gunhilda, the daughter of king Wertgeorn and of the sister of king Canute, who was left a widow after the

[81] Ramsey.

[82] "Qui et Manni," are the words in the text; but they are most probably not the correct reading.

death of earl Hacun and Harold, with her two sons, Hemming and Turkil, was expelled from England. Proceeding to Flanders, she resided for some time at a place which is called Bruge,[83] and then went to Denmark.

In the year 1045, Brithwold, bishop of Wiltshire,[84] departed this life, and was succeeded by Herman, the king's chaplain, a native of Lorraine. In the same year, Edward, king of the English, assembled a very strong fleet, at the port of Sandwich, against Magnus, king of Norway, who was making preparations to invade England ; but a war being waged against himself by Sweyn, king of the Danes, it put an end to the expedition.

In the year 1046, on the tenth day before the calends of April, being the Lord's day, Living, bishop of the Wiccii,[85] and of Devonshire and Cornwall, died ; after whose death the bishopric of Crediton and Cornwall was immediately given to Leofric, a Briton,[86] the king's chancellor ; and Aldred, who was first a monk of Winchester, and afterwards abbut of Tavistock, received the bishopric of the Wiccii.[87] In this year Osgod Clapa was banished from England. Magnus, king of Norway, the son of king Olaf the Saint, having put to flight Sweyn king of the Danes, subdued the country of Denmark.

In the year 1047, the snow fell, in the west of England, in such vast quantities, that it even broke down the woods. Aldwin, bishop of Winchester, departed this life, on which Stigand was raised to the see. Sweyn, king of the Danes, sent ambassadors to Edward, king of the English,[88] on which earl Godwin advised the king to send him at least fifty ships, equipped with soldiers ; but because this advice did not seem good to earl Leofric and all the people, he was not willing to send him any. After this, Magnus, king of Norway, attended with a large and powerful fleet, fought a battle with Sweyn, and, after many thousands had been slain on both sides, expelled him from Denmark ; after which, he reigned over that country as well, and compelled the Danes to pay him a small tribute, and not long after, died.

[83] Bruges.

[84] Bishop of Ramesbury ; which see was afterwards removed to Salisbury.

[85] Worcester. [86] A native of Wales.

[87] The meaning is, that the bishopric of Worcester was divided into two ; that of Crediton being formed from it.

[88] The text has here, " Norreganorum," of the Norwegians," evidently a mistake.

In the year 1048, Sweyn regained possession of Denmark, and Harold Harfager, who was the son of Siward, king of Norway, and, on the mother's side, brother of Saint Olaf, and on the father's side, uncle to king Magnus, returned to Norway, and shortly after sent ambassadors to Edward, king of the English, and offered to him, and received in return, assurances of peace and friendship. On the calends of May, being the Lord's day, there was a great earthquake at Worcester, in the county of the Wiccii, at Derby, and at many other places; a mortality among men and animals prevailed throughout many of the provinces of England, and fires in the air, commonly called woodland[89] fires, destroyed towns and crops of standing corn in the province of Derby, and some other provinces.

In the year 1049, Leo began to reign,[90] the hundred and fifth pope; he was the pope who composed the new Gregorian chaunt. The emperor Henry collected an innumerable force against Baldwin, earl of Flanders, especially because he had burned his palace at Nimeguen, and, most beauteous as it was, destroyed it. Pope Leo took part in this expedition, and a great number of noblemen and grandees of many nations. Sweyn, king of the Danes, as the emperor had commanded him, was there also with his fleet, and on this occasion took the oaths of fealty to the emperor, who sent also to Edmund, king of the English, and requested that he would not allow Baldwin to escape, if he should attempt to do so by sea. In consequence of this, the king went with a large fleet to the port of Sandwich, and remained there until the emperor had obtained of Baldwin every thing he required.

In the meantime, earl Sweyn, the son of earl Godwin and Gytha, who had formerly left England, (because he was not allowed to marry Edgiva, abbess of the monastery of Leominster, whom he had debauched), and had gone to Denmark, returned with eight ships, and, dissembling, declared that he would, in future, continue faithful to the king. Earl Beorn, who was the son of the Danish earl Ulph, the uncle of Sweyn, the son of Spralling, the son of Urse, promised him that he would obtain his request of the king, and that his earldom should be restored to him.

Therefore, after earl Baldwin had made peace with the emperor, the earls Godwin and Beorn, with the king's permission, came with forty-two ships to Pevensey; but the rest of the

89 Silvaticus.　　　90 Leo the Ninth.

fleet he ordered to return home, retaining only a few ships
with him.   When word was brought to the king that Osgod
Clapa lay at Ulps with twenty-nine[91] ships, he recalled as
many as he could of the ships that he had sent away; on
which, Osgod, having fetched away his wife, whom he had
sent to Bruges, returned to Denmark with six ships; but
the others, going to Essex, returned, carrying off no little
booty from the neighbourhood of Eadulph's Promontory.
But in returning, they were overtaken by a violent storm,
which sank them all, except two, that were taken in the parts
beyond sea, when all were slain who were found on board of
them.   While these things were going on, earl Sweyn came
to Pevensey, and with deceitful intent, requested his cousin,
earl Beorn, to go with him to the harbour of Sandwich, and,
as he had promised, reconcile the king to him.

Beorn, trusting in his relationship, and taking with him but
three companions, set out with him; on which, Sweyn took him
to Bosanham,[92] where his ships were, and putting him on board,
instantly ordered him to be strongly fettered, and kept him
there with him until he came to Dartmouth, where having
slain him, and thrown him into a deep ditch, and covered him
with earth, the six ships left him; two of which were shortly
afterwards taken by the men of Hastings, who, having slain
those on board of them, carried the ships to Sandwich, and
there presented them to the king.   Sweyn, however, flying to
Flanders, with two ships, remained there until Aldred, the
bishop of Worcester, brought him back, and reconciled the king
to him.

In the same year, at the request of the abbat Herimar, a
man of exemplary piety, Saint Leo the pope came to France,
having in his retinue the governor and all the dignitaries of
the city of Rome, and dedicated the monastery of Saint Remigius, the apostle of the Franks, which had been built at
Rheims, with the greatest pomp; and afterwards held a
great synod of archbishops, bishops, and abbats, in that city,
which lasted six days; to which synod was sent, by Edward,
king of the English, Aldwin, a monk of Ramsey, and abbat
of the monastery of Saint Augustine.

In the year 1050, Machetad, the king of Scotland, sent money

[91] The Anglo-Saxon Chronicle says thirty-nine.
[92] Bosham, in Sussex.

to Rome, for the purpose of distribution. Edsy, archbishop
of Canterbury, departed this life, and was succeeded by Robert,
bishop of London, a Norman by birth. Herman, bishop of
Wiltshire,[93] and Aldred, bishop of Worcester, set out for Rome.
In the year 1051, Alfric, who was also called Putta, archbishop of York, died at Southwell, and was buried at Medes-
hamburgstede,[94] being succeeded by Kinsy, the king's chaplain.
In this year, king Edward freed the English from the heavy tax,
in the thirty-eighth year after his father, king Egelred, had
first ordered it to be paid for the Danish soldiers.

After these things, in the month of September, Eustace the
Elder, earl of Boulogne, who had married the sister of king
Edward, (Goda by name, arrived at Canterbury with a few
ships. Here[95] his soldiers, while stupidly and awkwardly in
quest of lodgings for themselves, killed one of the citizens;
on which, a fellow-citizen of his, being witness of this,
avenged him, by slaying one of the soldiers. On this, the
earl and his men, being greatly enraged, slaughtered a great
number of men and women with their arms, and trod down
children and infants under their horses' hoofs. But when
they saw the citizens running together to resist them, disgracefully taking to flight, they escaped with difficulty, after seven
of their companions had been slain, and fled to king Edward,
who was then at Glavorne.[96]

Earl Godwin being indignant at such things taking place
in his earldom, and greatly inflamed with anger, in his own
earldom, that is to say, in Kent, Sussex, and Wessex, and
his eldest son Sweyn in his, namely Oxford, Gloucestershire, Herefordshire, Somersetshire, and Berkshire, and his
other son Harold in his, namely, the provinces of Essex,
East Anglia, Huntingdon, and Grantebrigge,[97] collected an innumerable army; which however did not escape king Edward.
Consequently, sending messengers in all haste to Leofric, earl
of the Mercians, and Siward, earl of Northumbria, he begged
them to make haste and come to him with all they could as-
semble, as he was placed in great jeopardy.

93 Of Ramesbury.   94 Peterborough.
95 The Anglo-Saxon Chronicle and Matthew of Westminster represent
this as taking place at Dover, after the return of Eustace from Canterbury,
where he had stopped to refresh himself.   The Anglo-Saxon Chronicle
places the event in 1048.   96 Gloucester.   97 Cambridge.

However, they came at first with a few only ; but when they knew how the matter stood, they sent through their earldoms swift messengers on horseback, and collected a large army.   In like manner, earl Rodulph, son of Goda, sister of king Edward, collected as many as he could in his earldom.   In the meantime, Godwin and his sons, after the nativity of Saint Mary, coming with their forces into the province of Gloucester, pitched their camp at a place which is called Langeto, and sending ambassadors to the king at Gloucester, under the threat of making war, demanded the surrender of earl Eustace, and his allies as well, both Normans and men of Boulogne, who had taken possession of the castle on the hill of Dover.

In consequence of this, the king was for the moment greatly alarmed, and, being afflicted with great anguish, was utterly at a loss to know what to do ; but when he understood that the army earls Siward, Leofric, and Rodulph were approaching, he determinedly made answer that he would on no account give up Eustace and the others who were demanded ; on hearing which, the messengers returned empty-handed.   After their departure the army entered Gloucester, being prepared for battle with such hostile and resolute spirit, that they wished to engage immediately with earl Godwin's army, if the king would permit them.   But, inasmuch as the best men in all England were assembled together on his side and theirs, it seemed to earl Leofric and some others, to be the more prudent part not to begin a battle with their fellow-countrymen ; but they proposed that, exchanging hostages, the king and Godwin should, on a day named, meet at London for a conference.

This counsel being approved of, and messages interchanged, and hostages given and received, the earl returned into Wessex ; but the king assembled a more numerous army from the whole of Mercia and Northumbria, and led it with him to London.   On the other hand, Godwin and his sons came to Southweore,[98] with a great multitude of the men of Wessex ; but, as his army had gradually diminished, he did not dare to come to the conference with the king, but on the approach of night, took to flight.   Wherefore, next morning, the king in council, and by the unanimous consent of his army, pronounced sentence of banishment against him and his five sons ; on which he, with his wife Githa, and Tosti,

[98] Southwark.

with his wife Juthitha, daughter of Baldwin, earl of Flanders, and two other of his sons, Sweyn and Girth, repaired to Tornege, where his ships were in readiness. Hastily placing on board as much gold and silver and other precious things as they were able to carry, and embarking with all speed, they directed their course to Baldwin, earl of Flanders. Moreover, Harold and Leofwin, his sons, going to Bristol, embarked on board a ship which their brother Sweyn had provided for himself, and crossed over to Ireland. The king, on account of the anger which he entertained against her father Godwin, repudiated queen Edgitha, and sent her ignominiously with a single attendant to Werewell, where he gave her into the custody of the abbess.

After these things had thus happened, William, duke of the Normans, with a multitude of his subjects, came to England, and, with his attendants, was honorably entertained by king Edward, who afterwards dismissed him, on his return to Normandy, with great and numerous presents.

In the year 1052, Elfgiva, or Emma, the former queen, and wife of kings Egelred and Canute, departed this life at Winchester, on the second day before the nones of March, and was buried there. In the same year, Griffin, king of Wales, ravaged a great part of the province of Hereford; the people of the province, and a considerable number of Normans, went out from the castle against him, but, after slaying many of them, he gained the victory, and carried off with him considerable spoil. This battle was fought on the same day that, thirteen years before, the Welch had slain Edwin, the brother of earl Leofric.

Shortly after this, earl Harold and his brother Leofwin returned from Ireland, and entering the mouth of the Severn with a great number of ships, landed at the confines of Somerset and Devon, and laid waste many towns and fields in those parts. Against them a great number of the people of Somerset and Devon went out, but Harold defeated them, slaying more than thirty noble thanes of their number, together with many others; after which he returned to his ships with the spoil, and then sailed round Penwithsteort.[99]   Upon this, king Edward, with all expedition, sent forty ships, supplied with provisions and picked soldiers, to the port of Sandwich, and ordered them to

[99] Land's End.

await the approach of earl Godwin, and be on the look-out;
but, in spite of this, unknown to them all, returning with a
few ships, he landed in Kent, and secretly sending messengers,
enticed to his assistance the people of Kent, and afterwards
the people of Sussex, Essex, Surrey, and all the mariners of
Hastings and of all the parts near the sea-shore, besides some
others; all these with one voice declared that they were ready
to live or die for him.

When this became known to the king's fleet that lay at the
port of Sandwich, it set out in pursuit of him, on which he
took to flight, and escaped, concealing himself in whatever place
he could. But the king's forces returned to the port of Sandwich, and from there repaired to London. On learning
this, earl Godwin returned to the Isle of Wight, and sailed
near the shore until his sons Harold and Leofwin came with
their fleet; and when they had met they desired from plunder
and rapine, only, when necessity demanded it, taking provisions for their troops. Enticing to their assistance all the
people they could in the vicinity of the sea-shore and in
other places, and picking up all the mariners they met with,
they steered their course towards the port of Sandwich, their
arrival at which place was reported to king Edward, who
was at this period staying at London. Despatching messengers with all speed, he sent word to all who had not revolted from him, that they must come to his assistance with
the greatest haste; but being very slow in their movements,
they did not come in time.

In the meantime, earl Godwin coming up the Thames with
his fleet against the tide, on the day of the exaltation of the
Holy Cross, being the second day of the week, came to South-
weorc,[1] and waited there until flood-tide. Meanwhile, by
means of messengers, he convened certain of the citizens
of London whom he had previously brought over by various
promises, and caused nearly all of them to wish entirely
as he would have them. After this, all things being arranged
and set in order, on the flood-tide coming, with all speed
they heaved their anchors, and no one on the bridge opposing them, sailed up the river close to the south shore. The
land forces also came, and putting themselves in battle
array on the bank of the river, presented a dense and terrible

line of battle; after which, the fleet turned towards the north shore, as it was its intention to surround the king's fleet. For the king had both a fleet and a numerous land army; but because both with the king and with Godwin there were very few who had any spirit (so greatly did almost all the English abhor fighting against their own kindred and fellow-countrymen), the consequence was, that all the more prudent men on either side, effecting a reconciliation between the king and the earl, bade the army lay aside their arms. The following morning the king held a council, and fully restored to Godwin and his wife and all his sons, with the exception of Sweyn, their former honors.

He, being moved with penitence, because, as previously mentioned, he had slain his cousin Beorn, journeyed from Flanders to Jerusalem, barefoot, and on his return thence, having contracted a disease from the excessive cold, died in Lycia. Edgitha, also, his queen, the daughter of the earl, the king received with due honor, and restored her to her former dignity.

Peace and concord being thus established, to all the people they promised good laws, and banished all the Normans who had instituted unjust ones, and had pronounced unjust judgments, and had given the king bad counsel against the English. Some few, however, namely, Robert Le Dragon, and his son-in-law, Richard the son of Scrobi, Alfred, the king's master of the horse, Aufrid, surnamed Ceokesfot, and some others whom the king loved more than the rest, and who had preserved their fidelity to him and all the people, they allowed to remain in England. But Robert, the archbishop of Canterbury, William, the bishop of London, and Ulph, the bishop of Lincoln, with difficulty escaping with their Normans, crossed the sea; however, on account of his virtues, William was shortly after recalled and reinstated in his bishopric.

Osborn, however, surnamed Pentecost, and his companion, Hugh, surrendered their castles, and, with the permission of earl Leofric, passing through his earldom, repaired to Scotland, where they were received by Machetad,[2] king of the Scots. In the same year, on the night of the feast of Saint Thomas the Apostle, there was a wind so strong and violent that it blew down many churches and houses, and broke numberless trees, or tore them up by the roots.

[2] The king who is more generally known as Macbeth.

In the year 1053, the brother of Griffin, king of South Wales, whose name was Rees, on account of the frequent depredations which he had committed, was slain by command of king Edward, at a place called Bulendun,[3] and his head was brought to the king at Gloucester, on the vigil of the Epiphany. In the same year, when the second day of the festival of Easter was being celebrated, a dreadful calamity befel earl Godwin at Winchester, while, as usual, he was sitting at table with the king. For, being suddenly attacked by a fatal malady, he sunk down on his seat bereft of speech: on seeing which, his sons, Harold, Tosti, and Girth, carried him into the king's chamber, hoping that, after a little while, he would recover from the attack; but he, being deprived of all strength, departed this life on the fifth day after, being the seventeenth day before the calends of May, and was buried in the old monastery there. He was succeeded in the dukedom by his son Harold, whose earldom was given to Algar, the son of earl Leofric.

In the year 1054, Siward, the valiant earl of Northumbria, by command of king Edward, invaded Scotland, with both an army of horse and a strong fleet, and fought a battle with Macbetad, king of the Scots; and, after many thousands of the Scots, and all the Normans, of whom mention has been made above, were slain, put him to flight, and gave the crown to Malcolm, son of the king of the Cumbrians, as king Edward had commanded. But in this battle his own son,[4] and many of the English and Danes, were slain.

On the death of Godwin, the abbat of Winchcomb, Alred, bishop of Worcester, on the feast of Saint Kenelm, appointed abbat in his room (Godric, the son of Godman, the king's chaplain. After this, the same bishop was dispatched on an embassy, with costly presents, to the emperor; by whom, and Herman, archbishop of Cologne, he was entertained with great honor, and remained with them a whole year; on the king's behalf, he also suggested to the emperor to send ambassadors to Hungary, and bring back his cousin, the son of king Edmund Ironside, and procure his return to England.

In the year 1055, Siward, earl of Northumbria, died at

York, and was buried at the monastery of Galmanho,⁵ which he had founded, and his earldom was given to Tosti, the brother of duke Harold.

A short time after this, a council was held in London, and king Edward outlawed earl Algar, the son of earl Leofric, without any blame on his part; who immediately went to Ireland, and, having procured eighteen piratical ships, returned, and going to Griffin, king of the Welsh,⁶ begged that he would aid him against king Edward; on which he, immediately collecting from the whole of his kingdom a numerous army, requested Algar, with his forces, to meet him and his army at a place named. Having met, they entered the province of Hereford, for the purpose of laying waste the territories of the English; whereupon the timid duke Rodulph, nephew of king Edward, collecting an army, met them two miles from the city of Hereford, on the ninth day before the calends of November. He ordered the English, contrary to their usage, to fight on horseback; but, just when they were about to engage, the duke, with his Franks and Normans, was the first to take to flight, which the English seeing, followed their leader's example.

Nearly the whole of the enemy pursued them, and slew of them four or five hundred men, and wounded a great number; after which, having gained the victory, king Griffin and earl Algar entered Hereford, and, having slain seven canons who had defended the doors of the principal church, and having burnt the monastery (which bishop Athelstan, the true worshipper of Christ, had built), with all its ornaments, and the relics of Saint Egelbert, the king and martyr, and of other Saints, and having slain some of the citizens and taken many prisoners, and spoiled and burnt the city, they enriched themselves with a vast amount of plunder.

After this, the king commanded an army to be levied in England, and, assembling it at Gloucester, gave the command of it to the valiant duke Harold, who followed them, and, boldly entering the territories of the Welch, pitched his camp beyond Straddele. But they, being aware that he was a brave man and a warlike commander, did not dare to join battle with him, but fled into South Wales; on discovering which, he dispatched

⁵ An abbey, afterwards incorporated with St. Mary's, at York.
⁶ North Wales.

thither the greater part of his army, and commanded them,
if necessity demanded it, manfully to resist the enemy. Returning with the rest of his troops to Hereford, he surrounded it with a deep trench, and fortified it with gates
and bars.

In the meantime, messages being interchanged, Griffin,
Algar, and Harold, and those who were with them, met at a
place which is called Billigesleage,[7] and, peace being granted
and received, agreed upon a lasting friendship between them.
This being settled, the fleet of earl Algar proceeded to
Chester, and there awaited the pay that had been promised
it; but he himself went to the king, and received back from
him his earldom. At the same period, Tremerin, the bishop of
Wales,[8] a religious man, departed this life. He had for a long
time been the coadjutor of Athelstan, bishop of Hereford, after
he himself had become unable to perform the duties of the
bishopric; for, during a period of thirteen years, he was deprived of his eyesight.

Herman, the bishop of the province of Wiltshire, being
annoyed because the king was unwilling to allow the transfer
of the see from the town which is called Ramnebirig[9] to the
abbey of Malmesbury,[10] resigned the bishopric, and, crossing
the sea, assumed the monastic habit at Saint Bertin's, and remained at the monastery there three years.

In the year 1056, the emperor Henry died at Rome, and
was succeeded by his son Henry. Athelstan, the bishop of
Hereford, a man of great sanctity, departed this life on the
fourth day before the ides of February, at the town which is
called Bosanbrig, and his body being taken to Hereford, was
buried in the church there, which he had built from the
foundation. He was succeeded by Leonegar, the chaplain of
duke Harold, who, in the same year, on the sixteenth day
before the calends of July, was slain at the place which is
called Glastingeberie,[11] together with his clergy, and the sheriff
Agelnoth, and many others, by Griffin, king of the Welsh.
He enjoyed the bishopric eleven weeks and four days.

After his death, the bishopric of Hereford was given in
charge to Aldred, bishop of Worcester, until a bishop should
be appointed. Afterwards, the same bishop, and the nobles

---

[7] Or Bilsley.   [8] Of Saint David's.   [9] Ramesbury.
[10] Roger of Wendover says Salisbury.   [11] Glastonbury.

Leofric and Harold, reconciled Griffin, king of the Welsh, with
king Edward. Earl Agelwin Oddo,[11*] the lover of churches,
the supporter of the poor, the defender of widows and orphans,[12]
the guardian of chastity, having received the monastic habit
a month before his death from Aldred, bishop of Worcester,
died on the second day before the calends of September, at
Deorhirst, but being honorably buried in the monastery of
Pershore, rests there. Algeric, the bishop of Durham, having of
his own accord resigned the bishopric, retired to his own monastery, which is called Burgh,[13] where he was educated, and became a monk, and lived there twelve years. He was succeeded
in the bishopric by his brother, Egelwin, a monk of the
monastery.

In the year 1057, the Clito Edward, son of king Edmund
Ironside, according to the command of his uncle, king Edward, came to England from Hungary, whither, as previously
mentioned, he had long before been sent into banishment.
For the king had determined to make him heir to the kingdom
in succession to himself; but, shortly after he had arrived,
he departed this life at London. Leofric, the praiseworthy
earl, and of happy memory, son of duke Leofwin, departed
this life at a good old age, at his own town, which is called
Bromleage,[14] on the second day before the calends of September, and was honorably buried at Coventry: which monastery,
among the other good works which he did in his lifetime, he
himself and his wife, the noble countess Godiva, a worshipper
of God, and a devoted lover of Saint Mary ever a virgin, had
built with their patrimonial possessions from the very foundation, and abundantly endowed it with lands, and so enriched
it with various ornaments, that in no monastery throughout
the whole of England could such a quantity of gold, silver,
jewels, and precious stones be found, as was at that period contained therein.

The monasteries, also, of Leominster and Wenlock, and of
Saint John the Baptist, and Saint Werburgh the Virgin, at
Chester, and the church which Eadnoth, bishop of Lincoln,
had built at the famous place which, in English is called

[11*] Earl of Devon.
[12] This seems to be intended as the meaning of the word " pupillorum"
here.   [13] Burgh, near Stamford.   [14] Bromley.

Stow Saint Mary,[15] in Latin the place of Saint Mary, they enriched with precious ornaments : the monastery of Worcester, also, they endowed with lands, and that of Evesham with buildings, and enriched it with various ornaments and lands. The wisdom of this earl, so long as he lived, greatly benefitted the kings and all the people of England : he was succeeded in his dignities by his son, Algar.

Hecca, the bishop of the South Saxons,[16] died, and in his place Egelric, a monk of Christ's church in Canterbury, was chosen bishop.

In the year 1058, Algar, earl of Mercia, was outlawed by king Edward the Second, but, by the aid of Griffin, king of the Welsh, and the assistance of a fleet of the Norwegians, which unexpectedly came to aid him, he speedily regained his earldom by force. Aldred, bishop of Worcester, with becoming honor, dedicated the church which he had built in the city of Gloucester, from the foundation, in honor of Peter the chief of the Apostles ; and afterwards, with the king's permission, appointed Wulstan, who had been ordained by himself a monk of Worcester, abbat there. Then, resigning the charge of the bishopric of Wiltshire,[17] which had been entrusted to him to govern, and restoring it to Herman, who has been previously mentioned, he went beyond sea, and set out for Jerusalem by way of Hungary, a thing that no archbishop or bishop of England is known to have done till then.

In the year 1059, Nicolas, bishop of the city of Florence, was elected pope, and Benedict was expelled.

In the year 1060, Henry, king of the Franks, departed this life, and was succeeded by his eldest son, Philip. Duduc, bishop of Wells, died, and was succeeded by Gisa, the king's chaplain ; they were both natives of Lorraine. Kinsy, archbishop of York, died at York, on the eleventh day before the calends of January, and being carried to the monastery which is called Burgh, was honorably interred there. In his room, Aldred, bishop of Worcester, was chosen archbishop, on the Nativity of our Lord ; and the bishopric of Hereford, which had also been conferred on him by reason of his zeal, was given to Walter, a native of Lorraine, the chaplain of queen Edgitha.

In the year 1061, Aldred, archbishop of York, set out for Rome with earl Tosti, and received the pall from pope Nicolas.

[15] In Lincolnshire.   [16] Of Selsey, in Sussex   [17] Ramesbury.

In the meantime, Malcolm, king of the Scots, boldly laid waste Northumbria, the earldom of his sworn brother, Tosti, having violated the peace[18] of Saint Cuthbert at Eilond. In the same year, pope Nicolas departed this life, and Alexander, being chosen the hundred and forty-ninth pope, succeeded him.

In the year 1062, Wulstan, a venerable man, was appointed bishop of Worcester. Beloved by God, he was a native of the province of Warwick in the kingdom of Mercia, and sprung of pious parents, Eastan being the name of his father, and Wulfgiva of his mother; he was trained in literature and the ecclesiastical duties, at the noble monastery which is called Burgh; indeed, both his parents were so extremely zealous in the cause of piety, that long before the end of their lives, making a vow of chastity, they separated from each other, and rejoiced to end their days in the holy garb of the monastic order. The young man, led by their example, his mother in especial persuading him to it, left the world, and in the same monastery at Worcester, in which his father before him had served God, received the monastic habit and ordination from the venerable Brithege, bishop of that church, by whom he was ordained both deacon and priest. Immediately, therefore, at the very onset, he embraced a life of severe discipline and entirely devoted to the practice of piety, and speedily became a wonderful example in watching, fasting, praying, and all kinds of virtues. In consequence of this, by reason of the rigidness of his morals, he was first chosen for some time master and guardian of the novices; after which, on account of his intimate acquaintance with ecclesiastical duties, he was, by the mandate of the seniors, appointed both chaunter and treasurer of the church.

Having now gained an opportunity of more freely serving God, by reason of the guardianship of the church being entrusted to him, he gave himself up wholly to a life of contemplation; both day and night he devoted himself either to prayer or to reading the Scriptures, and subdued his body by fasting two or three days together; he practised holy vigils to such an extent, that not only day and night, but even sometimes, a thing that we could hardly have credited, if we had not heard it from his own mouth, even four days and nights together

[18] Probably meaning that he had ravaged some of the lands belonging to the church of Saint Cuthbert, or the see of Durham.

he would pass without sleep, and thus incur danger through the brain being almost dried up, had he not hastened to satisfy nature by a hurried sleep. At length, when, by the power of nature he was compelled to sleep, he did not refresh his limbs in slumber by means of bed or bedclothes, but, upon a bench in the church, supporting his head with the book from which he was praying or reading, he would recline for a short time.

At length, on the death of Egelwin, prior of the monastery, this venerable man was chosen by bishop Aldred, prior and father of the fraternity. This office he discharged most laudably, far from relaxing the severity of his former life, but on the contrary increasing it in many ways, that he might thereby afford to the others an example of good living. Afterwards, in the course of some years, on the election of the abovenamed Aldred, bishop of Worcester, to the archbishopric of York, the unanimous consent both of the clergy and of the whole of the people fixed upon him, king Edward having given them leave to choose as their bishop whomsoever they pleased.

It so happened that, on this occasion, the legates of the Apostolic See were present at his election, namely, Armenfred, bishop of Sion, and another, who, having been sent by pope Alexander to Edward, king of the English, on ecclesiastical business, by the royal orders resided at Worcester throughout nearly the whole of Lent, waiting there for an answer to be given to their legateship, when a royal court was held at the ensuing Easter. These persons, while staying there, were witnesses of his laudable life, and not only gave their sanction to his election, but even encouraged in every way both the clergy and the people to that course, and by their authority confirmed the election.

He however, on the other hand, most obstinately refused, and exclaimed, that he was not worthy, and even affirmed with an oath that he would much more willingly assent to his decapitation than to the acceptance of so high an office.

When, therefore, he had been often attended by several religious men on this question, and could not by any means be persuaded to give his consent, he was at length severely rebuked for his disobedience and obstinacy, by Wulsy, a recluse, and a man of God, who was known then to have passed more than forty years of his life in solitude. Alarmed, also, by a Divine warning, with the greatest sorrow of heart he was compelled to give his consent, and having accepted the bishopric, was consecrated on the Lord's day on which was celebrated the nativity of Saint Mary,[19] and by his life and virtues shone forth as an illustrious bishop of the see of Worcester. He was consecrated, however, by Aldred, the archbishop of York, as at this period the episcopal duties of Stigand, the archbishop of Canterbury, were suspended by our lord the pope, because he had presumed to accept the archbishopric while Robert, the archbishop, was still living ; however, his canonical profession was made to Stigand, the abovenamed archbishop of Canterbury, and not to Aldred, who ordained him.

In addition to this, the archbishop of York, who ordained him, was by the agency of Stigand, and on account of the charges made by his followers, ordered to declare before the king and the nobles of the realm, that he from that time forward did not wish to claim any secular authority or ecclesiastical rights over him, either because he had been consecrated by him, or because before the consecration he had been a monk under him.[20] This ordination took place when he was more than fifty years of age, it being the twentieth year of the reign of king Edward, and the fifteenth of the indiction.

In the year 1063, Harold, the valiant duke of Wessex, by the command of king Edward, after the Nativity of our Lord, took with him a small body of horse, and set out from Gloucester, where the king was then staying, in great haste for Rhyddlan,[21] for the purpose of slaying Griffin, king of Wales, on account of the frequent ravages which he committed in the English territory, and the disgrace which he so frequently caused to his lord, Edward. But he, on learning beforehand the approach of Harold, embarked on board ship with his family, and with some difficulty made his escape. Harold, on finding that he had fled, set fire to his palace, and, burning his ships with their equipments, returned on the same day. But, about the Rogation Days, setting sail with a fleet from Bristol, he sailed round a great part of the coast of Wales, and was met by his brother, earl Tosti, with a body of horse, as the king had commanded, on which, joining their forces, they began to ravage those districts. The Welch being, consequently, compelled to do so, gave hostages, and made submission, and

---

[19] The 8th of September.
[20] When he was prior of the monastery of Worcester.
[21] In Flintshire.

promised that they would pay tribute, and outlawed their own king, Griffin.

In the year 1064, Griffin, king of the Welch, was slain by his people on the nones of August, and his head, and the head of his ship with its ornaments, was sent to duke Harold, who afterwards presented them to king Edward. After this, king Edward gave the country of the Welch to his brothers, Blethogent and Rithwalan; on which, to him, and to duke Harold, they took the oath of fealty, and that at their command they would be ready for them both by land and by sea, and would obediently render all things that had been rendered before from that land by its former kings.

In the year 1065, the venerable man, Egelwin, bishop of Durham, raised from his tomb the bones of Saint Oswin, formerly king of Bernicia, in the monastery which is near Tynemouth, four hundred and fifteen years after his burial, and with great honor enclosed them in a shrine.

Harold, the brave duke of Wessex, in the month of July, ordered a great building to be erected in the country of the Welch, at a place which is called Portaseith,[22] and many things for eating and drinking to be there collected, that his lord, king Edward, might be enabled to stay there some time, for the sake of hunting. But Caradoc, the son of Griffin, king of the South Welch, whom a few years previously Griffin, king of the North Welch, had slain on invading his kingdom, came thither on the day of Saint Bartholomew the Apostle, with all he could muster, and slew nearly all the workmen together with those who inspected them, and carried off all the good things that were collected there.

After this, on the fifth day before the nones of October, being the second day of the week, the thanes of Northumberland, Dunstan, son of Agelnoth, and Gloniern, son of Eardulph, came from Gamelbarn to York, with two hundred soldiers; and, in revenge for the shameful death of the Northumbrian nobles, the thanes Cospatric (whom queen Egitha, for the sake of her brother Tosti, had ordered to be treacherously assassinated in the royal palace, on the fourth night of the Nativity of our Lord), and Gamel, the son of Orm, and Ulph, the son of Dolphin, whom, in the preceding year, earl Tosti had treacherously ordered to be slain at York, in his

22 Portheswet, near Chepstow.

own chamber, while a treaty of peace existed between them, as also by reason of the exorbitant tribute which he had unjustly levied from the whole of Northumbria, on the same day, first slew his Danish household servants, Amund and Ravensweare, whom they stopped in their flight outside of the walls of the city, and, on the following day, two hundred men of his court, on the northern side of the river Humber, and then broke open his treasury, and, carrying off all that was there, took their departure.

After this, almost all the people of that earldom, assembling together, met Harold, the duke of Wessex, and the other persons whom, at the request of Tosti, the king had sent to them for the purpose of making peace, at Northampton. First there, and afterwards at Oxford, on the day of the Apostles Saint Simon and Saint Jude, on Harold and many others attempting to reconcile them to earl Tosti, they all with one voice refused, and pronounced him an outlaw, together with all those who had encouraged him to enact unjust laws, and, after the feast of All Saints, with the aid of earl Edwin, expelled Tosti from England; on which, together with his wife, he forthwith repaired to Baldwin, earl of Flanders, and passed the winter at Saint Omer. By the king's command, Morcar was appointed earl over the people of Northumbria.

After these things, king Edward began gradually to sicken, and, on the Nativity of our Lord, held his court at London, as well as he was able, and with great glory caused the church, which he himself had erected from the foundation, in honor of Saint Peter the chief of the Apostles, to be dedicated on the day of the Holy Innocents.

In the year from the incarnation of our Lord 1066, king Edward the Peaceful, son of king Egelred, that honor to the English, departed this life at London, in the fourth year of the indiction, on the vigil of the Epiphany of our Lord, being the fifth day of the week, after having held the kingly authority over the Anglo-Saxons twenty-three years, six months, and twenty-seven days; and, on the following day, he was buried with royal honors, and most bitter was the grief of all then present, and attended with plenteous tears.

After his burial, the viceroy Harold, son of earl Godwin, whom, before his decease, the king had appointed his successor, was elevated to the throne by all the chief men of Eng-

land, and was on the same day, with due honor, consecrated
king by Aldred, the archbishop of York.

Respecting the miracles which God, who is ever wonderful
and glorious in his Saints, deigned to work for Saint Edward,
the king and confessor, during his life, a few words are here an-
nexed.   On a certain day, while the said king lay prostrate in
prayer before the altar at Westminster, during the celebration
of the mass, he saw in a vision, as though the king of the
Danes had prepared a great ship, for the purpose of a hostile
invasion of England; but, when he was about to enter from
a boat into the larger ship, he slipped down between them
and sank, immediately on which his ship went to pieces.   On
seeing this miracle, the blessed king Edward smiled, and gave
exceeding thanks to God.   On this, the bishop, who was cele-
brating the mass, was afraid that the king had seen something
about him in the celebration thereof to cause his laughter.
Consequently, after the mass was finished, the bishop, having
called together earl Harold and, others of the king's nobles
who were then present, anxiously asked the king why he had
smiled during the celebration of the mass; on which, the king
related to him the vision he had seen; and the day and hour
being marked, they sent messengers to Denmark, and found
that it had happened to the king of the Danes just as king
Edward had predicted.

Another story relative to the same king.   One day, when the
before-named Edward, king of the English, was on a journey,
there met him John, the blessed Apostle and Evangelist, under
the form of a poor man, and begged alms of him.   As the king
had no money at hand to give him, he took his ring from off his
finger and gave it to him.   Now, on the same day, the same
blessed Evangelist appeared to a certain stranger, as he was
going forth from the holy city of Jerusalem, and said to him,
" Whence comest thou, and whither art thou going?"   To
which the stranger made answer, " I am from England, and I am
desirous of returning thither."   The Apostle then said to him,
" Dost thou know Edward, the king of England?"   On which he
made answer,   " My lord, I do know him."   The Apostle then
said to him, " Take this ring, and carry it to king Edward,
and tell him that the Apostle John sends him back this ring,
which he himself gave to him this day on the road as he
was walking; and may the good angel of the Lord accompany

K 2

thee, and grant thee a prosperous journey, Amen." On this, taking the ring and bidding him farewell, he saw the Apostle no more.

Now, on the same day, under the guidance of the Lord, to whom nothing is impossible, this stranger arrived in England, and, delivering the ring to the king, told him everything that had happened to him on the road, and how, on that day, he had returned from Jerusalem. Although this seemed to be impossible, still, in consequence of the assertions of sojourners who had been with him at Jerusalem, and who, a long time after this, returned into England, it was found to be the truth.

On another occasion it befell the same king Edward, that, on a certain day, he was taken by the queen and earl Harold to his treasury, to see a large sum of money which the queen and earl Harold, without the knowledge of the king, had collected for his necessities (namely, four pennies from every hide of land throughout each province of England, in order that the king might, by the day of the Nativity of our Lord, purchase clothes for the necessities of the soldiers and his servants); having entered the treasury, the queen and earl Harold accompanying him, he beheld the devil seated upon the money; on which the king said to him, "What dost thou do here?" Whereto the devil made answer, "I am here keeping guard over my money." Upon this, the king said to him, "I conjure thee by the Father, and the Son, and the Holy Ghost, tell me how it is that this money is thine." To this the devil made answer, and said, "Because it has been unjustly obtained out of the substance of the poor." During all this, those who attended him were standing astonished at hearing them talk, but seeing no one except the king; who afterwards said to them, "Restore this money to those from whom it was taken;" and his commands were immediately complied with.

Another story relative to this king. On a certain day of state, when Edward, the above-named king of the English, had been crowned at London and was clothed in royal vestments, and was going from his palace towards the monastery,[23] accompanied by a crowd of nobles, archbishops, bishops, clergy, and people, there sat in the way by which the king was

[23] Probably of Westminster.

about to pass, a certain leprous man, full of running sores. Those who went before rebuked him, and, wishing to remove him thence, bade him hold his peace; on which, the king said to them, " Allow him to sit there." When the king had approached him, the leper thus addressed him, " I conjure thee, by the living God, to carry me on thy shoulders into the church';" upon which the king, bowing down his head, ordered the leper to be placed on his shoulders. And it came to pass, that, when the king moved on, and prayed to the Lord that He would restore the leper to health, his prayers were heard, and the leper was made whole from that hour, praising and blessing the Lord.[24]

Harold, as soon as he had begun to reign, proceeded to abolish all unjust laws and to enact just ones, to become the zealous patron of churches and monasteries, to venerate and encourage the bishops, abbats, monks, and clergy, to show himself pious, humble, and affable to all, and to hold evil-doers in detestation. For he gave general orders to the dukes, earls, sheriffs, and thanes, to seize all thieves, robbers, and disturbers of the realm, and himself used every exertion, for the defence of the country, both by sea and land.

In the same year, on the eighth day before the calends of May, there appeared a comet, not only in England, but even, it is said, throughout the whole world. It made its appearance during seven days, and shone with extreme brightness; whence the saying;

> In the year one thousand sixty-six
> A comet all England's gaze did fix.[24*]

Shortly after this, earl Tosti, returning from Flanders, landed in the Isle of Wight, and, having compelled the islanders to find him tribute and provisions, took his departure and collected plunder near the sea-shore, until he came to the port of Sandwich. On hearing this, king Harold, who was then staying at London, ordered a considerable fleet, and an

---

[24] With this king originated the supposed efficacy of the royal touch for king's evil; which was supposed to be possessed by the royal family of England till the reign of queen Anne, the last who practised it.

[24*] This translation is about as good as the rhyming verses in the original :—

> Anno milleno, sexageno, quoque seno
> Anglorum metæ crinem sensére cometæ.

army of horse, to be levied, and himself made preparations to
set out for the port of Sandwich. When this was reported to
earl Tosti, taking with him some of the mariners who were well
inclined and some who were ill-wishers to him, he retreated,
directing his course to Lindesey, where he burned a great
number of towns, and put many men to death.

On learning this, Edwin, earl of Mercia, and Morcar, earl
of Northumbria, flew to their rescue with an army, and
drove him out of that country.   On his departure thence,
he repaired to Malcolm, king of the Scots, and remained with
him all the summer.   In the meantime, king Harold came
to the port of Sandwich, and there waited for his fleet, which,
when it had assembled, came to the Isle of Wight, and,
as William, duke of the Normans, the cousin of king Edward, was making preparations to invade England with
an army, all the summer and autumn he was awaiting his
arrival, and, besides, kept a land force in suitable positions
near the sea-shore.   However, on the approach of the nativity
of Saint Mary, their provisions failing, the fleet and the land
force returned home.

After this, Harold Harfager, king of Norway, and brother
of Saint Olaf, came with a very strong fleet, amounting to
more than five hundred large ships, and anchored suddenly at
Tynemouth ; on which earl Tosti met him, as they had
previously arranged, with his fleet, and, making all speed,
they entered the mouth of the river Humber, and then, sailing
against tide up the river Ouse, landed at a place which
is called Richale.   When this became known to king Harold,
he speedily moved his troops towards Northumbria ; but, before the king could come thither, the two brothers, earls
Edwin and Morcar, with a large army, had had an engagement
with the Norwegians on the northern bank of the river Ouse,
near York, on the vigil of Saint Matthew the Apostle, being
the fourth day of the week ; and had at the first onset, manfully fighting, slain great numbers.   But, after the battle had
lasted a long time, the English, being unable to sustain the
attack of the Norwegians, and having lost a great number of
their men, turned their backs, and far more were drowned in
the river than slain in the battle.

The Norwegians having gained the victory, and having
taken one hundred and fifty hostages from the city of York,

returned to their ships, having left there a hundred and fifty of their own men as hostages. But, on the fifth day after this, that is to say, on the seventh day before the calends of October, being the second day of the week, Harold, king of the English, attended by many thousands of soldiers fully armed, arrived at York ; and, meeting the Norwegians at a place called Stamford Bridge, slew king Harold Harfager and earl Tosti with the edge of the sword, together with the greater part of their army, and, although it was most keenly contested, gained a complete victory : but to his son Olaf, and to Paul, earl of the Isle of Orkney, who had been sent with part of the army to guard the ships, he gave liberty to return to their country with twenty ships and the remnant of their army, having first received from them hostages and oaths for their future good behaviour.

WILLIAM THE ELDER.

In the meantime, while these things were going on, and the king supposed that all his enemies were crushed, word was brought to him that William, duke of Normandy, had arrived with an innumerable multitude of horsemen, slingers, archers, and foot, and that he had levied strong bodies of auxiliaries from the whole of England, having landed at a place which is called Penvesca.[25]   Upon this, the king with the greatest haste moved his army towards London ; and although he was well aware that in the two battles above-mentioned the bravest men of the whole of England had fallen, and that the centre of his army had not yet come up, he did not hesitate to meet the enemy with all possible speed in Sussex ; and, at the distance of nine miles from Hastings, where he had pitched his camp, on the eleventh day before the calends of November, being Saturday, and the day of Saint Calixtus the pope and Martyr, he engaged with them, before the third part of his army was drawn up ; but, as the English had been drawn up in a confined spot, many withdrew from his ranks, and but very few remained with him with undaunted hearts.

Still, from the third hour of the day[26] until nightfall, he made a most determined resistance against the foe, and

[25] Pevensey.   [26] Nine in the morning.

defended himself so bravely, and with such consummate valour, that the enemy could hardly get the better of him. But, alas! after very great numbers had fallen on both sides, at twilight he himself fell; the earls Girth and Leofwine, his brothers, also fell, and most of the nobles of England; on which duke William with his men returned with all speed to Hastings. The length of Harold's reign was nine months and as many days.

But in order that the origin may be known of the grounds on which William invaded England, the circumstances which had transpired a short time before this period shall be briefly related.

When the disagreement arose between king Edward and earl Godwin, as previously mentioned, the earl was driven into exile with his family from England. Afterwards, on his endeavouring to effect a reconciliation with the king, in order that he might be allowed to return to his own country, the king would by no means consent thereto, unless he first received hostages as a guarantee of his own security. In consequence of this, Wulnoth, son of Godwin, and Hacun, son of his son Sweyn, were given as hostages, and sent to Normandy in charge of duke William the Bastard, the son of Robert, son of Richard, his[27] mother's brother. Sometime after this, when earl Godwin was dead, his son, Harold, asked leave of the king to go to Normandy, and obtain the liberty of his brother and nephew, who were kept there as hostages, and to bring them back with him to their own country; on which the king made answer: "By me this shall not be done; but that I may not appear to wish to prevent you, I permit you to go wherever you like, and to try what you can effect: still I have a presentiment that your efforts will end in nothing but injury to the whole kingdom of England and disgrace to yourself; for I know that the duke is not so devoid of intelligence as to be willing on any account to entrust them to you, if he does not foresee some great profit to accrue therefrom to himself."

However, Harold embarked on board of a ship, which, with all on board of it, being driven by a violent tempest into a river of Ponthieu, which is called the Maia, according to the custom of the place he was claimed as a captive by the lord

[27] King Edward the Confessor.

of that district.   Harold, on being thrown into prison, having, however, bribed one of the common people with the promise of a reward, secretly gave him directions to inform the duke of Normandy of what had befallen him.   On hearing this, William immediately sent messengers in all haste, and told the lord of Ponthieu that Harold and his people must be sent to him immediately, free from all harm, if he wished to enjoy his future friendship in the same degree as hitherto ; he, however, being unwilling to send him, once more received a command from William that he must send Harold, otherwise he would find most assuredly, that William, duke of Normandy, would instantly come armed to Ponthieu for the purpose of taking him away with all his property, even to the utmost farthing.

Alarmed by these threats, he sent Harold with his companions, on which he was most honorably received by duke William, who, on hearing why he had left his country, made answer that he would be successful if it rested with him.[28]   He, therefore, kept Harold with him for some days, and showed himself very kind and courteous towards him, in order that by such conduct he might gain his feelings in support of his own objects.   At length he disclosed to him what his designs were, and stated that king Edward once, when in his youthful days, he was staying in Normandy, with himself then a youth, promised him upon his oath, that if he should become king of England, he would grant to him, in succession to himself, the hereditary right to the kingdom; and, in addition to this, he said : "And if you will engage to aid me in this matter, and to procure for me the castle of Dover, with the well of water there, and will give your sister in marriage to one of my nobles, and promise to send her to me at the time that shall be agreed on by us, and also, to accept my daughter in marriage, then you shall both receive your nephew safe and sound immediately, and, your brother, when I come to reign in England; and if, by your aid, I am firmly established in that kingdom, I promise that every thing that in reason you shall ask of me, you shall obtain."

Harold was sensible of danger either way, and did not see how he was to escape if he did not acquiesce in the wishes of William in every respect : he, therefore, gave his as-

[28] " Si in ipso non remaneret," hardly seems to be a correct reading here.

sent. But in addition to this, William, in order that everything might be definitively settled, having brought some relics of saints, led Harold to attest, by taking an oath upon them, that he would in deed fulfil everything that had been agreed upon between them.

These matters being concluded, Harold received his nephew and returned to his country; but when, in answer to the king's enquiries, he informed him of what had happened and what he had done, he answered, "Did I not tell you that I knew duke William well, and that, in consequence of your journey, great evils might result to this kingdom? I foresee that, by this conduct of yours, great misfortunes will befall our country; and I only pray that Divine Providence will grant that they come not in my day."

Shortly after, king Edward departed this life, and, as he had appointed previously to his death, Harold succeeded him in the kingdom. On this, duke William sent him word, that although, violating his oath, he had not observed his promise in other respects, still, if he would marry his daughter he would put up with what he had done, but, if not, he would without doubt assert his right to the promised succession to the kingdom by force of arms.

But Harold would neither say that he was ready to comply with the one alternative, nor that he feared the other; at which, William being indignant, was inspired with great hopes of conquering England by reason of this unjust conduct of Harold. Having, therefore, prepared a considerable fleet, he sailed for England, and a severe engagement taking place, Harold was slain in battle, and William being victorious, obtained the kingdom.

Some of the Franks still give an account of[29] the circumstances of this battle who were there present. But although there were various chances of success on the one side and the other, still, there was such great slaughter and disorder caused by the Normans, that the victory which they gained must without doubt be ascribed to the judgment of God, who by punishing the crime of perjury shows that he is a God who abhors unrighteousness.

On hearing of the death of king Harold, the earls Edwin

[29] " Adhuc" can hardly mean " at the present day," in allusion to oral testimony; as our author lived nearly a hundred years after the time of William the Conqueror.

and Morcar, who with their men had withdrawn from the battle, came to London, and taking their sister, queen Aldgitha, sent her to the city of Chester.   Aldred, archbishop of York, and these earls, together with the citizens of London, and the mariners, were desirous to make the Clito Edgar, grandson of king Edmund Ironside, king, and promised that they would fight for him.   But while many were making preparations to go forth to battle, the earls withdrew their aid from them, and returned home with their forces.

In the meanwhile duke William laid waste the provinces of Sussex, Kent, Southampton, Surrey, Middlesex, and Hereford; and did not cease burning towns and slaying men, till he came to the city which is called Beorcham.[30]   Here Aldred, the archbishop, Wulstan, bishop of Worcester, Walter, bishop of Hereford, the Clito Edgar, earls Edwin and Morcar, and five of the nobles of London, with many others came to him, and, giving hostages, made submission, and took the oaths of fealty to him.   He also made a treaty with them, but, in spite of it, allowed his army to burn the towns, and plunder them.

On the approach of the festival of the Nativity of our Lord, he marched with all his army to London, that he might be crowned there; and because Stigand, the primate of the whole of England, was charged with not having canonically received the pall, on the day of the Nativity, which in that year fell on the second day of the week, he was consecrated with due honor at Westminster, by Aldred, the archbishop of York; but first, as the same archbishop requested him to do, before the altar of Saint Peter the Apostle, in the presence of the clergy and the people, he promised on oath, that he would be ready to defend the holy churches of God and their rulers, and that he would justly and with royal foresight rule over all the people subject to him, enact and observe just laws, and utterly discountenance rapine and unjust judgments.

In the year 1067, on the approach of Lent, king William returned to Normandy, taking with him Stigand, archbishop of Canterbury, Agelnoth, abbat of Glastonbury, the Clito Edgar, the earls Edwin and Morcar, Walter, a noble earl, son of earl Siward, Agelnoth, a native of Canterbury, and many

---

[30] Berkhampstead.

others of the chief men of England, also his brother Odo, bishop of Bayeux, and William FitzOsbern, whom he had made earl of the province of Hereford ; and leaving garrisons in England, he ordered the fortresses throughout the country to be strengthened.

In this year, Wulsy, bishop of Dorchester, departed this life at Winchester, but was buried at Dorchester.

At this period, there was a certain very powerful thane, Edric surnamed "the Woodsman,"[31] son of Alfric, the brother of Edric Streona, whose lands, because he disdained to surrender to the king, the men of the castle at Hereford, and Richard the son of Scrob, frequently laid waste ; but as often as they attacked him, they lost many of their knights and esquires. Therefore, having called to his aid the kings of the Welch, namely Bleothgent and Riward, about the time of the Assumption of Saint Mary, the said Edric laid waste the province of Hereford, as far as the bridge over the river Lug,[32] and carried off a great quantity of plunder.

Afterwards, on the approach of winter, king William returned to England from Normandy, and imposed on the English an intolerable tribute, and then, going into Devonshire, hostilely attacked the city of Exeter, which the citizens and some English thanes held against him ; on which he laid siege to it, and speedily took it by storm. However, the countess Githa, the mother of Harold king of England, and sister of Sweyn king of Denmark, flying with many others from the city made her escape and went to Flanders; but the citizens with assurances of friendship submitted to the king.

In the year 1068, there were two popes at Rome, namely, the bishop of Parma, who was expelled, and the bishop of Lucca, who continued to be pope.

After Easter, the countess Matilda came from Normandy to England, and on the day of Pentecost, Aldred, archbishop of York, consecrated her queen. After this, Marleswein and Cospatric, and the other nobles of Northumbria, in order to avoid the king's severity, and fearing lest like some others they might be placed in confinement, taking with them the Clito Edgar, his mother Agatha, and his two sisters Margaret and Christiana, went by ship to Scotland ; and, with the per-

---

[31] " Silvaticus :" probably corresponding to our surname " Atwood." He is more generally called Edric the Outlaw.
[32] The Avon.

mission of king Malcolm, passed the winter there.   On this, king William came with his army to Nottingham, and having strengthened the castle, proceeded to York, and fortifying the two castles there, placed in them five hundred soldiers, giving orders for the castles to be strengthened in the city of Lincoln and other places.

While these things were going on, the sons of king Harold, Godwin and Edmund the Great, returning from Ireland landed in Somersetshire; where being met by Eadnoth, who had been master of the stables[33] to king Harold, with some troops, a battle was fought, in which he, with many others, was slain.   Having gained the day, they collected considerable spoil in Devonshire and Cornwall, and then returned to Ireland.

In the year 1069, being the third year of his reign, king William sent earl Robert Cummin against the Northumbrians of the country north of the Tyne; for they had all united in one determination, not to submit to the rule of a foreigner, and had resolved either to slay him, or else, all of them, to fall by the edge of the sword.   On his approach, Egelwin, bishop of Durham, met him, and warned him to be on his guard against treachery; but he, thinking that no one dared this, despised the warning, and, entering Durham with a large body of soldiers, allowed his men to act with hostility in all quarters, even to slaying some peasants belonging to the church; still, he was received by the bishop with all kindness and honor.   But the Northumbrians hastening onward all night, at daybreak broke through the gates with the greatest violence, and slew the followers of the earl in every direction, they being quite unprepared for the attack. The contest was waged most fiercely, the soldiers being struck down in the houses and streets, and the combatants attacked the house of the bishop in which the earl was entertained; but finding that they could not endure the darts of those who defended it, they burned the house together with those who were therein.   So great was the multitude of the slain, that nearly every spot in the city was filled with blood, and out of seven hundred men only one escaped.   This slaughter took place on the fifth day before the calends of February, being the fourth day of the week.

[33] "Stallarius."   There is some doubt as to the correct meaning of this word.

In this year, shortly before the nativity of Saint Mary, the sons of Sweyn, king of Denmark, Harold, Canute, and their uncle earl Osborn, came from Denmark with two hundred and forty ships, and landed at the mouth of the river Humber. Here they were met by the Clito Edgar, earls Alde and Marleswein, and many others, with a fleet which they had assembled; earl Cospatric also came with all the forces of the Northumbrians, and with one accord they determined to oppose the Normans. Being greatly distressed at their approach, Aldred, archbishop of York, was attacked with a severe illness and ended his life, as he had requested of God, in the tenth year of his archiepiscopate, on the third day before the ides of September, being the sixth day of the week; he was buried in the church of Saint Peter, on the eighth day after, being Saturday, the thirteenth day before the calends of October.

The Normans, who garrisoned the castles, fearing lest the houses which were in their vicinity, might be used by the Danes for the purpose of filling up the fosse, began to set them on fire; and the flames, increasing, raged throughout all the city, and together with it, burned the monastery of Saint Peter. But the Divine vengeance most speedily exacted a heavy retribution at their hands; for, before the whole city was destroyed, a Danish fleet came on the second day of the week to the aid of the besiegers, and the Danes making an attack upon the castles on the one side, and the Northumbrians on the other, stormed them on the same day; more than three thousand of the Normans being slain, the Danes sparing the lives of William de Malet, who was then sheriff of the province, with his wife and two children, and of Gilbert de Ghent with a few others, repaired to their ships with their innumerable forces, and the Northumbrians returned home.

When king William was informed of this, being greatly enraged, he swore that he would pierce the whole of the Northumbrians with a single spear, and shortly afterwards, having assembled an army hastened with feelings of extreme irritation to Northumbria, and did not cease throughout the whole winter to ravage it, slay the inhabitants, and commit many other acts of devastation.

In the meantime, sending a message to Osborn, the Danish earl, he promised that he would privately present him with no small sum of money, and give his army free licence to seize provisions in the neighbourhood of the sea-shore, upon condition that, after the close of winter, they should depart, without any further hostilities.   To these propositions Osborn, being greedy for gold and silver, to his great disgrace, assented.   While the Normans, in the preceding year, were laying waste England, throughout Northumbria and some other provinces, but in the present and succeeding year, throughout almost the whole of England, but especially Northumbria and the provinces adjoining to it, a famine prevailed to such a degree, that, compelled by hunger, men ate human flesh, and that of horses, dogs, and cats, and whatever was repulsive to notions of civilization ; some persons went so far as to sell themselves into perpetual slavery, provided only they could in some way or other support a miserable existence ; some departing from their native country into exile, breathed forth their exhausted spirits in the midst of the journey.

It was dreadful to behold human corpses rotting in the houses, streets, and high roads, and as they reeked with putrefaction, swarming with worms, and sending forth a horrid stench ; for all the people having been cut off, either with the sword or famine, or else having through hunger left their native country, there were not sufficient left to inter them. Thus, during a period of nine years, did the land, deprived of its cultivators, extend far and wide a mere dreary waste.   Between York and Durham there was not one inhabited town ; the dens of wild beasts and robbers, to the great terror of the traveller, were alone to be seen.

While the king was doing these things in the neighbourhood of York, Egelwin, bishop of Durham, and the chiefs of the people, being fearful that, on account of the death of the earl[35] at Durham and the slaughter of the Normans at York, the sword of the king would involve both innocent and guilty in a like destruction, unanimously disinterred the holy and incorruptible body of the blessed father Cuthbert and took to flight, on the third day before the ides of December, being the sixth day of the week.   They first rested at Girwine,[36] next at Bethlingtun,[37] the third time at Tughale,[38] and the fourth at

[35] Robert Cummin.   [36] Jarrow, in Durham.
[37] Bedlington, in Northumberland.   [38] Tughall, in Northumberland.

Ealande. Here, towards nightfall, their further progress was impeded by the sea being at high water, when lo! suddenly withdrawing, it left them free access, so that when they hastened on, the waves of the ocean followed in the rear, at a similar pace, and when they sometimes moved more slowly, the waves did not overtake them by speeding on at a faster pace, but, as soon as they had touched the shore, behold! the sea flowed back again and covered all the sands as before.

In the meantime, the king's army, dispersing in all directions, between the rivers Tees and Tyne, found nothing but deserted houses, and a dreary solitude on every side; the inhabitants having either sought safety in flight, or concealed themselves in the woods and among the precipices of the hills. At this period also, the church of Saint Paul the Apostle, at Girwine, was destroyed by fire. The church of Durham was deprived of all its guardians and all ecclesiastical care, and had become like a desert, as the Scripture says, a refuge for the poor, the sick, and the feeble. Those who were unable to take to flight, turning aside thither, sank there under the influence of famine and disease. The resemblance of the cross, which was the only one of the church ornaments remaining there, (as on account of its large size it could not be easily removed by them in their haste) was robbed of its gold and silver, which were torn off by the Normans.

On this, the king, who was not far off, hearing of the deserted state of the church, and the spoliation of the crucifix, was very indignant, and gave orders for those to be sought for who had been guilty of it. Shortly after, he happened to meet these very persons, and on seeing them turn out of the public road, immediately felt convinced that these men were conscious of having committed some misdeed; whereon, being seized, they immediately made discovery of the gold and silver which they had taken from off the crucifix. On this, he immediately sent them for judgment to the bishop and those who were with him, who were now returning from their flight; but they, acquitting them of the charge, let them escape with impunity. For, upon the approach of spring, the king having returned to the country south of the Humber, bishop Egelwin, after having, with all his people, passed three months and some days at Ealande, returned to the church of Durham, with the treasure of the holy body of Saint Cuthbert.

In the year 1070, at the season of Lent, by the advice of William, earl of Hereford, and some others, king William ordered his followers to search the monasteries throughout the whole of England; and the money which, on account of his severity and extortion, the wealthier English had deposited there, he ordered to be taken from them.

Bishop Egelwin, having returned from flight, as already mentioned, now meditated in his mind a perpetual exile. For, seeing the affairs of the English in a state of confusion on every side, and fearing that the sway of a foreign nation, to whose language and manners he was a stranger, would press with severity upon himself, he determined to resign his bishopric, and to provide for himself, as he best might, in a foreign land. Having, therefore, provided a ship, and put all necessaries on board, he was waiting for a fair wind in the harbour of Wearmouth.

At the same time there were some other ships there; on board of which were the Clito Edgar with his mother Agatha, and his two sisters, Margaret and Christiana, Siward Barn, Marleswein, and Elfwin, son of Norman, and many besides; who, after the attack on the castles at York, on the return home of the Danes, dreading the vengeance of the king for having aided them, were preparing to fly to Scotland and waiting for a fair passage thither.

At this period, a countless multitude of Scots, under the command of king Malcolm, passing through Cumberland, and making their way towards the east, fiercely laid waste the whole of Teesdale [39] and its neighbourhood, far and wide. Having come to a place which, in the English language, is called Hundredesfelde, and in the Latin "Centum Fontes" (*the hundred springs*), and having slain there some of the English nobles, the king, retaining with him part of his army, sent home the other part, with an infinite amount of spoil, by the road by which they had come. In doing this, his crafty design was, that the wretched inhabitants who, in their fear of the enemy, had for safety concealed themselves and their property in whatever hiding-places they could find, might suppose that the whole of the enemy's forces had departed, and that he might suddenly come upon them after they had, with a feeling of security, returned to their towns and homes;

[39] The vicinity of the river Tees.

which, accordingly, happened to be the case. For, having laid
waste part of Cleveland, he suddenly ravaged Heorternisse,
and thence making a fierce incursion upon the lands of Saint
Cuthbert,[40] deprived all of the whole of their property, and
some even of their lives.

In addition to this, he consumed the church of Saint Peter
the Apostle, at Wearmouth, with flames which were kindled by
his men in his own presence; other churches also he burned
to the ground, together with those who had taken refuge in
them. While riding near the banks of the river, and from
an elevated spot looking down upon the cruelties inflicted by
his men upon the wretched English, and satiating his mind
and his eyes with this sight of horror, word was brought to
him that the Clito Edgar and his sisters, comely young women
of royal blood, with many others, very wealthy fugitives from
their country, had taken refuge in that harbour. On this,
after interchanging courtesies with them, he kindly addressed
them when they came, and gave to them and all their attendants, with the strongest assurances of peace, an asylum in
his dominions for as long a period as they should think fit.
Amid these depredations inflicted by the Scots, earl Cospatric,
who, as already mentioned, had purchased the earldom of
Northumbria of king William for a sum of money, having
obtained the aid of some active allies, ravaged Cumberland
with dreadful havoc; and then, having laid waste the country
with fire and sword, returned with a large quantity of
spoil, and shut himself and his followers within the strong
fortifications of Bebbanburgh;[41] whence frequently sallying
forth, he greatly weakened the enemy's strength. At this
period Cumberland was subject to king Malcolm; not by right-
ful possession, but in consequence of having been subjugated
by force.

Malcolm, on hearing what Cospatric had done (while he
was still looking at the church of Saint Peter burning amid
the flames kindled by his own men), could hardly contain himself for anger, and commanded his men no longer to spare
any individual of the English nation, but either to strike them
to the earth and slay them, or, making them prisoners, carry
them off, doomed to the yoke of perpetual slavery. The
troops having received this sanction, it was dreadful even to

---

[40] In the north of Northumberland.   [41] Bamborough.

witness the cruelties they were guilty of towards the English. Some aged men and women were decapitated with the sword; others, like swine intended for food, were pierced through and through with lances; infants were torn from the breasts of their mothers, thrown aloft into the air, and on falling, received upon the points of lances, sharp weapons being thickly planted in the ground.

The Scots, more savage than wild beasts, took delight in these cruelties, as though a spectacle of games; and thus did the age of innocence, destined to attain heaven, breathe its last, suspended between heaven and earth. But the young men and young women, and whoever besides seemed adapted for toil and labour, were driven away in fetters in front of the enemy, to endure a perpetual exile in captivity as servants and handmaids. Some of these, while running before those who drove them on, became fatigued to a degree beyond what their strength could endure, and, as they sank to the ground on the spot, the same was the place of their fall and of their death. While beholding these scenes, Malcolm was moved to compassion by no tears, no groans of the wretched creatures; but, on the contrary, gave orders that they should be perseveringly driven onward in their course.

In consequence of this, Scotland became filled with menservants and maid-servants of English parentage; so much so, that even at the present day not only not even the smallest village, but not even the humblest house is to be found without them.

After the return of Malcolm to Scotland, bishop Egelwin having set sail with the view of proceeding to Cologne, a contrary wind arose and drove him back upon the coast of Scotland, which also, after a speedy passage, brought thither the Clito Edgar with his above-named companions. On this, king Malcolm, with the full consent of his relations, married Margaret, the sister of Edgar, a woman ennobled by her royal birth, but much more ennobled by her wisdom and piety, through whose zeal and untiring efforts the king himself, laying aside his barbarian manners, became more virtuous and more civilized. By her he had six sons—Edward, Edmund, king Edgar, Ethelred, king Alexander, king David, and two daughters, Matilda, queen of the English, and Mary, who became the wife of Eustace, earl of Boulogne.

L 2

In the same year, a great synod was held at Winchester, on the octave of Easter, by command of king William, who was there present; it was also sanctioned by our lord Alexander, the pope, who gave the authority of the Apostolic See thereto, through his legates, Hermenfred, bishop of Sion, and the cardinal priests, John and Peter. At this synod Stigand, archbishop of Canterbury, was deprived of his archbishopric on three grounds, namely; because he had wrongfully held the bishopric of Winchester together with the archbishopric; because, in the lifetime of archbishop Robert, he had not only held the archbishopric, but even for some time, at the celebration of the mass, had made use of his pall which remained at Canterbury, when he himself had been violently and unjustly expelled from England; and because he had received the pall from Benedict, who had been excommunicated by the holy Church of Rome, for having gained the papacy by means of bribery. His brother Agelmar, the bishop of East Anglia,[42] was also deprived there, as were also some abbats; all which was done by the agency of the king, in order that as many of the English as possible might be deprived of their honors; in whose place he might appoint persons of his own nation, for the purpose of strengthening his possession of the kingdom which he had recently acquired.

For this reason, also, he deprived of their honors certain bishops and abbats, whom, as no evident reason existed, neither synods nor secular laws condemned; and, placing them in confinement, kept them there to the end of their lives, being merely influenced, as already mentioned, by suspicion on account of the kingdom he had newly acquired.

At this synod, also, while the rest, being sensible of the king's feelings, were afraid lest they should be deprived of their dignities, the venerable man, Wulstan, bishop of Worcester, resolutely demanded restoration of a considerable quantity of property belonging to his see which had been retained in his possession by archbishop Aldred, when he was removed from the see of Worcester to that of York, and which, after his death, had come into the king's hands; and both asked for justice to be done by those who presided over the synod, and demanded it of the king. But the church of York, as it then had no pastor to speak for it, was dumb; judgment was

---

[42] Bishop of Helmham, in Norfolk.

therefore given that the claim should remain in its present
state until an archbishop was appointed, who might defend his
church, and there would be a person to make answer to his
charge; so that, after the charges and answers had been considered, judgment might be given with more fairness and certainty. Accordingly, on the present occasion, the claim stood
over for a time.

On the day of Pentecost, in this year, the king, being then
at Windsor, gave the archbishopric of the church of York to
Thomas, a venerable canon of Bayeux, and the bishopric of
Winchester to Valceline, his own chaplain : and, by his command, on the following day, Armenfred, the above-named
bishop of Sion, held a synod, John and Peter, the cardinals
before-mentioned, having returned to Rome.

At this synod Agelric, bishop of the South Saxons,[43] was
degraded in an uncanonical manner; and shortly after, for no
fault on his part, the king placed him in confinement at
Mearlesberge.[44] A considerable number of abbats were also
deposed; after whose deposition, the king gave to his chaplains
Arfract, the bishopric of East Anglia,[45] and to Stigand, that
of the South Saxons; to some of the Norman monks he also
gave abbeys; and, as the archbishop of Canterbury had been
deposed, and the archbishop of York had recently died, by the
king's command Valceline was ordained on the eighth day
after Pentecost by the same Armenfred, bishop of Sion, the
legate of the Apostolic See.

On the approach of the feast of Saint John the Baptist, earl
Osborn departed for Denmark with the fleet that had lain
in the river Humber during the winter, but his brother,
Sweyn, outlawed him on account of the money, which, contrary to the wishes of the Danes, he had received from king
William. At this period the most valiant man, Edric, surnamed the Woodsman,[46] was reconciled to king William.
After this, the king summoned from Normandy Lanfranc, the
abbat of Caen, a Lombard by birth, a man of the greatest
learning in every respect, well skilled in all the liberal arts
and in the knowledge of both divine and secular literature,
and most prudent in counsel and in the management of temporal matters, and, on the day of the Assumption of Saint

[43] Bishop of Selsey.   [44] Marlborough.
[45] Of Helmham.   [46] Silvaticus.

Mary, appointed him archbishop of Canterbury, and, at the feast of Saint John the Baptist, being the Lord's Day, had him consecrated at Canterbury. His consecration was performed by Giso, bishop of Wells, and Walter, bishop of Hereford, who had both been ordained at Rome by pope Nicolas, at the time when Aldred, archbishop of York, received his pall. For these bishops had avoided receiving ordination from Stigand, who then held the see of Canterbury, as they knew that he had received the pall in an uncanonical manner. Herman, bishop of Salisbury, with some others, was also present at his consecration, shortly after which, Lanfranc consecrated Thomas, archbishop of York.

These matters completed, the claim of the venerable Wulstan, bishop of Worcester, was again considered, Thomas having been now consecrated archbishop, to speak for the church of York; and, a synod being held at a place which is called Pedreda,[47] before the king and Lanfranc, archbishop of Canterbury, and the bishops, abbats, earls, and principal men of England, by the aid of the grace of God, the matter was there concluded, although Thomas, the archbishop of York, and his supporters, used every possible device, though far from being based upon the truth, to lower the church of Worcester, and to subject her to the church of York, and strove in every way to make her a dependant thereof. However, by the just judgment of God, and the most positive evidence of writings much defaced and almost worn to pieces, Wulstan, the man of God, not only regained the possessions that he had claimed and demanded, but, also, by the gift of God and the concession of the king, obtained that extent of liberty which had been bestowed upon her by the first founders king Ethelred and Saint Hosher, earl of the Wiccii, and by Cenred, Ethelbald, Offa, Saint Kenulph the father of Kenelm the Martyr, and their successors after them, and those who reigned over the whole kingdom of England, namely, Edward the Elder, Ethelstan, Edmund, Edred, Edgar father of king Edward the Martyr, and those who had succeeded them.

In the year from the incarnation of our Lord, 1071, Lanfranc and Thomas went to Rome, and received the pall from pope Alexander. The earls Edwin and Morcar, finding that king William wished to place them in confinement, secretly fled

47 Petherton, in Somersetshire.

from his court, and for some time remained in open rebellion against him. However, on finding that their attempts were not crowned with success, Edwin determined to go to Malcolm, king of the Scots, but, being treacherously attacked on the road by his own people, was slain. Morcar and Hereward, however, a man of the greatest bravery, with many others, repaired by ship to the Isle of Ely, intending to winter there; whither Egelwin, bishop of Durham, and Siward, surnamed Barn, returning by sea from Scotland, also came. But, when the king heard of this, with the help of his sailors, he cut them off from all exit on the eastern side of the island, and, on the western side, ordered a bridge to be constructed two miles in length. On seeing that they were thus enclosed, they ceased making resistance, and all, with the exception of Hereward and a few who made their escape through the fens, surrendered to the king; who shortly afterwards placed bishop Egelwin in confinement at Abingdon, where the same winter he ended his life; but as to Earl Morcar and the rest, he distributed a part of them in various places of confinement throughout England, and having first deprived them of their hands or their eyes, let go the rest. The king then appointed Walcher, a member of the church of Liege, to the bishopric of Durham, and he was accordingly consecrated at Winchester. He had come to this country on the king's invitation, being a person of illustrious family, graceful manners, and endowed with the recommendations of divine and secular knowledge. Eilaf, one of the king's household servants, very high in office, together with other men of rank, escorted him to York, where earl Cospatric met him by the king's command, and escorted the bishop as far as Durham; he arrived at the church of his see at the period of Mid-Lent.

In the year 1072, after the Assumption of Saint Mary, king William, having in his train Edric, surnamed the Woods-man,⁴⁹ set out for Scotland with a fleet and an army of horse, for the purpose of subjugating it; for Malcolm, king of the Scots, had greatly offended him in having, as already mentioned, so dreadfully ravaged his territories the year before. But when the king of the English had entered Scotland, king Malcolm met him at a place which is called Abernithie, and did homage to him." On his return thence, king William deprived earl Cospatric of his dignity, making it a charge against him that

⁴⁹ He is also called in history the Outlaw, and the Forester.

he had counselled and aided those who had slain the earl[49] at Durham, and had taken part with the enemy when the Normans were slain at York. After his deprivation, Wal-theof was raised to the earldom, to which he was entitled both on his father's and his mother's side, being the son of earl Siward, by Elfrida, the daughter of Ealdred, who was formerly earl.

At this period, that is to say, when the king was returning from Scotland, he built a castle at Durham, where the bishop and his people might enjoy security from the incursions of the enemy; and, as some of the Normans disbelieved that the blessed Cuthbert either was a Saint, or that his body was kept there, at the feast of All Saints, while the bishop was cele-brating the mass, the king ordered his two chaplains to enter the sanctuary, and to open the tomb and examine, both by seeing and touching, whether the holy body was deposited there. For the king had previously declared that, if it was not there, all the elders should be put to death. Upon this, all being in great consternation, the chaplains were just about to perform his commands. Now at this period, the cold weather was very severe; but, in the meantime, the king began to feel overpowered by an intolerable heat, and to perspire most copiously, and to be attacked with an excessive trembling; so, at once sending to his chaplains, he ordered them not to presume to touch the tomb.

Immediately after this he mounted his horse, and ceased not to ride at its utmost speed till he reached the river Tees. From that time forward he held this Saint in the highest esteem, and confirmed the more favored laws and customs of that church, which it had received in time past, for perpetual observance, and in addition thereto, gave and granted, and by charter confirmed to God and Saint Cuthbert, and the prior and monks there serving God, for a pure and perpetual alms-giving, his royal manor consisting of the vill of Hemming-burgh, with all the lands, of Brakenholm, with all the lands thereto adjoining, together with the church of the vill afore-said, and all things thereto, pertaining in wood and plain, in moor and meadow, in forest and marsh, together with the water-mills and ponds, with merc[50] and merc,[51] and sac,[52] and

49 Robert Cummin.
50 The right of holding markets.   51 Probably right of piscary.
52 The lord's right of trying litigated causes among his vassals, and levying fines.

soke,⁵⁰ and tol,⁵¹ and them,⁵² and infangtheof,⁵³ and all the right boundaries thereof, together with all their rights and customs, as fully, quietly, and freely, as ever Saint Cuthbert fully and quietly held his other lands, together with all the royal customs and liberties which the king himself held therein, when, after the conquest of England, he held the same in his own hands, and with the same boundaries, with which he himself, or Tosti before him, or Siward, had held the said manor.

Bishop Walcher and earl Waltheof were afterwards on the most friendly and cordial terms, insomuch that, sitting together with the bishop, at the synod of the priesthood, he humbly and obediently would carry out whatever was enjoined by the bishop in his earldom, for the correction of Christian manners.

In the year from the incarnation of our Lord 1073, all points agreed, as to the course of the sun and moon, with the fifteenth year of the reign of Tiberius, in which our Lord was baptized, that is to say, the day of the Baptism was on the eighth day before the ides of January, being the Lord's day and Epiphany; the second day of the week was the commencement of His Fast for forty days; and thus, from the time of the Baptism of our Lord in the fifteenth year of the reign of Tiberius, there had been a revolution of two great cycles, that is to say, of one thousand and sixty-four years.

In this year, William, king of the English, with the especial assistance of the English whom he had brought with him from England, subjugated the city which is called Mans, and the province⁵⁴ belonging thereto. The Clito Edgar came to Normandy from Scotland by way of England, and was reconciled to king William. Earl Waltheof, sending a strong body of Northumbrians, took a bloody revenge for the death of his grandfather earl Aldred; for the swords of some men whom he had placed in ambush cut off the sons of Carl who had slain him, while they were at a banquet at Setringetun.

In the year 1074, Hildebrand, who was also called Gregory, archdeacon of Rome, was elected pope, and consecrated. The

⁵⁰ A somewhat similar right to the last. In the text it is erroneously printed "sosciene," for "socam."
⁵¹ The right to levy import duties.
⁵² The right of a lord to follow his servants on the lands of another.
⁵³ The right of apprehending malefactors.   ⁵⁴ Of Maine.

pope holding a council, according to the decrees of Saint Peter the Apostle, and of Saint Clement and other holy fathers, by edict forbade the clergy, and especially those consecrated to the divine mysteries,[55] to have wives, or to cohabit with women, except such as the Nicene synod or other canons excepted. He also decreed that, in conformity with the sentence of Simon Peter, not only the buyer and seller of any office, such for instance as that of bishop, abbat, prior, dean, or titleman of a church, but whoever abetted them, should receive the condemnation of Simon Magus.[59] For the Lord hath said, " Freely have ye received, freely give."

Three poor monks being sent by the Divine Spirit from the province of the Mercians, that is to say, from Evesham, came to York, in the province of the Northumbrians, and requested Hugh Fitzbaldric, who at that time held the shrievalty, to provide them with a guide on their journey, as far as the place which is called Munkeceastre,[60] that is to say, the " city of the monks," which place is now called New-castle. Being escorted thither, and having staid there for some time, on finding there no ancient vestige of the servants of Christ they removed to Jarrow, where, the ruins hardly disclosing what it had been in ancient times, there were to be seen many monastic edifices with half-ruined churches; here they were received with the greatest kindness by bishop Walcher, who supplied them with all necessaries.

Aldwin was the chief of them, both by reason of age and his exemplary manners, while Elfwine was the second, and Reinfrid the third ; by these three persons, three mon-asteries were refounded in the province of the Northum-brians ; one at Durham, near the hallowed and incorruptible body of the father Cuthbert, in honor of the holy Virgin Mary ; another at York, in honor of the same Mary, the mother of God, where this noble monastery, on its foundation, had for its first abbat Stephen, its second Richard, its third Geoffrey, the fourth being the present dignitary, Severinus. The third of these monasteries was restored at a place which was formerly called Streinschalh, that is to say, " the bay of the sea," and is now called Withebi,[61] of which Benedict is the present abbat. Of late years, after the most dreadful devastations of the

58 Those in priests' orders.   59 As being guilty of simony.
60 The Saxon name of Newcastle-on-Tyne.   61 Whitby, in Yorkshire.

pagans had with fire and sword reduced the churches and monasteries to ashes, Christianity being almost extinguished, there were scarcely any churches left, and those few covered with twigs and thatch; but no monasteries had been anywhere rebuilt for two hundred years. Thus did belief in religion wax faint, and all religious observances entirely die away; the name of a monk was a thing unheard-of by the people in the provinces, who were struck with amazement when by chance they beheld any one devoted to the monastic life, and clothed in the garb of a monk. But on the above-named three persons coming to dwell among them, they themselves also began to change their brutish mode of living for the better, to give them all possible assistance in restoring the sacred places, rebuilding the half-ruined churches, and even building new ones in the spots where they had previously existed. Many persons also abandoned a secular life, and assumed the monastic habit; few, however, of these were provincials; they were mostly persons from the remote districts of England, who, being allured by the report of their character, repaired thither, and zealously attached themselves to them.

Of these, Turgot, afterwards bishop of the Scots, was one. He, being sprung from a family by no means among the lowest ranks of the English, was one among a number of hostages, who, when England was totally subjected to the Normans, had been placed in confinement in Lincoln castle, which was the place of safe keeping for the whole of Lindesey. Having bribed the keepers with a sum of money, he secretly, to the hazard of his friends, fled to certain Norwegians, who were then at Grimsby, loading a merchant-ship for Norway, on board which the ambassadors of king William, who were about to proceed to Norway, had procured a passage.

When the ship, speeding on at full sail, had lost sight of land, behold! the run-away hostage of the king came forth from the lower part of the ship, where the Norwegians had concealed him, in the sight of all, and caused astonishment among the ambassadors and their attendants. For he had been sought in every spot, and the king's tax-gatherers had made their search in that very ship; but the cunning of those who concealed him had contrived to deceive the eyes of the searchers. Upon this, the ambassadors insisted upon their furling their sails, and by all means steering back the ship towards the

English shore, in order to take back the run-away hostage of
the king. This was stoutly resisted by the Norwegians, whose
wish it was that they should steer onward in the course they
had so prosperously begun; upon which a division arose, and
prevailed to such a degree that each party took up arms against
the other. But as the force of the Norwegians was superior,
the boldness of the ambassadors very speedily subsided, and
the nearer they approached to land, the more did they humble
themselves to the others.

Upon their arrival there, the runaway youth behaved himself becomingly and modestly, showed himself grateful to the
nobles and principal men, and came under the notice of king
Olaf, who being of a very pious turn of mind, was in the
habit of reading holy books, and giving his attention to literature amid the cares of state. He would also frequently stand
by the priest at the altar, and assist him in putting on the holy
vestments, pouring the water upon his hands, and with great devotion performing other duties of a similar nature. Accordingly,
on hearing that a clerk had come over from England, a thing
that seemed somewhat unusual at that period, he employed him
as his own master in learning the Psalms; in consequence of
which he lived in extreme affluence, the bounty of the king and
nobles flowing in upon him apace. His mind, however, was
often smitten, in a spirit of compunction, with contempt for
the world, and, whenever he was able, he would withdraw
himself from the banquets of the revellers, and take delight
in solitude, praying to God with tears that he would direct
him in the paths of salvation. But, inasmuch as religious
aspirations, when subjected to delay, frequently change, his
mind by degrees fell away from this state, and in consequence
of the success which attended his pursuits, the pleasures of
this world had too great attractions for him.

But he, who, when invited, was unwilling to come of his
own accord, at a future time, by compulsion, entered the house
of his heavenly Father. For some years after, he was returning
home by ship with a large sum of money; but when out at
sea, the vessel was wrecked in a most violent storm, and his
companions perishing, he lost the whole of his property, having,
with some five or six others, with the greatest difficulty
saved his life. Coming to Durham for the purpose of offering
up his prayers, he informed bishop Walcher of every thing

that had happened to him, and stated to him that it was his
fixed purpose to assume the monastic habit. On this the
bishop received him with all humility, and, sending him to
Aldwin, of whom mention has been made above, said : " It is
my prayer and my command, that you will receive this my
son, and, clothing him in the monastic habit, will teach him
to observe the monastic rule of life." Aldwin on receiving him,
submitted him to the regular probation, and when he had
passed through that state conferred upon him the monastic
habit, and so trained him by precept and example, that after
his own decease, by order of bishop William, he succeeded him
as prior of the church of Durham, which for twenty years,
less twelve days, he zealously governed. But in the year
when Ranulph was made bishop, who succeeded William,
Alexander the Eighth, king of the Scots, having asked the
assent of Henry, king of the English, thereto, he was chosen
bishop of the church of Saint Andrew.

In the same year in which pope Hildebrand held the above-
named council, Roger, earl of Hereford, son of William, earl of
the East Angles, contrary to the command of king William,
gave his sister in marriage to earl Rodulph. The nuptials
being celebrated with the utmost magnificence, amid a large
concourse of nobles at a place in the province of Grantebridge,[62]
which is called Ixning, a great number there entered into a
conspiracy against king William, and compelled earl Waltheof,
who had been intercepted by them by stratagem, to join the conspiracy. He, however, as soon as he possibly could, went to
Lanfranc, the archbishop of Canterbury, and received absolution from him at the holy sacrament, for the crime that he had,
although not spontaneously, committed ; by whose advice, he
also went to king William, who was at the time staying in
Norway, and disclosing to him the whole matter from beginning to end, threw himself entirely upon his mercy.

In the meantime, the chiefs above-mentioned, being determined to promote the success of this conspiracy, repaired to
their castles, and began, with their supporters, to use all possible endeavours in encouraging the rebellion. But the venerable Wulstan, the bishop of Worcester, with a great body of
soldiers, prevented the earl of Hereford from fording the river
Severn and meeting earl Rodulph, with his army, at the place

appointed. Wulstan was also joined by Egelwin, the abbat of Evesham, with all his people who had been summoned to his assistance, together with Urso, the sheriff of Worcester, and Walter de Lacy, with his troops, and a considerable multitude of the lower classes. But earl Rodulph having pitched his camp near Grantebridge, Odo, bishop of Bayeux, the king's brother, and Geoffrey, bishop of Constance, having collected a great body both of English and Normans and prepared for battle, opposed him.

On seeing that his attempts were thus thwarted by the multitude that opposed him, he secretly fled to Norwich, and entrusting the castle to his wife and his knights, embarked on board ship, and fled from England into Brittany; on which, being pursued by his adversaries, all of his men whom they could overtake they either put to death, or else inflicted upon them various kinds of punishments. After this, the nobles besieged the castle of Norwich, until, peace being made by the king's sanction, the countess, with her people, was allowed to leave England. These events having happened, in the autumn the king returned from Normandy, and placed earl Roger in confinement, and in like manner threw earl Waltheof into prison, although he had besought his mercy.

Edgitha, the former queen of the English, died this year at Winchester, in the month of December, on which her body was, by the royal command, conveyed to London, and honorably buried at Westminster, near that of her lord, king Edmund. Here, at the ensuing Nativity of our Lord, the king held his court, and some of those who had uplifted their necks against him he banished from England, and others he mangled, by putting out their eyes, or cutting off their hands; earls Waltheof and Roger, condemned by a judicial sentence, he committed to closer custody.

In the year 1075, earl Waltheof, by command of king William, was unrighteously led outside of the city of Winchester, and there cruelly decapitated with an axe, and buried in the ground on the spot; but in course of time, God so ordaining it, his body was raised from the earth, and carried with great honor to Croyland, and with great pomp buried in the church there. While he was still in possession of life in this world, on being placed in close confinement, he unceasingly bewailed what he had done amiss, and most zealously endea-

voured to make his peace with God by means of watchings and
prayers and fastings and almsgiving; his memory men have
tried to bury in the earth, but we are to believe that in truth
he rejoices with the Saints in heaven, the above-named archbishop Lanfranc, of pious memory, having faithfully attested it,
from whom, on making confession, he had received absolution.
He asserted that he was innocent of the charge on which he
was accused, namely, that of joining in the aforesaid conspiracy, and that what he had been guilty of in other respects, he had, like a true Christian, bewailed with the tears
of repentance; and Lanfranc declared that he himself should be
blessed, if, after the end of his life, he should be able to enjoy
his happy repose.   After him, the care of the earldom of Northumbria was entrusted to Walcher, bishop of Durham.

After these transactions, the king led his army into Brittany,
and besieged the castle of earl Rodulph, which is called Dol,
until Philip, king of France, forced him to retire.

At this period, as the secular clergy chose rather to submit
to be excommunicated, than to put aside their wives, pope
Hildebrand, in order that he might, if possible, chastise them
by means of others, ordered in the following words that no
person should hear mass performed by a married priest :

"Gregory, the pope, who is also called Hildebrand, the
servant of the servants of God, to all throughout the realms
of Italy and Germany, who show due obedience to Saint
Peter, the Apostolic benediction.   If there are any priests,
deacons, or sub-deacons, who are guilty of the crime of fornication, we do on behalf of Almighty God, and by the authority
of Saint Peter, forbid them entrance into the church, until
such time as they shall amend and be repentant.   But if any
shall prefer to persist in their sinful course, no one of you
is to presume to listen to them while officiating; inasmuch as
their blessing is changed into a curse, and their prayers into
sinfulness, as the Lord beareth witness by his prophet, saying,
' Your blessings I will curse,' " &c.[62]

In the year 1076, Sweyn, king of the Danes, a man greatly
devoted to literature, departed this life, and was succeeded by
his son, Harold.

In the year 1077, Robert, the eldest son of king William,
because he was not allowed to take possession of Normandy,
which, before his arrival in England his father had given to

[62] Mal. ii. 2.

him in the presence of Philip, king of the Franks, fled to France, and, with the aid of king Philip, frequently committed great depredations in Normandy, burning towns and slaying men, and thus caused no little trouble and anxiety to his father.

In the year 1078, after the Assumption of Saint Mary, Malcolm, king of the Scots, laid waste Northumbria, as far as the great river Tyne; and having slain many persons and captured more, returned home with a large amount of spoil.

In the year 1079, king William, while attacking his son Robert before the castle of Gerbolitred, which king Philip had given to him, being wounded by him in the arm, was thrown from his charger, but immediately, on Robert recognizing his voice, he dismounted, and bade him mount his own horse, and so let him depart; on which, many of his men having been slain, and some taken prisoners, and his son William and many others wounded, he took to flight. The venerable man Robert, who had received priests' orders, at the hands of the most reverend Wulstan, the bishop of Worcester, was ordained bishop of Hereford, at Canterbury, by Lanfranc, the archbishop. This took place on the fourth day before the calends of January, being the Lord's day.

In the year 1080,[63] Walcher, bishop of Durham, a native of Lorraine, and a man distinguished for his virtues, was, without reason, murdered by the Northumbrians, at a place which is called Gateshead,[64] that is to say, the "goat's head," on the day before the ides of May, being the fifth day of the week; which act was done in revenge for Liulph, a man of noble birth and high rank.

This person, by hereditary right, was entitled to many possessions throughout England; but, because in those times the Normans were incessantly giving loose in every direction to their savage propensities, he betook himself with all his family to Durham, as he was sincerely attached to the memory of Saint Cuthbert. His wife was Agitha, daughter of earl Aldred, by whom he had two sons, Uctred and Morcar. The sister of this Agitha was Elheda, the mother of earl Waltheof; for which reason that earl entrusted his little cousin, Morcar, to

63 This event is placed by Roger of Wendover in the year 1075. He gives a very different account of the circumstances attending it.

64 Gateshead.

the monks of Jarrow, to be nurtured by them in the love of God. At this time earl Waltheof himself was at Tynemouth; which place, together with the little child, he placed at the disposal of the monks. Liulph, the child's father, was greatly beloved by the bishop; so much so, that without his advice he would by no means transact or dispose of the more weighty questions of his secular business. For this reason his chaplain, Leofwine,[65] whom he had raised to such a pitch of favour that hardly anything in the bishopric and earldom[66] was done without his opinion being first consulted, was inflamed by the stings of envy, and being, in consequence of his elevation, greatly inflated with excessive pride, arrogantly set himself in competition with the above-named Liulph.

In consequence of this, he treated some of his judgments and opinions with the utmost contempt, and used every possible endeavour to render them of no effect; in addition to which, he would frequently wrangle with him before the bishop, even using threats, and often provoke him to anger by the use of contemptuous expressions. On a certain day, when Liulph had been invited by the bishop to take part in his counsels, and had given his opinion as to what was legal and just, Leofwine obstinately opposed him, and exasperated him by the use of contumelious language. Because Liulph on this occasion answered him more sharply than usual, Leofwine withdrew himself hastily from the court of justice, and, calling aside Gilbert (to whom, being his relative, the bishop had entrusted the earldom of Northumbria to manage as his deputy), earnestly entreated him to avenge his wrongs and put Liulph to death as soon as he possibly could effect it.

Gilbert immediately yielded to his iniquitous requests, and, having assembled together his own men at arms, together with those of the bishop and the said Leofwine, proceeded on a certain night to the house where Liulph was then staying, and most

[65] The name of this person, who is called Leobin by William of Malmesbury, affords a singular illustration of the extreme incorrectness of the text. In the same page it is written "Leodwinus," "Leothwinus," "Leolwinus," "Leofwinus," and "Leolfwinus." This faultiness, however, is far from being confined to proper names.

[66] It has been already stated that, after the unfortunate end of earl Waltheof, the earldom of Northumberland was given in charge to the bishop of Durham. Bracton informs us that the bishop of Durham had as full power in the county of Durham as the king had in his own palace.

iniquitously slew him and nearly all his household, in his own house. On hearing of this, the bishop heaved a sigh from the inmost recesses of his heart; and, taking his hood from off his head, and throwing it on the ground, immediately said in mournful accents, to Leofwine, who was then present, "By your factious designs, and most short-sighted contrivances, Leofwine, these things have been brought about. Therefore, I would have you know for certain, that both myself, and yourself, and all my household, you have cut off by means of the sword of your tongue."

On saying this, he instantly betook himself to the castle, and immediately sending messengers throughout all Northumbria, commanded all to be informed that he was not an accomplice in the death of Liulph, but that, on the contrary, he had banished Gilbert, his murderer, and all his associates, from Northumbria, and would be prepared to exculpate himself before a court of ecclesiastical jurisdiction. After this, having interchanged messages, he and the relatives of those who were slain, having mutually given and received assurances of peace, appointed a place and day on which to meet and come to a better understanding. On the appointed day they met at the place named, but as the bishop declined to plead his cause in the open air, he entered the church there, together with his clergy and those of his knights who were of higher rank, and while a council was being held, several times sent out of the church such of his own followers as he thought fit, for the purpose of making peace with them. The people, however, would by no means accede to his requests, for they believed it to be a matter beyond a doubt that Liulph had been slain by his command; for, the night after the death of his relative,[68] Leofwine had not only entertained Gilbert and his associates at his house, in a friendly and hospitable manner, but even the bishop himself had shown him favour and hospitality just as before.

In consequence of this, all those of the bishop's party who were found outside of the church were first slain, only a few escaping by flight; on seeing which, the bishop ordered his relative, the

---

[68] "Propinqui sui." This is probably an incorrect reading. We have been previously informed that Gilbert was a relative of the bishop; but it does not appear that Liulph was related to the bishop or to Gilbert. It may, however, mean "of his neighbour."

above-named Gilbert, whose life was sought, to go out of the church, in order that his death might satisfy the fury of the enemy. On going out, some knights followed him close for the purpose of defending him, but being instantly attacked by the enemy on all sides with swords and lances, they were killed in an instant; however, they spared two English thanes, in consequence of their being of the same blood with themselves. They also slew Leofwine, who had so often given the bishop advice to their disparagement, with some others of the clergy, directly they came out.

For when the bishop understood that their fury could by no means be appeased, unless Leofwine, the head and author of all this calamity, was slain, he begged him to go out of the church; and when he could by no means prevail upon him to do so, the bishop himself went to the door of the church, and begged that his own life might be spared, and on their refusal, covered his head with the border of his garment and went out of the door, and instantly fell dead, pierced by the swords of the enemy. After him they ordered Leofwine to come forth, and, upon his refusal, set fire to the roof and walls of the church; on which, preferring to finish his life rather by being burnt than being slain with the sword, he endured the flames for some time; but, after he had been half roasted alive, he sallied forth, and, being cut to pieces, paid the penalty for his wickedness and died a shocking death.

To avenge the horrible deaths of these persons, king William, in the same year, ravaged Northumbria, sending thither Odo, bishop of Bayeux, with a large body of soldiers. In the autumn of the same year, the same king William sent his son, Robert, against Malcolm, king of the Scots; but after he had proceeded as far as Egelbereth, he returned without completing his object, and founded Newcastle upon the river Tyne.

William succeeded to the bishopric of Durham on the fifth day before the ides of November, and on the fourth day before the nones of January, was consecrated at Gloucester, by Thomas, the archbishop of York.

At Pentecost, in this year, the emperor Henry, being at Mentz, determined upon the deposition of pope Hildebrand, and, on the nativity of Saint John the Baptist, appointed Wibert, bishop of the city of Ravenna, pope in his stead.

In the year 1081, the emperor Henry marched with an

M 2

army to Rome against the pope, but, having laid siege to the city, was unable to effect an entrance.

In the year 1082, after much slaughter and rapine had ensued between the emperor Henry and pope Hildebrand, on the night of Palm Sunday, a great number of persons were slain. King William placed in confinement in Normandy his brother, Odo, bishop of Bayeux.

In the year 1083, the emperor Henry stormed the city of Rome, and having taken it, established Wibert in the Apostolic See; on which, Hildebrand retired to Beneventum, and lived there till the day of his death, and Henry returned to Germany.

A disgraceful quarrel took place between the monks, and Turstin, the abbat, of Glastonbury, a man unworthy to be named, and possessed of no prudence, whom king William, taking from the monastery of Caen, had appointed abbat of that place. Among other doings, in his folly, he treated the Gregorian chaunt with contempt, and attempted to compel the monks to leave it off, and learn the chaunt of one William, of Feschamp, and sing it; this they took to heart, because they had, both in this particular and in the other offices of the church, grown used to the practices of the Roman Church. Upon a certain day, when they did not expect it, he rushed into the chapter-house, with an armed body of soldiers, and pursued the monks, who in their extreme terror had fled into the church, even to the altar; and there the soldiers, piercing the crosses, and images, and shrines of the Saints with darts and arrows, even went so far as to slay one monk while embracing the holy altar, who fell dead pierced with a spear; another also fell at the verge of the altar, transfixed with arrows; on which, being compelled by necessity, the monks stoutly defended themselves with the benches and candle-sticks belonging to the church, and, though grievously wounded, succeeded in driving all the soldiers beyond the choir. The result was, that two of the monks were killed and fourteen wounded; some of the soldiers were also wounded.

Upon this, an inquisition was held, and as the principal fault lay clearly on the abbat's side, the king removed him, and replaced him in his monastery in Normandy. A number of the monks were also, by the king's command, dispersed

among the bishoprics and abbacies, and there kept in confinement. After the king's death, the same abbot repurchased
the abbey from his son, king William, for a sum of five hundred pounds of silver, and wandering about for some years
among the possessions of that church, at a distance from the
monastery itself, just as was befitting a homicide, died in misery.

The monks assembled[69] at Durham, by command of king William the Younger, on the seventh day before the calends of
June, being the sixth day of the week.

On the fourth day before the nones of November, being the
fifth day of the week, queen Matilda departed this life in Normandy, and was buried at Caen.

"Thomas,[70] by the grace of God archbishop of York, to the
bishops and abbats, both those who now hold the said offices in
England also as those who shall succeed them hereafter, and
to all the archbishops, his successors for ever in the see of York,
greeting: Inasmuch as it is our office to perform the duties of
religion to all, so in especial are we bound to pay pious respect
to those Saints of God, from whose bounty it is manifest
that we have received especial benefits. Therefore, we having
been chastened with the scourge of God, and having been
parched in an incredible manner during a period of two
years with weakness from the attacks of fever; and whereas
all the physicians declared that it was evident that death
alone would be the termination of our sufferings, and that there
were no means by which they might counteract the evil effects
of this prolonged weakness. Wherefore, being warned in a
vision, groaning and weeping I passed a night at the tomb of
Saint Cuthbert, where, being wearied out with disease and
fatigue, I was overcome with sleep; upon which Saint Cuthbert appeared to me in a vision, and touching each of my
limbs with his hands, rendered me, when I awoke, whole
from all infirmity; and whereas, at the same time, he commanded me to be duteous to him in all respects, and requested
that all things whatsoever in my diocese he or his should possess, should be free and discharged from all burdens whatso-

[69] This seems to allude to the monks of Glastonbury, who had been
driven from the abbey by William the First, and placed in confinement;
otherwise, the event is not inserted in its proper place.
[70] There is probably an omission here, nothing being stated by way of
introduction to this letter.

ever; and inasmuch as, having been aided by the mercies of the blessed confessor, I have been the more duteous to him, as it was more especially my bounden duty to pay him the greatest homage.—And whereas William, bishop of Durham, has brought a letter of pope Gregory the Seventh, from the Apostolic See, to the council of king William sitting at Westminster, and, with the consent of all, has obtained leave to remove the secular clergy from his church and substitute monks therein. Wherefore, greatly rejoicing at all these things, according to the precept of the abovenamed pope, and according to the command of our lord king William, and out of the love I am bound to owe to Saint Cuthbert, with the consent and permission of the chapter of York, and with the confirmation of the whole synod, I have given and granted, and by this present deed confirmed, and have afterwards, with my own hand, presented at the altar unto Saint Cuthbert, the letter underwritten, which is addressed to Saint Cuthbert and his bishop, and all the monks his servants—Know then, all persons, both present and to come, that I, Thomas, archbishop of York, in obedience to the precept of pope Gregory the Seventh, and with the ratification of our lord king William, and with the attestation thereto of the whole council of England, and with the consent of the chapter of York, do give and do grant unto God and Saint Cuthbert, and to all his bishops in succession, and to all the monks who shall be there in time to come, that all churches whatsoever, which at the present time they may happen to possess in my diocese, or which hereafter they shall canonically obtain by royal grant or gift of the faithful, or which they shall build upon their own lands, they shall hold free and entirely acquitted for ever by me and all my successors, of all claims which belong to me or to my successors. Wherefore, I will and command that they shall hold all their churches in their own hands, and possess them without molestation, and freely place in them their own vicars, who shall only consult me and my successors as to the faithful cure of souls, but them us to all other alms-deeds and benefits :—and further, I do grant, confirm, and command, that they, as well as their vicars, shall be for ever free and acquitted from all synodals,[71] and from all aids, impositions, rents, exactions, or hospices,[72] both as regards myself and my deans and archdeacons, as well as the vicars and servants of us all. I do also forbid, under penalty of excommunication, that any person shall annoy them or their clergy, upon any pretence whatever, or compel them to go to synods or chapters, unless they shall be willing so to do of their own accord. But if any one shall have any complaint against them or theirs, let him repair to the court of Saint Cuthbert at Durham, that he may there receive such redress as he is entitled to. For, all the liberties and dignities which I or my successors shall be entitled to in our own churches or in our lands, we do freely grant for ever unto them and Saint Cuthbert in all their churches and lands, and without any deceit or gainsaying, I do, on behalf of myself and my successors, confirm the free and quiet possession thereof."

In the year 1084, pope Hildebrand, who was also called Gregory, departed this life. William, king of the English, levied upon every hide of land throughout England the sum of six shillings.

In the year 1085, Edmund, abbat of Pershore, a man of remarkable virtue, departed this life on the seventeenth day before the calends of July, being the Lord's day. In the same year, Canute, son of Sweyn, king of the Danes, prepared, with a strong fleet and the aid of his father-in-law, Robert, earl of Flanders, whose daughter he had married, to invade England; whereupon, king William, having levied many thousand soldiers throughout the whole of Gaul, foot and archers, and taking some from Normandy, in the autumn returned to England, and dispersing them throughout the whole kingdom, commanded the bishops, abbats, earls, barons, sheriffs, and royal bailiffs to supply them with provisions. But when he learned that his enemies were checked,[73] he sent back part of his army, and part he retained with himself throughout the whole of the winter, and held his court at Gloucester during the Nativity of our Lord; in which place he gave bishoprics to his three chaplains, namely, that of London to Maurice, that of Thetford to William, and that of Chester to Robert.

---

[72] "Hospitio." A right on the part of certain persons to demand entertainment in religious houses.

[73] Because there was a mutiny in the Danish fleet, which ended in the king being slain by his soldiers.

In the year 1086, king William caused the whole of England to be described, of how much land each of his barons was possessed, how many knight's fees, how many carucates, how many villains, how many animals, and even how much ready money, each person possessed, throughout the whole of his kingdom, beginning from the highest down to the lowest, and how much rent each property could return:[74] the whole of the country being in a state of disturbance in consequence of the numerous murders occasioned thereby. After this, in the week of Pentecost, at Westminster, where he was holding his court, he knighted his son Henry, and shortly after ordered the archbishops, bishops, abbats, earls, barons, and sheriffs, with their soldiers, to meet him at Salisbury, on the calends of August; and on their coming thither, he compelled their knights to swear fealty to him against all men.

At this period, the Clito Edgar, having obtained leave of the king, passed over the sea with two hundred soldiers, and went to Apulia. His sister, Christiana, entered a monastery which has the name of Romsey, and assumed the habit of a nun. In the same year there was a murrain among animals, and a great pestilence in the air.

In the year 1087, the relics of Saint Nicolas were transferred from Myra to the city of Bar. In this year, Aldwin, prior of Durham, departed this life. A raging fire consumed many cities, and the church of Saint Paul, together with the largest and best part of London.

On Saturday, the sixth day before the ides of July, the Danes, in a certain church, conferred the honor of martyrdom on their king, Canute. In this year, Stigand, bishop of Chichester, Scotland, abbat of Saint Augustine's, Alfy, abbat of Bath, and Turstine, abbat of Pershore, departed this life. In the same year, before the Assumption of Saint Mary, king William entered France with an army, and burned with fire a city which is called Mantes, and all the churches therein, and two recluses, and then returned into Normandy. But, upon his return, a dreadful pain in the intestines attacked him; and, becoming weaker and weaker every day, when, as his illness increased, he saw that the day of his death was approaching, he released from confinement his brother, Odo, the bishop of Bayeux, earls Morcar and Roger, Siward, surnamed

74 These returns were entered in what is called Doomsday-book.

Barn, and Wulnoth, the brother of king Harold, whom he had kept in confinement from his childhood, and all besides whom he had imprisoned, either in Normandy or England. After this, he gave the kingdom of England to his son William, and, to his eldest son, Robert, who was then in exile in France, he left the dukedom of Normandy And then, being fortified with the heavenly viaticum,[75] after having reigned over the English nation twenty years, ten months, and twenty-eight days, he parted with his kingdom and his life, on the fifth day before the ides of September, and, having been there interred, rests at Caen, in the church of Saint Stephen the Proto-martyr, which he had built from the foundation, and amply endowed.

WILLIAM THE YOUNGER.

On this, his son, William, repaired to England with all haste, taking with him Morcar and Wulnoth, but, shortly after his arrival at Winchester, he consigned them to the same strict confinement as before; after which, on the sixth day before the calends of October, being the Lord's day, he was consecrated king at Westminster, by Lanfranc, archbishop of Canterbury. Then, returning to Winchester, he distributed the treasures of his father, as he himself had commanded, throughout England; that is to say, to some of the principal churches ten golden marks, to some six, and to some less.   To each of the churches situate in country places [76] he ordered five shillings to be given, and crosses, altars, shrines, text-books,[77] candlesticks, chalices, pipes,[78] and various ornaments, embellished with gold, silver,

[75] The consecrated wafer, administered to the dying, "in articulo mortis."

[76] The words are " in villis sitis." The allusion is to the parish churches throughout the country.

[77] This seems the best translation for "textos," which means the book of the Gospels, which was generally adorned with gold and jewels, and kept in the treasury of the monastery, and laid on the altar on Saints'-days and Sundays.

[78] " Fistulas." Allusion is made to the pipes which (in the early centuries of the church, when the Holy Eucharist was administered to the laity in both kinds,) were used by the communicants for the purpose of sucking the wine out of the cup. The object of this seems to have been that, by the use of several pipes, more than one might partake of it at the same time.

and precious stones, to be distributed among the most deserving churches and the monasteries.

His brother Robert, also, on his return to Normandy, bounteously divided among the monasteries, churches, and the poor the treasures which he found, in behalf of the soul of his father; and, after having knighted them, allowed Duncald,[79] the son of Malcolm, king of the Scots, and Ulph, the son of Harold, the former king of the English, whom he had released from confinement, to depart.

In the year 1088, a great dissension arose among the nobles of England. For a portion of the Norman nobility was in favour of king William; but the other, and larger part espoused the cause of Robert duke of Normandy, and desired to invite him to govern the kingdom, and either deliver up William alive to his brother, or, putting him to death, deprive him of his kingdom. The chiefs in this execrable affair were Odo, bishop of Bayeux, who was also earl of Kent, Geoffrey, bishop of Constance, Robert, earl of Mortaigne,[80] Roger, earl of Shrewsbury, and the chief men of eminence throughout the whole kingdom, with the exception of arch-bishop Lanfranc. This abominable deed they privately discussed during Lent, and, immediately after Easter, began to ravage the country each in his own neighbourhood, and plunder and pillage it, at the same time providing their castles with fortifications and provisions. Geoffrey, bishop of Constance, and Robert de Mowbray repaired to Bristol, where they laid a very strong castle, and laid waste all the country as far as the place which is called Bathun.[81]

The nobles also of Hereford and Shrewsbury, with a multitude of people from Wales, proceeded as far as Worcester, laying waste and destroying with fire everything before them. They intended, also, to have taken the church and the castle, which latter was at that period entrusted to the charge of the venerable bishop Wulstan. When the bishop heard of this he was greatly distressed, and, considering what plan he should adopt, had recourse to his God, and entreated Him to look down upon His church and His people, thus oppressed by their enemies. While he was meditating upon these things, his household sallied forth from the castle, and took and slew five hundred of them, and put the rest to flight.

79 V. r. Duncan.   80 Half-brother of William the First.   81 Bath.

Roger Bigot entered the castle of Norwich, and spread devastation throughout the country.[82] Bishop Odo, through whom these evils had arisen, proceeded into Kent, and laid waste the royal vills, and ravaged the lands of all those who preserved their fealty to the king and gained possession of the castle of Rochester.

On hearing of these things, the king caused the English to be assembled together, and, pointing out to them the treachery of the Normans, entreated them to give him their assistance, on condition that, if they should prove faithful to him in this emergency, he would grant them better laws, such as they should make choice of; he also forbade all unjust taxes, and returned to all their woods and right of venison ; but, whatever he promised, he soon withdrew. The English however, then assisted him faithfully.   Accordingly, the king assembled his army for marching on Rochester, where he supposed his uncle, bishop Odo, was; but, when they came to Tunbridge, they found the castle closely shut against the king. However, the English, boldly storming it, destroyed the whole castle, and those who were in it surrendered to the king. After this, the king with his army directed his course towards the castle of Pevensey ; for bishop Odo had withdrawn from Rochester and fled to that castle, whither the king, with a large army, followed him, and besieged the castle for six entire weeks.

While these things were going on in England, Robert, duke of Normandy, had assembled a considerable force, and was preparing to send it to England, intending shortly to follow, as though making sure of England through the agency of bishop Odo and the others, who were his partisans there.   But William the Younger had now taken measures of defence by sea with his cruisers, which slew many of them on their passage to England, and sank others at sea; so much so, that no man can tell the number of those who perished.

During the period of these transactions at sea, bishop Odo, and those who were with him, being compelled by hunger, surrendered the castle of Pevensey, and promised, on oath, that they would leave England and not enter it again, except

[82] The words after "Norwich" here are adopted from the Anglo-Saxon Chronicle ; as the text has " et omnes vicit in malum," words which admit of no sense whatever, and are clearly erroneous.

with the leave of king William; they also engaged that they
would first deliver up the castle of Rochester. But, when
Odo had come to Rochester with the king's men, who, on
the king's behalf, were to receive possession of the castle,
he was immediately placed in confinement together with them,
by those who were in the castle. Some persons assert that
this was done by the cunning contrivance of the bishop. However, in this castle there were some valiant knights, and almost
all the nobility of Normandy. There was also there, Eustace
the Younger, earl of Boulogne, and many of the nobles of
Flanders. When the king heard of this, he came with his
army to Rochester, and laid siege to the city; upon which,
after a short time, those who were in it surrendered; and
thus the bishop, who was almost a second king of England,
irrecoverably lost his dignity. But, on arriving in Normandy,
he immediately received charge of the whole province[3] from
duke Robert. William, bishop of Durham, and many others
also, took their departure from England.

In the year 1089, Lanfranc, the archbishop of Canterbury,
departed this life, on the ninth day before the calends of July,
being the fifth day of the week. In the same year, on the
third day before the ides of August, being Saturday, about the
third hour of the day, there was a very great earthquake
throughout England.

In the year 1090, William the Younger, king of England,
with the intention of taking Normandy from his brother Robert
and subjecting it to his own dominions, first took the castle of
Walter de Saint Valery, and the castle which has the name
of Albemarle, and, afterwards, several other castles, and placed
knights in them, who committed ravages throughout Normandy. On seeing this, and discovering the faithlessness of
his own people, duke Robert sent ambassadors to Philip, king
of the Franks, his liege lord, who thereupon came into Normandy, and the king and the duke laid siege to one of the
castles which was garrisoned by his brother's troops. On this
being told to king William, he secretly sent a considerable
sum of money to king Philip, and, entreating him to desist from
besieging it, succeeded in his object.

[3] These words are succeeded by the following detached sentence,
" cujus ordinem causæ libellus in hoc descripsus ostendit." It is evidently
corrupt, and capable of no exact translation; though it probably means,
" the reasons for which will appear from what is previously stated."

In the year 1091, King William the Younger went over to
Normandy in the month of February, with the design of
taking it from his brother Robert; but, while he was there,
peace was made between them by treaty, on condition that
the duke should with good faith deliver up to the king
the earldom of Eu,[81] Feschamp, the abbey of Mount Saint
Michael, and Keresburg,[82] with the castles which had revolted
from him, and that the king should reduce to subjection to
the duke the province of Maine and the castles of Normandy,
which were then making resistance to him. It was also
agreed that the king should restore their lands in England
to all the Normans who had lost them by reason of their
fidelity to the duke, and should also give to the duke as much
land in England as was then arranged between them. In
addition to this, they came to an understanding that if the
duke should die without a son lawfully born in wedlock, the
king should be his heir; and, in like manner, if the king
should happen to die, the duke should be his heir. Twelve
barons on the king's side and twelve on the duke's guaranteed
this treaty by oath.

In the meantime, while these matters were being treated of,
their brother Henry,[83] having raised all the troops he could,
with the aid of some of the monks in the place, took possession of Mount Saint Michael, laid waste the king's lands,
and took prisoners some of his men, and spoiled others. In
consequence of this, the king and the duke, assembling an army,
besieged the Mount during the whole of Lent, and had frequent
skirmishes, and lost some men and horses. But the king,
growing wearied of the protracted siege, retired without
coming to terms, and, shortly after, dispossessed the Clito
Edgar of all the honors which the duke had conferred upon
him, and banished him from Normandy.

In the meantime, in the month of May, Malcolm, king of
the Scots, invaded Northumbria with a large army. If he
could only find provisions, his object was to make further
inroads and commit acts of violence upon the people of England. But God ordained it otherwise; and, therefore, he was
impeded in his designs. The king, on hearing of this, re-

82 Of course he would naturally be displeased at the little regard paid
to his interests in the compact then being made.

turned to England with his brother Robert in the month of August, and shortly after, set out for Scotland with a considerable fleet and an army of horse, with the object of waging war against Malcolm; on coming to Durham, he restored bishop William to his see, three years on that very day after he had left it; that is to say, on the third day before the ides of September.

But before the king had reached Scotland, a short time previous to the feast of Saint Michael, nearly the whole of his fleet was lost, and many of his horse perished through hunger and cold; after which, king Malcolm met him with his army in the province of Loidis.[67] On seeing this, duke Robert sent for the Clito Edgar, whom the king had banished from Normandy, and who was then staying with the king of the Scots, and, by his assistance, made peace between the two kings, upon the understanding that Malcolm should pay homage to him, as he had paid homage to his father, and that king William should restore to Malcolm the twelve towns which he had possessed in England under his father, and pay yearly twelve golden marks. But the peace that was made between them lasted only a short time. The duke also reconciled the king to Edgar.

On the ides of October, being the fourth day of the week, a violent flash of lightning struck the tower of the church of Winchelcomb, and made a wide opening in the wall, close to the roof; it split asunder one of the beams, and giving a severe blow to the image of Christ,[88] hurled the head to the ground, and broke the right thigh. The image, also, of Saint Mary, which stood near the cross, was struck by the flash, and fell to the ground; after which, there followed a great smoke, with an excessive stench, which filled the whole church and lasted until the monks of the place, chaunting psalms, had gone round the buildings of the monastery with holy water and incense, and relics of the Saints.

In addition to this, on the sixteenth day before the calends of November, being the sixth day of the week, a violent whirlwind, coming from the south, blew down more than six hundred houses in London, and a considerable number of churches. It attacked the church which is called Saint Mary at Arches, and killing two men there, lifted the roof with the rafters aloft, and after carrying it to and fro in the air, at length fixed six of

67 Leeds.   88 On a crucifix.

the rafters in the same order in which they had been originally
inserted in the roof, so deep in the ground, that of some of
them only the seventh, of some the eighth part, was visible;
and yet they were seven or eight and twenty feet in length.

After this, the king returned from Northumbria through
Mercia into Wessex, and kept the duke with him till nearly
the Nativity of our Lord, but was not willing to fulfil the
treaty that had been made between them. The duke being
greatly annoyed at this, on the tenth day before the calends of
January, returned to Normandy with the Clito Edgar.

At this period, according to the reports in England, there
were two so-called popes of Rome, who, disagreeing as to
their right to the title, divided the church of God into two
parties; these were Urban, who was formerly called Odo,
bishop of Ostia, and Clement, whose former name was
Wibert, archbishop of Ravenna; this matter, not to speak of
other parts of the world, had so greatly occupied the attention
of the church of England for many years, that from the time
that Gregory, also called Hildebrand, departed this life, up to
the present period, it had refused to pay obedience or make
submission to any pope; Italy and France, however, acknowledged Urban as the vicar of Saint Peter.

In the year 1092, the greater part of the city of London
was destroyed by fire. On the nones of April, being the
second day of the week, Osmund, bishop of Salisbury, with
the assistance of Valcelline, bishop of Winchester, and of John,
bishop of Bath, dedicated the church which he had built within the castle of Salisbury. Bishop Remigius also, who, with
the sanction of king William the Elder, had changed the seat of
his bishopric from Dorchester[91] to Lincoln, wished to dedicate
the church which he had built there, and which was well worthy
of the bishop's chair, as he perceived that the day of his
death was close at hand. But Thomas, the archbishop of York,
firmly opposed him, and asserted that the church was built in
his province. King William the Younger, however, in consideration of a sum of money which Remigius gave him, gave
orders to the bishops of nearly the whole of England to
meet together on the seventh day before the ides of May and
consecrate the church; but, two days before the time appointed,

[91] In Oxfordshire.

by the secret dispensation of God, bishop Remigius departed from this world, and the dedication of the church stood over for the present. After this, the king set out for the province of Northumbria, and rebuilt the city which in the British language is called Carleil,[95] and in Latin, Luguballia, and erected a castle there ; for this city, with some others in those parts, had been destroyed two hundred years before, by the pagan Danes, and had remained desolate from that time until the present period.

In the year 1093, king William the Younger was attacked by a severe illness at a royal town which is called Alvestan, on which he repaired with all haste to Gloucester, and there lay ill throughout the whole of Lent. Thinking that he should shortly die, at the suggestion of the barons, he promised the Almighty to correct his mode of living, no longer to sell churches or put them up for sale, but to protect them with his kingly power, to destroy unrighteous laws, and to enact righteous ones. The archbishopric of Canterbury, which he had kept in his own hands, he gave to Anselm, the abbat of Bec, who was then in England, and the bishopric of Lincoln to his chancellor, Robert, surnamed Bloet.

A new church was commenced to be built at Durham, on the third day before the calends of August, being the fifth day of the week, bishop William, and Malcolm, the king of the Scots, and the prior Turgot, on that day laying the first stone of the foundation. On the day of the feast of Saint Bartholomew the Apostle,[96] Malcolm, the king of the Scots, came to Gloucester, to meet king William the Younger, as had been previously arranged between their ambassadors, in order that, according

[92] Carlisle. Holinshed has the following remark upon a passage in Matthew of Westminster. " Here have I thought good to advertise you of an error in Matthew of Westminster, crept in either through misplacing the matter by means of some exemplifier, either else by the author's mistaking his account of years, as 1072 for 1092, referring the repairing of Carlisle unto William the Conqueror, at what time he made a journey against the Scots in the said year 1072. And yet not thus contented ; to bewray the error more manifestly, he affirmeth that the king exchanged the earldom of Chester with Rafe or Ranulf de Micenis, alias Meschines, for the earldom of Carlisle, which the said Meschines held before, and had begun then to build and fortify that town ; whereas it is certain that Ranulf de Meschines came to enjoy the earldom of Chester by way of inheritance."

[93] V. r. The ides.

to the wish of some of the chief men of England, peace might
be renewed and there might exist a lasting friendship between
them; they separated, however, without coming to terms.
For William, in his excessive haughtiness and pride, con-
temptuously refused to see Malcolm or to treat with him. In
addition to this, he also wished to force him to make redress
in his own court solely according to the judgment of his own
barons, but Malcolm utterly declined to do so, unless the conference were held upon the confines of the two kingdoms, where
the kings of the Scots had been in the habit of making redress
to the kings of England, and in conformity with the opinion of
the nobles of both kingdoms. Shortly after these events, a very
wonderful sign appeared in the sun.

In the same year, Roger, earl of Shrewsbury, Guido, abbat
of Saint Augustine's, and Paulinus, abbat of the church of
Saint Alban, departed this life. This Paulinus, having by
means of the violent conduct of earl Robert,[94] effected an entrance into the church of Tynemouth, in spite of the prohibition of the monks of Durham, who had been the possessors of
it, was there attacked with an illness, and died on his way home
at Seteringtun.[94*] On the day of the feast of Saint Brice,[95]
Malcolm king of the Scots, and Edward, his eldest son, were
slain in Northumbria with their men, by the soldiers of Robert
earl of Northumbria; in whose death the judgment of God is
distinctly visible, from the fact that he and his men perished in
the same province which he had been in the habit, at the dic-
tation of avarice, of laying waste.

For, on five occasions he had afflicted it with dreadful ravages,
and had carried off its wretched inhabitants in slavery; the first
time in the reign of king Edward, when Egelwin was bishop
of Durham, at the period when Tosti, the earl of Northumbria,
had gone to Rome; the second time in the reign of king
William, the above-named Egelwin being still bishop, on
which occasion, Cleveland was laid waste; the third time, in
the reign of the same king William, when Walcher was
bishop of Durham, at which period he proceeded as far as the
river Tyne, and after having slaughtered multitudes of men
and burned many places, returned with a large amount of booty;

[94] De Mowbray.
[94*] Called Colewich by Roger of Wendover, who calls the abbat Paul.
[95] Thirteenth of November.

the fourth time, in the reign of king William the Younger, when William was bishop of Durham, on which occasion, with an innumerable army, he came as far as Chester,[96] with the full intention of proceeding further; but a small body of troops uniting against him, he returned with all speed from very fear.

The fifth time, having collected all the troops he possibly could, he invaded Northumbria, with the intention of reducing it to utter desolation, but was slain near the river Alne,[97] by Morell,[98] a most valiant knight, together with his eldest son, Edward, whom he had appointed his successor in the kingdom. A portion of his army died by the sword of the enemy, and those who escaped the sword were drowned in the inundations of the rivers, which were at that time unusually swollen by the winter rains. The body of this king and most blood-thirsty butcher, there being none of his own people to cover it with earth, two of the country-people placed in a cart, and buried it at Tynemouth ; and thus it came to pass that in the very place where he had deprived multitudes of life, liberty, and possessions, by the judgment of God, he himself lost his life and possessions.

On hearing of his death, Margaret, queen of the Scots, was affected with such violent grief, that she suddenly fell extremely ill; immediately upon which, sending for the priests, she entered a church, and having confessed to them her sins, caused herself to be anointed with oil, and to be provided with the heavenly viaticum, entreating the Lord with most urgent and repeated prayers, that he would not allow her any longer to remain in this world of misery. Her prayers were heard, for on the third day after the king's death, she was released from the bonds of the flesh, and, as we have reason to believe, passed to the joys of everlasting salvation. For, during her life, she shewed herself a most devoted follower of piety, justice, peace, and charity ; assiduous in her prayers, she mortified her body by watching and fasting, enriched churches and monasteries, and loved and honored the servants and handmaids of God ; she broke bread to the hungry, clothed the naked, gave lodging,

[96] Chester-le-street, in Durham.
[97] In the vicinity of Alnwick, in Northumberland.
[98] V. r. Merkell. The Anglo-Saxon Chronicle says that he was steward to earl Robert.

food, and raiment to all strangers who came to her, and loved God with all her heart.

After her death, the Scots chose [99] as their king, Dufenald, the brother of king Malcolm, and expelled from Scotland all the English who belonged to the royal court. On hearing of this, Duncan, the son of king Malcolm, who was at that time in the service[1] of king William, requested him to give him his father's kingdom; and, on his prayer being granted, swore fealty to him, and immediately repaired with all haste to Scotland, accompanied by a multitude of English and Normans, and, expelling his uncle, Dufenald,[2] from the kingdom, reigned in his stead. Shortly after, some of the Scots meeting together, cut off nearly the whole of his men; on which, with a few others, he made his escape. However, they afterwards allowed him to reign over them, on condition that he should no more introduce Englishmen or Normans into Scotland, or allow them to serve under him.

At this period, a meeting was held of nearly all the bishops of England, among whom Thomas, the archbishop of York, held the chief place; and on the second day before the nones of December they consecrated Anselm, abbat of Bec, archbishop of Canterbury. In the same year, William, earl of Eu, being overcome by his inordinate greediness for money, and allured by the magnitude of the honors promised him, revolted from his natural lord, Robert, duke of Normandy, to whom he had sworn fealty, and, coming to England, after acting the part of a guilty seducer,[3] acknowledged himself a subject of king William.

In the year 1094, Robert, duke of Normandy, by ambassadors, informed king William that he should renounce the treaty

[99] The Anglo-Saxon Chronicle also mentions this election. Upon the passage, Mr. Ingram, the Translator, observes, " From this expression, it is evident that, though preference was naturally and properly given to hereditary claims, the monarchy of Scotland, as well as of England, was in principle elective. The doctrine of hereditary, of divine, of indefeasible right, is of modern growth."

[1] "Militabat." The Anglo-Saxon Chronicle says that he had been given by his father as a hostage to king William.

[2] The name which we call "Donald."

[3] "Ut seductor maximus." He had probably seduced others from their loyalty to duke Robert; if, indeed, the reading here is correct, which is very doubtful.

which they had made; he also called him a perjured and perfidious man, if he should refuse to observe the compact which had
been made between them in Normandy. In consequence of this,
about the calends of February, the king went to Hastings, and
while staying there, caused the church of Battle[4] to be dedicated in honor of Saint Martin; there he also deprived Herebert,[5] bishop of Thetford, of his pastoral staff; for he had
secretly intended to go to pope Urban, to seek absolution from
him, on account of the bishopric which he had purchased for
himself, and the abbey he had bought for his father, Robert,[5*] from king William, for a thousand pounds. After
this, at mid-Lent, the king went over to Normandy, and, a
truce being agreed on, held a conference with his brother, but
parted from him without coming to terms.

After this, they again met in the field of Mars; when those
who, on oath, were to effect a reconciliation between them,
laid all the blame on the king; on which he would neither
admit his fault, nor observe the treaty. Being greatly enraged
in consequence, they separated without coming to terms.
The duke took his departure for Rouen, but the king returned
to Eu, and there took up his quarters, and levied soldiers
on every side; to some of the Norman nobles he gave gold, silver, and lands, and to some he promised them, in order that they
might revolt from his brother Robert, and subject themselves,
together with their castles, to his sway. Having accomplished
all these matters to his wish, he distributed his soldiers among
the castles which he had either previously held, or had then
gained possession of.

In the meantime, he took the castle which is called Bures, and
of the duke's knights which he found therein, some he sent in
captivity to England, and some he kept in confinement in Nor-

> [4] Battle Abbey, which had been commenced by William the Conqueror.
> [5] This was Herbert de Losinga; whose letters, which were supposed
> to be lost, have recently been discovered. Roger of Wendover gives a
> different version of this story; he says, " In 1094, Herebert, surnamed
> Losinga, was abbot of Ramsey, but he now by purchase procured himself
> to be made bishop of Thetford; but afterwards, in penitence for his crime
> he went to Rome, where he resigned his simoniacal staff and ring into
> the hands of the pope; but by the indulgence of the Holy See, he re-
> ceived the same back again, and returning home, transferred his see to
> Norwich, where he established a congregation of monks."
> [5*] His father was, probably, one of the secular clergy.

mandy; and, harassing his brother in every way, used his utmost exertions to deprive him of his patrimony. Accordingly, Robert, being compelled by necessity, brought his liege lord, Philip, king of the Franks, into Normandy with an army; on which the king laid siege to the castle of Argenton, and on the very same day, without any bloodshed, took seven hundred of the king's knights, together with twice as many esquires, together with all the garrison of the castle, and ordered them to be kept in close confinement, until each should ransom himself, after which, he returned to France.

Duke Robert, however, besieged a castle which is called Holm, until William Peverel and eight hundred men who defended it surrendered to him. When this became known to the king, he sent messengers to England, and ordered twenty thousand foot soldiers to be sent to Normandy to his assistance; who being assembled at Hastings, for the purpose of crossing the sea, by the king's orders, Ranulph took from them the money that had been given them to purchase provisions, namely, ten shillings from each man, and, ordering them to return home, sent the money to the king. In the meantime, the whole of England was afflicted with oppressive and unceasing taxes, and a great mortality of the people both in this and the following year.

In addition to this, first the people of North Wales, and then those of South Wales, throwing off the yoke of servitude by which they had been long oppressed, and lifting up their necks, struggled to regain their liberty. Accordingly, a great multitude having assembled together, they stormed the castles that had been founded in West Wales, and, in the provinces of Chester, Shrewsbury, and Hereford, burned the towns on every side, carried off plunder, and slew multitudes of English and Normans. They also stormed the castle in the Isle of Anglesey, and reduced it to subjection.

In the meantime, the Scots treacherously slew their king, Duncan, and some other persons, by the advice and entreaty of Dufenald, and then chose him again for their king. Shortly after, King William returned to England, on the fourth day before the calends of January, to wage war against the Welch, and immediately proceeded with his army into Wales, where he lost many men and horses.

' "Scutaris."

In the year 1095, at the middle of the seventh hour, on the night of Saturday, the eighteenth day of the month of January, Wulstan, the bishop of Worcester, was removed from this world; a venerable man, and one of most exemplary life, who from his youth had entirely devoted himself to his religious duties, and who, bent upon gaining the glory of the heavenly kingdom, with great devotion and humility of mind had carefully served God with the utmost zeal, and departed after many struggles of pious agony. This took place in the year, from the first day of the world, according to the assured account contained in the Holy Scriptures, five thousand two hundred and ninety-nine,[7] in the four hundred and seventy-sixth year of the present great year[8] from the beginning of the world, in the one thousand and eighty-fourth from the Passion of our Lord according to the Gospels, in the one thousand and sixty-sixth year according to the Chronicle of Bede, in the thousand and sixty-first year according to Dionysius,[9] in the year from the arrival of the Angles in Britain seven hundred and forty-five, from the arrival of Saint Augustine four hundred and ninety-eight, from the death of Saint Oswald the archbishop, one hundred and three, in the thirty-second year of the eleventh great Paschal cycle, in the five hundred and tenth year of the tenth from the beginning[10] of the world, in the fourth year of the second Solar cycle,[11] in the third year of the Bissextile cycle, in the third year of the second Nineteen year cycle, in the tenth year of the second Lunar cycle,[12] in the third year of the cycle of Indiction, in the eighteenth lustrum of his age, and in the third year of the seventh lustrum[14] of his pontificate.

In a wondrous manner, at the very hour of his departure, he appeared in a vision to his friend, Robert, the bishop of Hereford, to whom he was especially attached, at a town

7 According to the computation mostly used in the middle ages, our Saviour was born A.M. 4204.

8 This seems to be a cycle of nearly eleven years.

9 Dionysius, the Areopagite; whose supposed writings were much read in the middle ages.

10 This is, probably, a cycle of five hundred and thirty-two years.

11 The cycle of the sun, or of Sundays, is a period of twenty-eight years.

12 This would almost appear to be really the same cycle as the last; as the cycle of the moon, or of nineteen years, or of the golden number, is the same thing. Possibly the figures are incorrectly stated.

13 A cycle of eleven years.

14 These lustra consist of five years each.

called Cricklade, and ordered him to make haste to Worcester, to bury him.   The ring, also, with which he had received
the pontifical benediction, God would allow no one to draw
from off his finger, lest, after his death, the holy man should
appear to have deceived his friends, to whom he had frequently
foretold that he would not part with it, either in his lifetime or
at the day of his burial.

On the day before the nones of April, it seemed at night as
though stars were falling from heaven.   Walter, bishop of
Albano, legate from the Holy Church of Rome, being sent by
pope Urban, came to England before Easter, to bring the pall
to king William, for which he had sent the year before; which,
according to order, was, on the Lord's day, being the fourth
day before the ides of June, taken by him to Canterbury, and
laid upon the altar of our Saviour, and then assumed by
Anselm, and suppliantly kissed by all, as a mark of reverence
to Saint Peter.

On the sixth day before the calends of July, being the third
day of the week, Robert, bishop of Hereford, a man of extreme
piety, departed this life.   The above-named Wulstan, bishop
of Worcester, appeared to him in a vision, on the thirty-second
day after he had departed from this world, and sharply rebuked
him for his negligence and heedlessness, admonishing him to
use his best endeavours to amend both his own life and those
of his flock, with the utmost vigilance : if he did this, he affirmed that he would soon obtain pardon of God for all his
sins, and added, that he would not long retain his seat in the
chair in which he then sat, but that, if he should choose to be
more vigilant, he would be enabled to rejoice with himself in
the presence of God.   For both of these fathers had been most
zealous in their love of God, and most attached to each other ;
therefore we have reason to believe that he who was the first to
take his departure from this world unto God, felt an anxiety
for his most beloved friend, whom he had left in this world,
and used his best endeavours that he might, as soon as possible,
together with himself, rejoice in the presence of God.

At this period, Robert de Mowbray, earl of Northumbria,
and William de Eu, with many others, attempted to deprive king William of his kingdom and life, and to make
Stephen de Albemarle, his aunt's son, king, but were dis-
appointed.   For, on learning this, the king levied an army

throughout the whole of England, and, during two months, besieged the castle of the above-named earl Robert, at Tynemouth; and, having in the mean time taken a certain small fortress, he captured almost all the earl's bravest soldiers, and placed them in confinement, and then, laying siege to the castle, took it, and placed in custody the earl's brother, and the knights whom he found there. After this, over against Bebbanburg,[14*] that is to say, the city of Bebba, whither the earl had fled, he erected a castle, and called it "Malvoisin,"[15] and, having placed soldiers therein, returned to the country south of the Humber. After the king's departure, the garrison of Newcastle[16] promised earl Robert that they would allow him to enter it if he came secretly. Being overjoyed at this, he went forth on a certain night for that purpose, with thirty knights; on learning which, the knights who garrisoned the castle followed him, and, through messengers, made known his departure to the garrison of Newcastle. Not aware of this, on a certain Sunday, he made the attempt to carry out his plans, but failed, having been thus detected; on which, he fled to the monastery of Saint Oswin, the king and martyr;[17] where, on the sixth day of the siege, he was severely wounded in the thigh, while fighting with his adversaries, many of whom were also wounded, and many slain. Some of his men were also wounded, but all were captured, and he himself took refuge in the church; from which, being dragged forth, he was placed in confinement.

In the meantime the Welch stormed the castle of Montgomery, and slew there some of the men of Hugh, earl of Shrewsbury; at which the king being exasperated, he immediately commanded an expedition to be directed against it; and, after the feast of Saint Michael, led an army into Wales, and there lost many men and horses. On his return thence, he ordered earl Robert to be taken to Bamborough, and his eyes to be put out, unless his wife and his neighbour, Morel,[18] would surrender the castle. Compelled by this necessity, they surrender-

14 * Bamborough.   15 "Bad neighbour."
16 "Novi castelli" must mean the fortress of Newcastle, which had been lately erected, and not the new castle of Malvoisin, although Holinshed seems so to understand it; the present passage will not, however, admit of that construction being put upon it.   17 At Tynemouth.
18 The Anglo-Saxon Chronicle says that this Morel was his steward.
"Propinquus" may possibly mean "relative" here.

with surrendered the castle. The earl, being placed in close confinement, was led to Windsor; on which, Morell disclosed to the king the causes of the conspiracy taking place.

In the year 1096, William, bishop of Durham, died at Windsor, the royal palace, on the fourth day before the nones of January, being the second day of the week, but was buried at Durham, in the chapter-house there, on the northern side, having on the south the body of bishop Walcher; in the middle rests the body of Turgot, formerly bishop of the Scots, and prior of that church.

On the octave of the Epiphany, a council was held at Salisbury, and the king ordered William de Eu, who had been conquered in single combat, to be deprived of his eyes and his virility, and William Deandri, his sewer, his aunt's son, who had been privy to his treason, he ordered to be hanged; earl Odo of Champagne, who was the father of the above-named Stephen, and Philip, son of Roger earl of Shrewsbury, and some others, who had a guilty knowledge of the plot, he placed in confinement.

In this year, pope Urban came into France, and a synod was held at Clermont,[19] during Lent. He exhorted the Christians to set out for Jerusalem, for the purpose of waging war against the Turks, Saracens, Turcopoles,[19*] Persians, and other pagans, who at that period had overrun Jerusalem, and, having expelled the Christians, were in possession of Judæa. Immediately after his exhortation, at the same synod, Raymond, earl of Saint Gilles, and many others with him, assuming the emblem of the cross of Christ, engaged to undertake this pilgrimage in the cause of God, and to do what he had invited them to do : on hearing of which, other Christians in Italy, Germany, France and England, vying with each other, made preparations for the same expedition. The chiefs and leaders of these were Adimar, bishop of Puy, with a great number of other prelates, Peter the Hermit, Hugh the Great, brother to Philip, king of the Franks, Godfrey, duke of Lorraine, Stephen, count of Chartres, Robert, duke of Normandy, Robert, earl of Flanders, the two brothers of duke Godfrey,

[19] This council at Clermont, in Auvergne, continued from the 18th to the 28th of November, A.D. 1095, and not in 1096.

[19*] Turcopoles are supposed to have been the children of Christian mothers and Turkish fathers.

namely, Eustace, earl of Boulogne, and Baldwin, Raymond, the above-named earl, and Reimond, the son of Robert (Guiscard; and with these followed an immense multitude of people of all languages.

On the seventeenth day before the calends of July, being the Lord's day, Sampson was consecrated bishop of Worcester, in the church of St. Paul, at London, by Anselm, the archbishop of Canterbury. After this, Robert, duke of Normandy, having determined to set out for Jerusalem with the rest, sent ambassadors to England, and requested his brother William to renew the treaty of peace between them, and to lend him ten thousand marks of silver and receive from him the dukedom of Normandy as a security; upon which, the king, being desirous to comply with his request, gave orders to the nobles of England that each one should, to the best of his ability, supply him with money with all possible haste. Accordingly, the bishops, abbats, and abbesses, broke up the golden and other ornaments of the churches; the earls, barons, and sheriffs stripped their soldiers and villains, and supplied the king with no small amount of gold and silver. In the month of September the king crossed the sea and made peace with his brother, giving him six thousand six hundred and sixty-six pounds of silver, and receiving from him Normandy in pledge.

In the year 1097, William, king of the English, returned to England at the season of Lent, and, after Easter, set out a second time[20] for Wales, with an army of horse and foot, with the intention of destroying all persons of the male sex. However, he was unable to take or slay hardly any of them, but lost some of his own men, and a great number of horses. After this, he sent the Clito Edgar to Scotland, with an army, in order that, after expelling his uncle, Dufenald, who had usurped the throne, he might make his cousin Edgar, the son of king Malcolm, king in his stead.

On the thirteenth day before the calends of July, being Saturday, the Christians took the city of Nice. On the third day before the calends of October, and the fifteen days following, a comet appeared. Some persons at this period affirmed that they had seen in the heavens a wonderful sign, like a fire burning in the shape of a cross.

[20] This was his third expedition. See under the years 1094 and 1095.

Shortly after this, a misunderstanding arose between the king and Anselm, the archbishop of Canterbury, because, from the time he was made archbishop, he had not been allowed to hold a synod and correct the evils which had sprung up throughout England; on which he crossed the sea, and remaining for a time in France, afterwards proceeded to pope Urban at Rome. About the time of the feast of Saint Andrew, the king set out from England for Normandy. On the second day before the calends of January, Baldwin, abbat of the monastery of Saint Edmund, a man of exemplary piety and of French extraction, departed this life.

In the year 1098, on the third day before the nones of January, being Sunday, Valkeline, the bishop of Winchester, departed this life. In the spring of this year, William the Younger, king of the English, subdued the city which is called Le Mans, and by force reduced a great part of that province to subjection. In the meantime, Hugh, earl of Shrewsbury, and with him Hugh, earl of Chester, made a descent upon the island of Mevania, which is usually called Anglesey, with a body of troops, and slew many of the Welch whom they there captured, and of others they cut off the hands or feet, and then, depriving them of their virility, put out their eyes. A certain priest also, named Kenred, a man of advanced age, from whom the Welch had received advice in their affairs, they dragged out of his church, and, having deprived him of his virility and put out one of his eyes, cut out his tongue; but, on the third day after, by the Divine mercy, his speech was restored to him.

At this period, Magnus, king of Norway, son of king Olaf, the son of king Harold Harfager, wishing to add the islands of Orkney and Anglesey to his realms, came thither,[21] with a few ships; but, on his making an attempt to land, Hugh, earl of Shrewsbury, accompanied by a great number of armed knights, met him on the sea-shore; and, according to general report, being struck by an arrow from the king's own hand, was slain on the seventh day after he had exercised his cruelty on the above-named priest.

On the third day before the nones of July, being the fourth day of the week, the city of Antioch was taken by the Christians; a few days after which, the spear with which, while

21 To the isle of Anglesey.

suspended on the cross, the Saviour of the world was pierced, was, through the revelation of the Apostle Andrew, the most meek of the Saints, discovered in the church of Saint Peter the Apostle. Being encouraged on finding this, on the fourth day before the calends of July, being the second day of the week, the Christians, carrying it with them, marched forth from the city, and, engaging with the pagans, put to flight Corbaran, the commander of the soldiers of Soldan, the king of Persia, and the Turks, Arabs, Saracens, and many other nations, at the edge of the sword, and, after slaying many thousands, by the aid of God gained a complete victory.

Throughout the whole of the night of the fifth day before the calends of October in this year, there was an extraordinary brightness. In the same year, the bones of Canute, the king and martyr, were raised from the tomb, and, with due honor, placed in a shrine. Roger, the duke of Apulia, having assembled a great army, laid siege to the city of Capua, which had revolted against his authority. Pope Urban, attended, according to his command, by Anselm, the archbishop of Canterbury, set out for the council which he had appointed to be held at Bari, on the calends of October. At this council, many points of the Catholic faith were discoursed upon by the successor of the Apostles, with great eloquence. Here also, a question being mooted on the part of the Greeks, who wished to prove, on the authority of the Evangelists, that the Holy Ghost proceeded only from the Father, the above-named Anselm treated and discoursed and explained so admirably on the subject, that there was no one at the meeting who did not pronounce himself satisfied thereby.

In the year 1099, in the third week after Easter, pope Urban held a great council at Rome, at which he excommunicated all laymen who gave investiture to churches, and all who received investiture from the hands of laymen, as well as all those who consecrated persons for the duties of the office so bestowed. He also excommunicated those who, to gain ecclesiastical honors, did homage to laymen; affirming that it seemed most shocking that hands which had attained a distinction so high that it was granted to none of the angels, namely, by their touch,²² to create the God who created all

²² " Signaculo;" probably in allusion to marking with the sign of the cross.

things, and in the presence of God the Father, to offer up his
own self for the salvation of the whole world, should be reduced to such a pitch of disgracefulness or folly as to become
the handmaids of those hands which by day and night are
defiled by obscene contact, or, used to rapine and the unrighteous
shedding of blood, are stained thereby; upon which, all shouted
with one consent, "So be it! So be it!" and thereupon the council
was concluded. After this, the archbishop[24] proceeded to Lyons.

William the Younger, king of the English, returned to England from Normandy, and, at Pentecost, held his court at
London, and gave the bishopric of Durham to Ranulph, whom
he had appointed manager of the affairs of the whole kingdom;
and, shortly afterwards, he was consecrated there by Thomas,
archbishop of York.

On the ides of July, being the sixth day of the week, Jerusalem was taken by the Christians; and, soon after, on the
eleventh day before the calends of August, Godfrey, duke of
Lorraine, was elected king by the whole army.   On the
fourth day before the calends of August, being the fifth day of
the week, pope Urban departed this life.   On the second day
before the ides of August, being the same day of the week,
the Christians fought a very great battle before the city of
Ascalon, with Lavedal,[25] the commander of the army and
second in rank in the whole kingdom of Babylon,[26] and, by
the exceeding bounty of Christ, gained a wondrous victory.
Paschal, a venerable man, who had been ordained priest
by pope Hildebrand, having been elected pope by the Roman
people, was consecrated on the following day. On the third
day before the nones of November, the sea overflowed the land,
and swept away a great number of towns and men, and oxen
and sheep innumerable.

In the year from the incarnation of our Lord 1100, pope
Clement, who was also named Wibert, departed this life.

William the Younger, king of the English, while engaged
in hunting in the New Forest, which in the English language
is called Itene,[27] was struck by an arrow incautiously aimed
by Walter, a Frank, surnamed Tyrell, and died, in conse-

---

[24] Probably Anselm.   [25] Roger of Wendover says that his bap-
tismal name was Emyreius, and that he was an Armenian, the son of
Christian parents; and that on his apostatizing, he changed his name for
that of Elafdal.   [26] Persia.   [27] More properly Utine.

quence, on the fourth day before the nones of August, being
the fifth day of the week, in the eighth year of the indiction. The body was carried to Winchester, and buried at
the old monastery there, in the church of Saint Peter. And
not undeservedly did this befall him, for, as popular rumour
affirmed, this was undoubtedly the great might of God and
his vengeance. For, in ancient times, that is to say, in the
days of king Edward and the other kings of England, his
predecessors, that same district flourished most abundantly
in inhabitants, and worshippers of God, and churches, but, by
the command of king William the Elder, the people being
driven away, the houses half destroyed, and the churches pulled
down, the land was rendered fit only for the habitation of
wild beasts; and this, according to general belief, was the
cause of the mishap; for it was the fact that, some time before, Richard, the brother of this same king William the
Younger, lost his life in the same forest; and a short time
previously, his cousin Richard, son of Robert duke of Normandy, while hunting there, was pierced by an arrow discharged by one of his knights, of which wound he died. In
the place, also, where the king fell, in former times a church
had been built, but, as previously stated, in his father's time,
it was levelled with the ground.

In the days of this king, as in part already mentioned,
there were many portentous signs beheld in the sun, moon, and
stars; the sea, also, frequently flowed beyond its usual limits
on the shore, and swept away men and animals, towns, and a
vast number of houses.   In a village which is called Berkshire,[25] just before the king's death, blood flowed from a spring
during a period of three weeks.[26]   The devil, also, showed
himself frequently, in a frightful shape, to many Normans in
the woods, and made many communications to them respecting the king and Ranulph and some other persons. Nor is this
to be wondered at, for in their time almost all equity on part
of the laws was silent, and all grounds for justice being suppressed, money alone held sway with the men in power.   In
fine, at this period, some persons paid more obedience to the
royal wishes than to justice; so much so, that Ranulph, con-

[25] Some words are evidently omitted in the text.   William of Malmesbury says that this took place at the village of Finchampstead, in the
county of Berks.   [26] William of Malmesbury says fifteen days.

tray to ecclesiastical law and the prescribed rules of his order (for he was a priest), first put up to sale abbacies, and then bishoprics, the holders of which were dead, having lately received the presentations from the king, to whom he paid yearly no small sum of money. The influence of this man became so extensive, and so greatly did his power increase in a short space of time, that the king appointed him judge and general manager of the whole kingdom.

Having secured this extent of power, in every quarter throughout England he inflicted some of the richest and most wealthy by taking from them their property and lands. The poorer classes he unceasingly oppressed by heavy and unjust taxes, and, in many ways, both before he received his bishopric and after, persecuted both great and small in common, and ceased not to do so up to the period of the king's death. For on the very day on which the king met with his death, he held in his own hands the archbishopric of Canterbury and the bishoprics of Winchester and Salisbury.

HENRY THE FIRST.

King William reigned fourteen years all but twenty-eight days, and was succeeded by his younger brother, Henry. Shortly after, on the nones of August, he was consecrated king at Westminster, by Maurice, the bishop of London; and, on the day of his consecration, he set free the holy church of God, which had been sold and let to farm in his brother's time; he did away with all bad customs and iniquitous exactions by which the kingdom of England was unrighteously oppressed; he also established unbroken peace in his kingdom, and commanded that it should be maintained. To all in common he restored the laws of King Edward, together with those amendments to them which his father had made : but the forests, which he had made and held, he retained in his own hands. Not long after this, on the seventh day before the ides of September, he placed Ranulph, the bishop of Durham, in confinement in the Tower of London, and recalled Anselm, archbishop of Canterbury, from Gaul.

In the meantime, Robert, earl of Flanders, and Eustace, earl of Boulogne, returned home first, and after them Robert, duke of

Normandy, with the wife whom he had married in Sicily. Shortly after this, Henry, king of the English, assembled the elders of England[30] at London, and took to wife Matilda, the daughter of Malcolm, king of the Scots, and of queen Margaret, and sister of the kings Edgar, Alexander, and David; on which she was consecrated queen, and crowned by Anselm, archbishop of Canterbury, on the Lord's day, being the day of the feast of Saint Martin.

Thomas, archbishop of York, a man whose memory was revered, and of exemplary piety, affable, and beloved by all, departed this life at York, on the Lord's day, being the fourteenth day before the calends of December, and was succeeded by Gerard, the bishop of Hereford.

In the year 1101, Louis, king of the Franks, visited the court of king Henry at London, at the time of the Nativity of our Lord. On the calends of February, Ranulph, the bishop of Durham, escaped from confinement, by means of extreme artfulness, and, crossing the sea, went to Robert, duke of Normandy, and persuaded him to make a hostile invasion of England. In addition to this, many of the powerful men in this country sent ambassadors to him, and begged him to come with all haste, offering him the crown and the kingdom. On the eighth day before the ides of June, the city of Gloucester, together with the principal monastery there and many others, was destroyed by fire.

In consequence of the above representations, Robert, duke of Normandy, having collected a vast number of knights, archers, and foot, assembled his ships at a place which, in the Norman language, is called 'Treport,'[31] on learning which, king William gave orders to his sailors to watch the seas, that no one might approach the English territory from the country of Normandy, and, having collected an innumerable army throughout the whole of England, he himself pitched his camp not far from Hastings, in Sussex; for he considered it a matter of certainty that his brother would land in that neighbourhood. But duke Robert, acting on the advice of bishop Ranulph, so wrought upon some of the king's sailors, by making them promises of different kinds, that, forsaking the fealty which they owed the king, they went over to him, and acted as his guides to England. All things, therefore, being in readi-

ness, together with his army, he embarked, and, about the
time of the feast of Saint Peter ad Vincula, landed at a
place called Portesmudh,[32] and immediately moving on his
army towards Winchester, encamped in a suitable spot.   On
learning his arrival, some of the chief men of England at
once, as they had previously arranged, went over to him, while
others, concealing their sentiments, remained with the king.
But the bishops, the common soldiers, and the English, with
resolute determination, sided with him, and were unanimously
prepared to go forth to battle in his cause.

However, the more prudent men on both sides, having held
a discreet conference among themselves, made peace between
the brothers on the following terms :—that the king was to pay
yearly to the duke three thousand marks of silver and restore
gratuitously to all the ancient dignities in England which they
had lost in consequence of their fidelity to the duke; and in
like manner, the duke was to restore them to those, who, for
the king's cause, had lost their dignities in Normandy, without
any recompense. On these terms being made, the king's army
returned home, and part of the duke's returned to Normandy,
while part remained with him in England.

In this year, Godfrey, king of Jerusalem, son of Eustace the
elder, earl of Boulogne, who had been previously the most
powerful duke of Lorraine, departed this life, and rests entombed
in the church of Golgotha.   After his death, the Christians
unanimously elected his brother, Baldwin, their king.   At
this period, Robert de Belesme, earl of Shrewsbury, the son
of earl Roger, commenced (with the view of opposing king
Henry, as the event proved,) to repair with a broad and high
wall the castle which Agelfleda, lady of the Mercians, in the
reign of her brother Edward the Elder, had formerly built on
the western side of the river Severn, at a place called Bridge;[33]
he also began to build another in Wales, at a place which is
called Carrocove.

In the year 1102, the above-named earl Robert de Belesme,
who also at that time ruled over the earldom of Ponthieu, and
was possessed of a considerable number of castles in Normandy, strongly fortified the city of Shrewsbury and the castle
there, as also the castles of Arundel and of Titchil,[34] with

---

[32] Portsmouth.   V. r. Moresmuth.   [33] Now Bridgenorth.
[34] Tickhill, in Yorkshire.

provisions, engines of war, arms, knights, and foot-soldiers, against king Henry. He also hastened, by every possible me-thod, working day and night, to complete the walls and towers of the castles of Bridge and Carrocove; the Welch also, and his own men, he encouraged by gifts of honors, lands, horses, and arms, and by various other presents, to become more zeal-ous and faithful to himself, and more ready to do what he wished.

These attempts, however, and his efforts were very soon stopped short. For his plots and intentions being, by means of certain information, discovered, the king pronounced him a public enemy. On this, at once assembling all the Welch and the Normans he possibly could at that moment, he and his brother Arnold laid waste part of the borough of Staf-ford, and carried away thence into Wales many beasts of burden and animals, together with some of the people. The king, however, without delay, laid siege first to his castle of Arundel, and, having erected castles around it, retired. He then ordered Robert, bishop of Lincoln, to lay siege to the castle of Tickill; while he himself, with an army levied throughout the whole of England, besieged the castle of Bridge, and ordered his people to construct engines of war and erect a castle there. In the meantime, by some trifling presents, he easily prevailed upon the Welch, in whom earl Robert placed great confidence, to disregard the oaths they had sworn to him, and entirely forsake him, and join in the attack against him. The consequence was, that, within thirty days, the city and all the castles were surrendered; and, having now subdued his enemy, Robert the king, ignominiously expelled him from England, and, shortly after, condemned his brother Arnold to a like fate, as a reward for his perfidious conduct.

After these events, king Henry being at London, with all the chief men of his kingdom, both ecclesiastics and those of the secular order, at Westminster he invested two of his clergy with bishoprics, appointing Roger, his chancellor, bishop of Salisbury, and Roger, his chief of the larder, bishop of Here-ford. Here, also, Anselm, archbishop of Canterbury, held a great synod, upon matters relating to the Christian reli-gion, the following prelates sitting there with him:—(Gerard,) archbishop of York, Maurice, bishop of London, William, bishop elect of Winchester, Robert, bishop of Lincoln, Samson, bishop of Worcester, Robert, bishop of Chester, John, bishop of Bath, Herbert, bishop of Norwich, Ralph, bishop of Chichester, Gundulph, bishop of Rochester, and the two who had lately received investiture, Roger and the second Roger. Osborn,[35] bishop of Exeter, being kept away by his infirmities, was unable to take part in the synod. At this synod, many abbats of French extraction, and some English, were deposed and deprived of their dignities, which they had unrighteously acquired, or had led a disgraceful life while enjoying them; namely, Guido, abbat of Pershore, Aldwin, abbat of Ramsey, the abbat of Middleton, Bodric, abbat of Burgh, Richard, abbat of Ely, and Robert, abbat of Saint Edmund's.

The above-named Roger, bishop elect of Hereford, was attacked with a malady, at London, and died; upon which, the queen's chancellor, Reinelm by name, was, with a similar investiture, substituted in his place. Henry, the king of the English, this year, gave Mary, the sister of queen Matilda, in marriage to Eustace, earl of Boulogne.

In the year 1103, a great disagreement arose between king Henry and archbishop Anselm, because the archbishop would not consent to the king conferring the investiture of churches, nor hold communion with those to whom the king had previously presented churches, as the successor of the Apostles had forbidden him and all others to do so. For this reason, the king ordered Gerard, the archbishop of York, to consecrate the bishops on whom the king himself had conferred investiture;[37] namely, William Giffard, and Roger, who had been his chaplain,[38] and to whom he had lately given the bishopric of Salisbury. Accordingly, Gerard obeyed the king's command; but, in the cause of justice, William Giffard disregarded it, and rejected the benediction of archbishop Gerard. In consequence of this, by the king's sentence, he was stripped of everything, and banished from the kingdom; the others, however, remained unconsecrated.

Shortly before this, Reinelm had returned to the king the bishopric of Hereford, because he was sensible that he had offended God, in having received the investiture of a church from the hand of any layman. After this, at Easter, the king

[35] V. r. Osbert.   [36] In Dorsetshire.   [37] By the ring and crozier.
[38] He has previously said that he was the king's chancellor.

o 2

held his court at Winchester; where, after receiving many injuries and divers affronts which he put up with, arch-bishop Anselm, at the king's request, set out for Rome on the fifth day before the calends of May, as had been arranged between him and the king, having in his company William, the bishop elect of Winchester, and some abbats who had been deprived of their abbeys, namely, Richard, abbat of Ely, and Aldwin, abbat of Ramsey.

Robert, duke of Normandy, came over to England to confer with the king, his brother; and, before he left England, gave up to him the three thousand marks of silver which the king, according to treaty, was to pay him each year. In the province which is called Berkshire, at a place the name of which is Hamstede, blood was seen[39] by many to spring out of the earth.

In the same year, on the third day before the ides of August, there was a violent storm of wind, which did such great mischief to the fruits of the earth throughout England that those who were then living had never seen the like at any previous time. In the year 1104, the venerable men, Walter, abbat of Evesham, and Serlo, abbat of Gloucester, departed this life; the former on the thirteenth day before the calends of February, the latter on the third day before the nones of March. At Pentecost, king Henry held his court at Westminster. In the same year, on the seventh day before the ides of June, being the third day of the week, four circles of a white color were seen around the sun, at about the sixth hour, one circle within another, just as though they had been painted there. All were astonished who saw this, as they had never before seen the like. In this year William, earl of Mortaigne, was deprived of all the lands he possessed in England. It is not easy to describe the misery which at this period the land of England endured, by reason of the king's exactions.

In consequence of the unbelief of certain abbats, in the pontificate of bishop Ranulph, the body of Saint Cuthbert the bishop was shown, and was, by Ralph, abbat of Seez,[41] after-

[39] This seems to be a repetition of the remarks mentioned under the year 1100, the name of the place being added. The Saxon Chronicle mentions it under this year; William of Malmesbury, as taking place in the reign of king William.

[41] A town in Normandy.

wards bishop of Rochester, and after that, archbishop of Canterbury, and the brethren of the church of Durham, by clear proofs, found uncorrupted, together with the head of Saint Oswald, the king and martyr, and the relics of Saint Bede, and many others of the Saints, in the presence of earl Alexander, the brother of Edgar, king of the Scots, and afterwards king. This disinterment took place four hundred and eighteen years five months and twelve days after his burial; being the sixth year of the reign of king Henry, and the sixth of the bishopric of Ranulph, and being from the beginning of the world, according to Bede and the Hebrew version, in the year five thousand three hundred and eight,[42] and according to the Seventy[43] interpreters, in the year six thousand three hundred and eight.

In the year 1105, Henry, king of the English, crossed the sea; and nearly all the chief men among the Normans, on his arrival, disregarding the duke, their liege lord, to whom they had sworn fealty, ran after the king's gold and silver, which he had brought from England, and delivered up to him the castles and fortified cities. He burned Bayeux, together with the church of Saint Mary there, and took Caen from his brother; after which, he returned to England, as he was unable to reduce the whole of Normandy to subjection, and in order that, supported by a large sum of money, he might return in the following year, and deprive his brother thereof, and render subject to himself the part that remained. However, William de Mortaigne, wherever he had the power, did injury to the king's property and men, on account of his own estates which he had lost in England.

In the year 1106, Robert, duke of Normandy, came to England, for the purpose of conferring with his brother, king Henry, whom he met at Northampton. On this occasion the duke begged him to restore the places he had taken from him in Normandy; with which request the king refusing to comply, the duke, being greatly enraged, crossed the sea to Normandy. In the first week of Lent, on the evening of the calends of March, being the sixth day of the week, a star of unusual appearance became visible, and, during twenty-five days, in

[42] According to the computation now used, A.M. 5108.
[43] The Septuagint.

the same manner, and at the same hour, was seen to shine between the south and the west. It seemed itself to be of small size and dim, but the brightness which was produced by it was very brilliant, and a train of light, just like a large beam, darted from the east and north into the star. Some affirmed that, at this period, they had seen more stars of unusual appearance. On the day of our Lord's Supper were seen two moons, shortly before daybreak, one in the east, the other in the west, both of them full; the same day being the fourteenth day of the moon.

In this year there was a shocking quarrel between Henry, emperor of Germany, and his son Henry; so much so, that they met in battle, and the father was slain by the son, after having reigned fifty years; upon which he was succeeded by his son the above-named Henry. Before the month of August, Henry, king of the English, crossed the sea and went to Normandy, on which nearly all the chief men of the Normans made submission to him, with the exception of Robert de Belesme and William de Mortaigne, and a few others, who adhered to duke Robert. At the Assumption of Saint Mary, Henry, king of the English, came to Bec, where he and archbishop Anselm holding a conference, became reconciled; and not long after, by the command and request of the king, the said archbishop returned to England. After this, the king assembled his army, and proceeding to a certain castle of the earl of Mortaigne, which is called Tenchebrai, laid siege to it. In the meantime, while the king was thus engaged, his brother Robert came upon him with his army, on the vigil of Saint Michael,⁴¹ and with him Robert de Belesme and William, earl of Mortaigne. A battle then taking place, king Henry gained the victory. On this occasion Robert, duke of Normandy, William, earl of Mortaigne, and Robert de Stuteville, with William Crispin and many others, were taken prisoners, while Robert de Belesme escaped by flight. In consequence of this success, king Henry subdued the whole of Normandy, and rendered it subject to his will, informing archbishop Anselm thereof by letter.

In the year 1108, Edgar, king of the Scots, departed this life, on the sixth day before the ides of January, and was succeeded by his brother Alexander. Normandy having now

⁴¹ Michaelmas eve.

been reduced to subjection by the king, Robert, duke of Normandy, and William, earl of Mortaigne, being first sent over to England as prisoners, the king himself returned to his kingdom before Easter. On the calends of August there was a meeting held at London of all the bishops, abbats, and nobles of the kingdom; and, during three days, in the absence of archbishop Anselm, there was a full discussion held between the king and the bishops upon the investitures of churches. Some of them urged, that the king ought to make them after the example of his father and brother, and not according to the precepts of and in obedience to the successor of the Apostles. But pope Paschal, standing firm in the opinion which had been promulgated from the papal chair, had conceded everything[45] which pope Urban had forbidden to be received as investitures, and by these means had made the king agree in his view on the subject of investiture.

After this, in the presence of Anselm, a great multitude being present, the king asserted and decreed that, from that time forward, no person should ever be invested in a bishopric or abbey by the king, or by any lay hand, in England, by the gift of the pastoral staff or of the ring; while Anselm conceded, that no person elected to a prelacy should be refused consecration to the dignity so received by reason of the homage which he should perform to the king. Gerard, archbishop of

[45] This passage, which might seem somewhat obscure, is probably explained by the more full account given by Roger of Wendover of what passed when Anselm and the deposed abbats appeared before the pope. " Pope Paschal received Anselm kindly : and, on a day appointed, William de Warewast, clerk and proctor for the king of England, brought forward his cause, and, amongst other things, firmly asserted that he would never resign the investiture of churches, even if he were to lose his kingdom, and confirmed this assertion with words of threatening import. To this the pope replied, ' If, as you say, your king would not give up the donation of churches to save his kingdom, neither would I, to save my life let him keep it.' Thus the king's business terminated, and archbishop Anselm began to intercede with the pope for the degraded bishops and abbats, that he would give them a dispensation to recover their lost dignities. Then the Holy See, which is never wanting to any one, if anything of a white or red colour passes between the parties, manfully restored the aforesaid bishops and abbats to their former dignities, and sent them back with joy to their own habitations." The allusion to the white or red colour refers to the power of silver or gold at the papal court, which was then open to great corruption.

York, placing his hand in the hand of Anselm, as he himself
desired, promised, upon his faith, that he would pay the same
obedience and be in the same subjection to him and his successors in the archbishopric, as he had promised to him when
about to be consecrated by him to the see of Hereford.

Walter Giffard, bishop elect of Winchester, Roger of Salisbury, Reinelm of Hereford, William of Exeter, and Urban
of Glamorgan, in Wales, came to Canterbury at the same time,
and were consecrated together by Anselm, on the third day
before the ides of August, being the Lord's day, the following
suffragans of his province assisting him in his duties: Gerard, archbishop of York, Robert, bishop of Lincoln, John,
bishop of Bath, Herbert, bishop of Norwich, Robert, bishop of
Chester, Ralph, bishop of Chichester, and Ranulph, bishop of
Durham. There was no one then living, who could remember in
past times so many pastors being elected and consecrated at
one time in England, except in the days of Edward the Elder,
when archbishop Plegmund consecrated seven bishops to seven
churches in one day.

In the same year, Maurice, bishop of London, Richard, abbat of Ely, Robert, abbat of Saint Edmund's, Milo Crispin,
Robert Fitz-Haimon, Roger Bigot, and Richard de Rivers
departed this life.

In the year 1108, Gundulph, bishop of Rochester, died on
the nones of March. Henry, king of the English, for the purpose of protection, enacted a law that, if any one should be
detected in the act of theft or larceny, he should be hanged.
He also enacted that base and spurious coin should be guarded
against with such strictness, that whosoever should be detected
coining spurious money, should lose his eyes and the lower
part of his body without any ransom; and, inasmuch as,
very frequently, while pennies were being coined,[46] they were
bent, or broken, and then rejected, he ordered that no penny
or obol,[47] which he also ordered to be made of a round form,
or even farthing, if it was a good one, should be rejected.
From this provision much good resulted to the whole king-

---

[46] "Eligebantur" is the word used here, probably by mistake for
"eligebantur," which may allude to the process of coining by ham-
mering out.

[47] Probably a small silver coin of three carats in weight.

dom, because the king thus exerted himself in secular matters to retrieve the troubles of the land.

In this year, Gerard, archbishop of York, departed this life, in whose place was elected Thomas, the cousin of Thomas, his predecessor. Philip, king of the Franks, departed this life, and was succeeded by his son Louis. Archbishop Anselm, at the king's request, consecrated Richard, the bishop of London elect, in his chapel at Paggaham, being assisted in the performance of this duty by William, bishop of Winchester, Roger, bishop of Salisbury, Ralph, bishop of Chichester, and William, bishop of Exeter, having first received from him the usual profession of obedience and subjection. After this, coming to Canterbury on the third day before the ides of August, he consecrated Ralph, abbat of Seez, a religious man, bishop of Rochester, in succession to Gundulph, William, bishop of Winchester, Ralph, bishop of Chichester, and Richard, bishop of London, assisting him in the performance of that duty; which same Richard, after the custom of his predecessors, on the same day presented a handsome gift to his mother church of Canterbury.

These are the provisions relative to archdeacons, priests, deacons, subdeacons, and secular clergy of whatever degree, which, in the year of our Lord's Incarnation 1108, Anselm, archbishop of Canterbury, and Thomas, archbishop elect of York, and all the other bishops of England, in the presence of the glorious king Henry, with the assent of his earls and barons, enacted :—" It is hereby decreed, that priests, deacons, and subdeacons, shall live in chastity, and shall have no women in their houses save only those who are connected with them by close relationship, according to the rule which the holy Synod of Nice has laid down. But those priests, deacons, and subdeacons who have, since the prohibition pronounced by the synod held in London, either retained their wives or married others, if they wish any longer to celebrate the mass, let them so entirely put them away from themselves as not to let them enter their houses ; nor are they themselves to go into the houses of such women, or knowingly to meet them in any house ; nor are any women of this description to live upon lands belonging to the church. But if for any proper reason it is necessary for either party to communicate with the other, having two lawful witnesses, let them converse together outside of the house. And if, upon the testimony of two or three lawful witnesses, or by the public report of the people of the parish, any one of them shall be accused of having violated this enactment, he shall clear himself, if he is a priest, by bringing six proper witnesses of his own order; if a deacon, four; if a subdeacon, two. But as for him, who shall not thus clear himself, he shall be deemed to be a transgressor of this holy enactment. And as for those priests who, despising the divine altar and the holy canons, have preferred to live with women, let them be removed from the holy office, deprived of all ecclesiastical benefices, and placed without the choir, being pronounced infamous; and he who, being a rebel and contumacious, shall not leave the woman, and shall presume to celebrate the mass, if, when called upon to make satisfaction, he shall neglect to do so, is to be excommunicated. The same sentence embraces the archdeacons and all the secular clergy, both as to leaving these women and avoiding cohabitation with them, and the severity of the punishment if they shall transgress these statutes. All archdeacons shall also swear that they will not receive money for tolerating the transgression of this enactment, nor suffer priests whom they know to be keeping women to chaunt the mass, or to have substitutes;[48] deans also shall swear to the same effect. The archdeacon, or deacon, who shall refuse to take oath to this effect, is to lose his archdeaconry or deanery. As to those priests, who, leaving the women, shall make choice to serve God and the holy altars, let them cease during forty days from the performance of their duties, and in the meantime employ substitutes in their places, such penance being imposed on them as to their bishops shall seem fit."

In the year 1109, Anselm, archbishop of Canterbury, departed this life at Canterbury, on the eleventh day before the calends of May, being the fourth day of the week, and on the following day, which was the Supper of the Lord, was buried with great honor. About the time of the Rogation Days, Henry, king of the English, returned to England, and at Pentecost held his court at Westminster; where Thomas, archbishop elect of York, was consecrated at London,[*] on the fifth day before the calends of July, by Richard, bishop of

48 " Vicaros," equivalent to " curates."   *** Westminster is generally considered by these writers as forming part of London.

London, and afterwards on the calends of August, being
Sunday, received, at York, from the hands of Cardinal Ulric,
the pall which the pope had sent him, and on the same
day consecrated Turgot, prior of Durham, to the bishopric
of Saint Andrew's in Scotland, which is called Cenrimunt.
In the same year, king Henry changed the abbacy of Ely
into an episcopal see, and made Hervey, bishop of Bangor,
bishop of that see. In the month of December a comet was
seen, near the milky circle, making its way with its train
towards the southern part of the heavens.

In the year 1110, Henry, king of the English, gave his daughter in marriage to Henry, king of Germany. In the same
year, different prodigies appeared throughout England. A very
great earthquake took place at Shrewsbury. The river at
Nottingham, which is called the Trent, was dried up for the
space of a mile from morning until the third hour of the
day, so much so, that men walked with dry feet upon its bed.
On the sixth day before the ides of July, a comet appeared,
and was seen to shine for a period of three weeks.

In the year 1111, Henry, king of Germany, came to Rome,
and taking pope Paschal prisoner, placed him in confinement,
but shortly after, when they were celebrating the festival of
Easter on the Campus Martius at the bridge on the Salarian
road,[49] was reconciled to him. In this year died Baldwin,
earl of Flanders, and was succeeded by his son Baldwin.
Henry, king of the English, removed the people of Flanders
who inhabited Northumbria, with all their chattels into Wales,
and gave them orders to colonize the district which bears the
name of Ros.[50]

The new monastery which had been built within the walls
of Winchester, through the influence of William, bishop of
Winchester the king ordered to be rebuilt without the walls,
and shortly after crossed the sea.

In the same year there was a most severe winter, a dreadful famine, a plague among men, and a murrain among animals,
both wild and domestic; there was also a very great mortality
among birds.

[49] A road near Rome, so called from having been used by the Sabines,
when fetching salt from the sea.

[50] The town of Denbigh. Henry either feared that these Flemings
would coalesce against him with the Scots, or placed them there for
the purpose of acting as a check upon the Welch.

In the year 1112, on the third day before the nones of May, being Sunday, Samson, the twenty-fifth bishop[51] of Worcester, departed this life. In October, Henry, king of the English, placed earl Hubert de Belesme in confinement at Cherbury.

In the year 1113, the city of Worcester was, on the calends of July, destroyed by fire, with the principal church and all the others, and the castle. One of the monks, a person of the greatest utility to the monastery, together with two servants and fifteen citizens, perished in the flames. In the month of July, Henry, king of the English, returned to England, and bringing with him earl Robert de Belesme from Normandy, placed him in close custody at Wareham. On the fourth day before the nones of October, two men of exemplary virtue departed this life; Thomas, the prior, and Coleman, a monk, of the venerable church of Saint Mary at Worcester, men of noble extraction. On the fifth day before the calends of January, being the Lord's day, Tenulph, the king's chaplain, received the bishopric of Worcester.

In the year 1114, on the eighth day before the ides of January, Matilda, daughter of Henry, king of the English, was married to Henry, the emperor of the Romans, at Mentz, and consecrated empress. On the sixth day before the calends of March, being the third day of the week, Thomas the Younger, archbishop of York, departed this life. When he was first taken ill, his medical men told him that he could not recover, except by means of carnal knowledge of a woman; on which he made answer, "Shame upon a malady which requires sensuality for its cure;" and being thus chosen by the Lord while of virgin purity closed his temporal life. On the sixth day before the calends of May, being the Lord's day, Ralph, bishop of Rochester, was elected at Windsor arch-bishop of Canterbury. On the third day before the nones of May, being the third day of the week, the city of Chichester, together with the principal monastery, was, through culpable carelessness, destroyed by fire.

On the day of the Assumption of Saint Mary, Turstin, the king's chaplain, was, at Winchester, elected to the archbishopric of York, and Arnulph, abbot of Burgh, was chosen bishop of Hereford. Henry, king of the English, after leading an army into Wales, before the feast of Saint Michael crossed the

51 He is by mistake called "Archiepiscopus," "archbishop."

sea. In this year, the river which bears the name of Medway, for a distance of some miles, receded so far from its bed, on the sixth day before the ides of October, that in the very middle of it not even the smallest vessel could make the slightest way. On the same day, the river Thames was also sensible of a similar decrease; for between the bridge and the royal tower,[52] and even under the bridge, so greatly was the water of the river diminished, that an innumerable multitude of men and boys forded it on foot, the water scarcely reaching to their knees. This ebb of the tide continued from the middle of the preceding night until dark on the following night. We have heard also on good authority that on the same day a similar low tide happened at Girvemnthe,[53] and other places throughout England.

In the year 1115, there was a most severe winter, so much so, that nearly all the bridges throughout England were broken by the ice. The emperor Henry, after besieging the city of Cologne and losing many of his men in a pitched battle, made peace, which he ratified by oath at the city of Neuss.[54] On the fifth day before the calends of July, being the Lord's day, Ralph, archbishop of Canterbury, received the pall from Anselm,[55] the legate of the holy Roman Church, at Canterbury, and on the same day was consecrated with great honor; at which place, also, were assembled the bishops of the whole of England. Teulph, bishop of Worcester, departed this life, and was succeeded by Wilfrid, bishop of Saint David's, in Wales; up to this time, the bishops of that see had been Welchmen, but he was succeeded by Bamard, the queen's chancellor. On the octave of the Apostles Saint Peter and Paul, a great council was held at Chalons, by Conon, a cardinal of the Roman church, at which he excommunicated those bishops who were not present at the council, and degraded some; some abbats also he deprived of their stalls and removed from their offices, forbidding them the performance of ecclesiastical duties.

In the month of July, Henry, king of the English, returned to England. Turgot, formerly prior of the church of Durham,

[52] The Tower of London.

[53] He probably means the vicinity of Jarrow ; in allusion to the large inlet of shoaly water, now called Jarrow Slake.

[54] A town or city of Germany, not far from Cologne.

[55] He was nephew to archbishop Anselm, then lately deceased.

and afterwards bishop of the Scots,[66] having returned to Durham, there departed this life. About the period of the feast of All Saints, Reinelm, bishop of Hereford, died, and was succeeded by Gosfrid, the king's chaplain. On the day of Saint Stephen the Martyr, Ralph, archbishop of Canterbury, ordained at that place Arnulph, abbot of Burgh, bishop of Rochester, and Gosfrid, the king's chaplain, bishop of Hereford.

In the year 1116, during the spring, Griffin, the son of Rees,[56*] carried off considerable booty into Wales, and burned some castles, in consequence of which, Henry, king of England, was unwilling to allow him to possess a particle of the lands of his father. On the fourteenth day before the calends of April, the earls and barons of the whole of England met at Salisbury. Here a trial took place relative to a dispute which had continued during a whole year, between Ralph, archbishop of Canterbury, and Turstin, archbishop elect of York. The latter, on being requested by the arch-bishop to do what was his duty to the church of Canterbury, and after the ecclesiastical usage, receive his benediction, made answer that he would willingly receive the benediction, but would on no account make the profession[58] which he required. On this, king Henry, perceiving that Turstin persisted in his obstinacy, openly protested that he must act after the manner of his predecessors, both as to making the profession, as also in other matters pertaining to the dignity of the church of Canterbury of ancient right, or else give up the archbishopric of York altogether, as well as the benediction; on hearing which, without previous consideration, Turstin renounced the archbishopric, and promised the king and the archbishop that he would not claim it again as long as he lived, nor would make any charge relative thereto, whoever might be substituted in his place.

At this time, Owen, king of the Welch, was slain. Henry, king of the English, crossed the sea, attended by Turstin, the archbishop elect of York, who hoped to obtain re-instalment into the see, and by the king's command receive the benediction from the archbishop, without the profession being exacted of him. The above-named Anselm, the legate of the Roman church who had brought the pall from Rome to the archbishop of Canterbury, returned from Rome about the month

[56] Of Saint Andrews.　　[56*] In Welch, Griffin ap Rice.　　[63] Of subjection to the see of Canterbury.

of August, and came to Normandy to king Henry, bringing letters from the successor of the Apostles, which directed him to act in England on behalf of the Apostolic see. This being soon spread abroad throughout the whole of England, by the advice of the queen and some of the nobles, Ralph, the arch-bishop of Canterbury, after the nativity of Saint Mary, crossed the sea, and went to the king whom he found staying at Rouen, and after having carefully conferred with him on the business on which he had come, taking each matter in its proper order, by the king's advice set out on his way to Rome. In the year 1117, by the command of king Henry, the new works at Cirencester were begun. In Lombardy, a great earthquake took place, and, according to the testimony of those who knew the fact, lasted for a period of forty days, during which time many buildings fell to the ground; and, a thing marvellous to be seen and spoken of, a certain town, of very considerable magnitude, was suddenly moved from its original site, and is at the present day to be seen by all at a place far distant. While some men of patrician rank at Milan were discoursing on matters of state, sitting beneath a certain tower, a voice from outside resounded in the ears of all, calling one of them by name, and begging him to come out immediately; on his delaying, a person appeared, and with entreaties, begged the man who had been called, to come forth; on doing which, the tower was suddenly overthrown, and in its dreadful fall buried all who were there.

On the calends of December, there was great thunder and lightning, which was followed by a vast deluge of rain and hail; on the third day before the ides of the same month, the moon appeared at first of the colour of blood, after which it became overshadowed. Robert, bishop of Chester, died.

In the year 1118, pope Paschal of holy memory departed this life, on the fourteenth day before the calends of February; and in his place was appointed one John, a native of Gaeta, who, changing his name, was called Gelasius. From his in-fancy he had been brought up as a monk, at the monastery of Monte Casino, and after he had grown up had assiduously fulfilled the duties of chancellor, during the ministration of the venerable successors of the Apostles, Desiderius, Urban, and Paschal.

Henry, king of Germany, who was also emperor of Rome,

on hearing that the pope was dead, flew to Rome, and nominated the bishop of Braga, who had been excommunicated at Beneventum by the same pope the previous year, to be pope, changing his name from Bourdin to Gregory; on which Gelasius retired from the city. On the day before the calends of May, Matilda, queen of the English, departed this life at Westminster, and was becomingly buried at the monastery there. At this period, many of the Normans, forsaking the fealty which they had sworn to king Henry, and having no fear of retribution, betook themselves to Louis, king of the Franks and his principal men, who were the enemies of their natural lord. In this year died Robert, earl of Mellent.

The above-named pope Gelasius came by sea to Burgundy, and his arrival soon became known throughout Gaul. On the seventeenth day before the calends of February, he sent a letter throughout Gaul to the archbishops, bishops, abbats, secular clergy, and principal men, complaining that he had been expelled with violence by the emperor from Rome, and that the bishop of Braga, an excommunicated person, had been thrust into the Apostolic See; at the same time, exhorting them to prepare themselves by their assistance in common to avenge the cause of the mother Church. These letters having been circulated throughout the provinces, all the men of influence were aroused, together with the middle classes, to go to meet the successor of the Apostles, and prepared with every possible effort to be present at the council, which he declared he would hold at Rheims at the time of Mid-Lent. In this year, a certain church having been dedicated at a town in England, called Momerfield, by Geoffrey, bishop of Hereford, as the people were returning home who had attended the dedication, after the serenity of the weather which had previously prevailed, on a sudden a most violent tempest arose, attended with thunder; some persons were struck with lightning and perished, while unable to get away from a place in which they had taken shelter. They were five in number, namely, three men and two women, one of which last was struck by a thunderbolt and killed, while the other woman was shockingly smitten from the navel down to the soles of her feet, and perished, enveloped in flames; the men alone with difficulty escaped with their lives, while their five horses were destroyed by the lightning.

In the year 1119, pope Gelasius died at Clugny, and was buried there; and in his place the cardinals and other Romans who had followed him, elected Guido, archbishop of Vienna, and gave him the name of Calixtus. While these transactions were going on in Burgundy, the Apostolate of the Roman Church was administered by the above-named Gregory. In consequence of the elevation of these two to the papacy, the world was shaken and divided into two factions, some giving their adhesion to the one, and some to the other; by reason whereof, the church was stricken with great scandal. On the fourth day before the nones of February, Geoffrey, bishop of Hereford, and, on the tenth day before the calends of September, Herbert, bishop of Norwich, departed this life. On the fourth day before the calends of October, being the Lord's day, at about the third hour of the day, a great earthquake took place at many places throughout England.

On the thirteenth day before the calends of November, pope Calixtus held a general council at Rheims; at this council there was a vast concourse of archbishops, bishops, abbats, and chief men of the various provinces, together with an immense multitude of the clergy and common people. There were counted there four hundred and twenty-four staffs of persons with pastoral honors; among whom was Turstin, the archbishop elect of York, who having with difficulty obtained the king's permission, had come thither in reference to his own business. But the king had previously sent his ambassador to the successor of the Apostles, for the purpose of telling him, among other things, not to consecrate the archbishop elect of York, or command or allow him to be consecrated by any other person than the archbishop of Canterbury, as used to be the custom. In answer to which, the successor of the Apostles replied: "Let not the king imagine that I would act in relation to the matter upon which he treats in any other way than he wishes, even though his request should be an unreasonable one: nor, indeed, has my inclination ever led me to wish to debase the ancient dignity of the church of Canterbury."

Moreover, on the morning of the Lord's day preceding the day of the appointed council, Turstin, having made preparations for his consecration to the archbishopric, the deputies of the archbishop of Canterbury charged that his consecration ought to be performed by the archbishop of Canterbury, according as the ancient usage and that observed up to the present time required ; in answer to which, the successor of the Apostles replied : "It is our wish to do no injustice to the church of Canterbury, but maintaining its dignity, we will do that which we purpose." Nevertheless, Turstin was consecrated by the successor of the Apostles, Ranulph, the bishop of Durham, who had been sent by the king to prevent his consecration, not having yet arrived; he, however, arrived some time after.

On the following day the council was held, and all persons taking their seats in the order of their ecclesiastical rank, and Louis, king of the Franks, and many other men of the highest station being there seated, by the consent of all the fathers, the statutes of enactment and of prohibition[59] were renewed, of which these are the five heads. "The laws which, by the sanction of the holy fathers, have been established in relation to simoniacal sin, we do also, by the judgment of the Holy Ghost and the authority of the Apostolic See, confirm. If any one therefore, shall, either by himself or by any person suborned thereto, buy or sell any bishopric, abbacy, priory, archdeaconry, presbytery, provostship, prebend, altar, or any ecclesiastical benefices, dignities, ordinations, consecrations, dedications of churches, clerical tonsure, seat in the choir, or any ecclesiastical duties, let both seller and buyer be subject to the peril of losing their dignities, offices, and benefices; and, unless he shall repent, let him be pierced by the point of anathema, and in every way cut off from the church of God, which he has injured. The investiture of bishoprics, abbacies, or any ecclesiastical possessions whatsoever, we do utterly forbid to be performed by lay hands; whoever, therefore, of the laity shall henceforth presume to give investiture, let him be subject to the penalties of anathema : and further, let him who has received such investiture be utterly, without hope of recovery thereof, deprived of the honor with which he has been invested. The universal possessions of the churches we do decree to be unshaken and inviolate for everlasting. But if any one shall take them away, or seize them, or by tyrannical power withhold the same, let him be smitten everlastingly with anathema, according to that decree of Saint Symmachus, which

[59] "Statuta de statuendis, et rescidenda de rescidendis."

begins, 'Let no bishop, no priest, no member of the clergy whatsoever, part with ecclesiastical dignities or benefices to any one, as though of hereditary right.' This, also, we do enjoin in addition thereto, that no payment shall be demanded for receiving baptism, chrism, holy oil, and burial. To priests, deacons, and subdeacons, we do utterly forbid the society of wives and concubines. And if any persons of this character shall be found, let them be deprived both of their ecclesiastical offices and benefices; and if they do not even then correct their uncleanness, let them be deprived of all communion with Christians."[60]

These decrees were sent to the emperor Henry, as he was not far distant, first from the council by persons of rank, and then by the successor of the Apostles himself, in order that, before the breaking up of the council, it might be ascertained whether, in the churches throughout his kingdom and each province subject to him, he would consent to canonical elections, that is to say, bishops and abbats being chosen by the church; and whether, to free consecrations, as is the case where those who are elected are consecrated where and by whom it is befitting;[61] and whether he would also consent that no lay person whatsoever should claim a right to the investiture in ecclesiastical matters, so that those elected might, through investiture with the pastoral staff and ring, enter through the door, that is, through Christ.

To these requests he made answer, that he would give up none of these particulars that belonged to him of right, and which the ancient customs of his ancestors had conferred upon him. At length, however, being prevailed upon by the authority of the general council, he conceded the first three points; but the last, namely, the right of investiture in ecclesiastical matters, he would not concede; in consequence of which, on the pope returning to the council, sentence of excommunication was pronounced against him. Some who were present at the council being indignant at this, the successor of the Apostles gave his commands that those who were offended thereat, should go forth and separate themselves from the society of their brethren, quoting the example of those seventy who, being offended as to eating the flesh of our Lord and

[60] Under the penalties of anathema.
[61] According to the rules of the church.

drinking his blood,[62] returned home, and no longer walked with him; and "inasmuch as," he said, "he who gathereth not with the Lord, scattereth; and he who is not with him, is against him, and that tunic which is not sewn together but woven, namely, the Holy Church, those who think with us are unwilling to have rent asunder, while those who differ from us are striving to rend it asunder." The successor of the Apostles having spoken to this effect, forthwith all were brought round to the same opinion, and sentence of excommunication was fulminated against the emperor Henry.

At length, some days after the council had broken up, Henry, king of the English, being offended at archbishop Turstin, because he had caused himself to be consecrated without his consent, and not in the way that ancient usage required, forbade him to return to any place in his dominions. After this, pope Calixtus came to Gisors, where the king of the English came to meet him, for the purpose of holding a conference. Many things were treated of between them, on account of which it was right that such great personages should meet; and, among the rest, the king obtained the pope's consent that he would grant him all the liberties his father had possessed in England and Normandy, and especially that he would allow no one to fill the office of legate at any time in England, unless he himself (on any important difference arising which could not be put an end to by the bishops of his kingdom) requested this to be done by the pope. All these points being settled for the present, the pope requested the king to become reconciled to Turstin, and in consideration of his love towards himself, his restoration to the archbishopric to which he himself had consecrated him. But the king confessed that he had vowed upon his faith that he would not do so, as long as he lived; to which the pope made reply: "I am the successor of the Apostles, and, if you do what I ask, will release you from the stringency of this oath." "I will discuss the matter," said the king, "and notify to you the result of my determination." Upon this, the pope withdrew, and the king, by messengers, gave him this answer upon the subject: "I will admit Turstin to the archbishopric upon condition, that he pay that obedience to the church of Canterbury which his predecessors did, otherwise, so long as I reign,

[62] In allusion to St. John, vi. 66.

he shall not preside over the see of York." Matters being thus concluded, the successor of the Apostles took his departure, and Turstin remained in France.

William, the son of king Henry and queen Matilda, a youth seventeen years of age, this year took to wife the daughter of the earl of Anjou. Baldwin, earl of Flanders, died of the effects of a wound which he had received at Eu.

In the year 1120, Henry, king of the English, and Louis, king of the Franks, after many losses on both sides, on a day appointed, held a conference; at which, peace having been made by mutual consent, by the command of king Henry, his son, William, did homage to the king of the Franks, and received under him the principality of Normandy; and thus, the kings departing in peace, the whole of the seditions which had raged throughout Normandy were suppressed, and those who had raised their arms against their lord, king Henry, having bowed their necks to his dominion, returned to obedience. And, inasmuch as archbishop Turstin had shown himself both vigilant and active in effecting a reconciliation between the kings, in consequence of his usefulness, he rendered the king's feelings more inclined to sanction his return. In addition to this, as the king was preparing to return to England, a letter came directed to him from the successor of the Apostles, enjoining him to receive archbishop Turstin, and, all other pretexts and excuses set aside, to restore him to his see. But in reply to this precept, the king deferred until his return to England what answer to give, in order that, having assembled his council there, he might consider with more mature deliberation what was to be done.

By the king's command, the chief men of Normandy did homage to his son William, a youth then just eighteen years of age; they also swore fealty to him, confirming it by oath. After this, all who had rebelled against him being either conquered or reconciled, and every thing prosperously concluded according to his wish, the fifth year after he had gone thither being not yet completed, the king returned to England by ship in better spirits than usual. To his son and all his retinue he had given a ship, a better one than which there did not seem to be in all the fleet, but as the event proved, there was not one more unfortunate; for while his father preceded him, the son followed somewhat more tardily, but with a still more unhappy result.   For the ship, when not far from land, while in full sail, was driven upon the rocks which are called Chaterase, and being wrecked, the king's son, with all who were with him, perished on the sixth day before the calends of December, being the fifth day of the week, at nightfall, near Barbeflet.[63] In the morning, the king's treasures which were on board the ship, were found on the sands, but none of the bodies of those lost.

There perished with the king's son, his illegitimate brother, earl Richard, together with the king's daughter,[64] the wife of Rotrou ; Richard, earl of Chester, with his wife, the king's niece, and sister of earl Tedbald, the king's nephew.   There also perished Othoel, the governor of the king's son, Geoffrey Riddell, Robert Muldint,[65] William Bigot, and many other men of rank ; also several noble women with no small number of the king's children ; besides one hundred and forty soldiers, with fifty sailors and three pilots.   A certain butcher was the only person who made his escape, by clinging to a plank of the wrecked vessel.   The king having had a fair voyage, on reaching England, thought that his son had entered some other port ; but on the third day he was afflicted with the sad tidings of his death, and at first, from the suddenness of the calamity, fainted away, as though a person of weak mind ; but afterwards, concealing his grief, in contempt of fortune he resumed his kingly spirits   For this son being the only one left him by lawful wedlock, he had named him heir to the kingdom in succession to himself.

In the year 1121, at the Purification of Saint Mary, having assembled the council of the whole of England at Windsor, Henry, king of the English, took in marriage Adeline, the daughter of Godfrey, duke of Lorraine.   Richard, the king's chaplain, was elected bishop of Hereford, and Robert Peche,[66] another royal chaplain, bishop of Coventry.   Herbert, almoner of Saint Peter's at Westminster, was chosen abbat of that place.   Edwin, a monk of the church of Canterbury, having been elected in the preceding year bishop of Saint Andrew's in Scotland, gave up his intention of ruling that see and re-

[63] Harfleur.
[64] Mary, the wife of Rotrou, earl of Perche.
[65] A misprint for Mauduit.
[66] V. r. Peccator—in English, "sinner ;" a curious name for a king's chaplain.

turned to his former place.   William Deschapelles, bishop of
Chalons, departed this life on the fifteenth day before the
calends of February, having assumed the monastic habit eight
days before his death.

There came a letter from pope Calixtus, relative to Turstin, directed to king Henry and Ralph, archbishop of Canterbury, in which he interdicted the latter from all sacerdotal and
episcopal duties; and both in the mother church of Canterbury,
and in the principal church at York, together with its provinces,
forbade the celebration of all divine offices together with the
burial of the dead, except the baptism of infants and the absolution of the dying,[67] unless within one month after the re-
ceipt of that letter, Turstin should be, without exacting the
profession of obedience, restored to his archbishopric.

In the same year, after Easter, pope Calixtus departed from
the city with a large body of men, and besieged the city of
Sutri, until he took both Bourdin the anti-pope and the place
itself, as the subjoined letter will more plainly show.

"Calixtus the bishop, servant of the servants of God, to his
dearly beloved brethren and sons, the archbishops, bishops, abbats, priors, and others, both clergy and laity, the faithful servants of Saint Peter throughout the Gauls, health, and the
apostolic benediction. Because the people have forsaken the law
of the Lord, and walk not in his judgments, the Lord visits their
iniquities with a rod, and their sins with stripes.   But retaining the bowels of paternal affection, those who put trust in his
mercy he does not repel; though for a long time, their sins
so requiring, the faithful of the church have been disturbed
by Bourdin, that idol of the king of Germany ; some indeed
have been taken captives, and others through starvation in
prison have been afflicted unto death.   Lately, however, after
celebrating the feast of Easter, when we could no longer pas-
sively endure the complaints of the pilgrims and of the poor,
we left the city with the faithful servants of the church, and
laid siege to Sutri, until the Divine power delivered the before-
named Bourdin, the enemy of the church, who had there made a
nest for the devil, as well as the place itself, entirely into our
hands.   We beg your brotherly love therefore, with us to
return thanks to the King of kings for benefits so great, and

[67] The original is " pœnitentias morientium ;" in allusion to the
administration of the " viaticum."

that you will remain most firmly in your obedience to the Catholic church, and in your duty to God, as you will receive from Almighty God, through His grace, the recompense for so doing, both here and hereafter. We beg also, that this our letter be sent from one to the other, all negligence laid aside. Done at Sutri, on the fifth day before the calends of May."

In this year, the daughter of Fulk, earl of Anjou, formerly the wife of William the son of king Henry, who had been drowned, was, at the request of her father, sent back by the king to her own country. The sons of the king of the Welsh, on hearing of the death of Richard earl of Chester, burning two castles and slaying many men, laid waste, with great ravages, some places in that earldom. King Henry, being indignant at this, having levied an innumerable army throughout all England, marched for the purpose of ravaging Wales; but, on his arrival at Snawedun,[66] the king of the Welch was reconciled to the king, appeasing him by presents and hostages, and, shortly after, the army returned home. At this period, king Henry having, by digging, made a long trench from Torksey as far as Lincoln, by turning into it the river Trent made a passage for shipping. Ranulph, bishop of Durham, also began a castle at Norham, on the banks of the river Tweed. On the vigil of the Nativity of our Lord, an unusual wind blew down not only houses, but even towers built of stone.

In the year 1122, king Henry was at Windsor during the festival of the Nativity, at Easter, at Northampton, and during Pentecost, at Windsor; whence he proceeded to London and Kent, and afterwards to Durham, in Northumbria. In the same year, died Ralph, archbishop of Canterbury, and John, bishop of Bath.

In the year 1123, during the festival of the Nativity, king Henry was at Dunstable, and thence proceeded to Berkhampstead. Here, a certain chancellor of the king, Ranulph by name, who had been afflicted with a malady for twenty years, but who had always gloried at court in his wickedness, being ready for all crimes, oppressing the innocent, and plundering the lands of many, while escorting the king to entertain him at his house, on coming to the top of a hill whence his castle could be seen, was so elated in spirits that he fell off his horse, and a monk galloped over him;[69] in consequence of which he was so crushed that he ended his life in a few days. The king went thence attended by Robert, bishop of Lincoln, on his road to Woodstock; where the bishop being attacked by a sudden malady, lost his speech, and, being carried to an inn, soon afterwards breathed forth his spirit.[70]

This happened on the tenth day of the month of January.

In the year 1124, at the feast of the Purification, the king gave the archbishopric of Canterbury to William de Curbuil, prior of the canons of Chiche.[71] After this, at Easter, king Henry, when at Winchester, gave the bishopric of Lincoln to Alexander, the nephew of Roger, bishop of Salisbury, justiciary of all England; he also gave the bishopric of Bath to Godfrey, the queen's chancellor, and about Pentecost, crossed the sea; on which a dispute arising, the earl of Mellent revolted from him; whereupon the king laid siege to his castle, the name of which is Pontaudemer, and took it.

In the year 1125, great success smiled on the king; for William de Tankerville, the king's chamberlain, fighting a pitched battle with him, took the above-named earl of Mellent prisoner, together with Hugh de Montfort, his brother-in-law, and Hugh FitzGervaise, and delivered them to the king; on which he placed them in confinement. In the same year died Teulph, bishop of Worcester, and Ernulph, bishop of Rochester.

In the year 1126, king Henry remained during the whole of the year in Normandy, and there gave the bishopric of Worcester to Simon, the queen's clerk, and that of Chichester to Seffrid, abbot of Glastonbury.[72] William, archbishop of

[69] The corresponding passage in Roger of Wendover's account is :—
"A monk of St. Alban's, whose lands he had unjustly seized on, involuntarily galloped over him."

[70] This circumstance is mentioned more fully in the Anglo-Saxon Chronicle. "It fell out on a Wednesday, being the fourth day before the ides of January, that the king rode in his deer-park, and Roger, bishop of Salisbury, was on one side of him, and Robert Bloet, bishop of Lincoln, on the other : and they rode there talking. Then the bishop of Lincoln sank down, and said to the king, 'My lord king, I am dying;' and the king alighted from his horse and took him between his arms, and bade them bear him to his inn, and he soon lay there dead."

[71] St. Osythe, in Essex. Ingram says that this priory was re-built A.D. 1118, for canons of the Augustine order, and that there are considerable remains of it.

Canterbury, also gave the bishopric of Rochester to John, his archdeacon. At Easter, John of Crema, a Roman cardinal, came over to England, and, after visiting the bishoprics and abbeys, not without great presents, at the nativity of Saint Mary held a solemn synod at London, where a great mishap befell him.

For, having at the synod spoken in the severest terms relative to the wives of the clergy, saying that it was the greatest wickedness to arise from the side of a harlot to make the body of Christ, while he himself had that same day made the body of Christ, he was, after nightfall, surprised in the company of a harlot. The thing being thus notorious throughout London, could not be denied; and thus the great honor in which he was held everywhere previously, was turned into the greatest disgrace. He returned home, therefore, by the judgment of God, in confusion and disgrace.

In the same year died Henry, emperor of the Romans, son-in-law of Henry, king of the English. But by some it is alleged that the same emperor, being led by a feeling of penitence for having killed his own father, after having gone on a certain night, according to his usual custom, to the bed of the empress Matilda, the daughter of Henry king of the English, the lights being put out and the servants having withdrawn, re-tired barefoot and dressed in woollen garments, leaving behind the imperial vestments, his wife, and his kingdom, and was never after seen, nor was it discovered what became of him. On this, the empress, taking with her the uncorrupted hand of Saint James the Apostle, and the imperial crown, returned to king Henry, her father. After the decease or departure of the emperor Henry, Lothaire succeeded to the throne. Henry, king of the English, being greatly rejoiced at gaining the hand of Saint James the Apostle, founded the noble abbey of Reddinges,[12] and enriched it with many valuables, and placed in it the hand of Saint James the Apostle; the imperial crown he placed in his own treasury.

The moneyers throughout almost the whole of England were, by king's order, seized for having secretly debased the coin, and, their right hands being first cut off, were then deprived of their virility. In this year there was a great famine, and so great was the dearness of provisions, that no one in our time

[12] Reading.

has seen the like, for a horse-load of corn was sold at the price
of six shillings. In this year, also, William, archbishop of
Canterbury, Turstin, archbishop of York, and Alexander, bishop
of Lincoln, went to Rome.

In the year 1127, during the Nativity, and Easter, and
Pentecost, king Henry remained in Normandy, and, having
made an honorable peace with the king of France, before the
feast of Saint Michael this most victorious king returned to
England, and brought with him his daughter the empress, the
widow of so great a man, as previously mentioned. In this
year, also, Robert, bishop of Chester, died.

In the year 1128, at the Nativity, king Henry held his
court at Windsor, and proceeded thence to London. During
Lent and Easter he was at Woodstock, where word was brought
to him that Charles, earl of Flanders, his most beloved friend,
had been, by the basest treachery, slain by his nobles in a
church at Brige,[73] and that the king of France had given
Flanders to William, the son of Robert Curthose, his nephew
and enemy, who, being now firmly established, had punished
all the traitors to Charles with many torments. Accordingly,
the king, being disturbed at these matters, held a council at
London at the time of the Rogation Days; and, in similar
manner, did archbishop William do the same at Westminster,
in the same city.

About Pentecost, the king sent his daughter to Normandy,
to be married to Geoffrey, son of the earl of Anjou, and afterwards, in August, the king himself followed. Richard, bishop
of London, departed this life, and the king gave the bishopric
to Gilbert, a man most learned in all subjects. At this time,
also, died Richard, bishop of Hereford.

In the year 1129, king Henry, having remained a whole
year in Normandy, marched in a hostile manner into France,
because the king of the Franks was supporting his nephew and
enemy; and encamping for eight days at Epernon, as securely
as though he had been in his own kingdom, he compelled
king Louis not to give aid to the earl of Flanders. While
here, on enquiring into the origin and career of the kingdom
of the Franks, king Henry was answered by a certain learned
man to the following effect :—

"Most powerful among kings, like most of the nations of

[73] Bruges.

Europe, the Franks derive their origin from the Trojans. For Antenor, flying with his people on the fall of Troy, built a city in the territories of Pannonia, called Sycambria. After the death of Antenor, they appointed as their leaders Turgot and Francion, from whom the Franks derive their name. (On their death, these were succeeded by Marcomer, who was the father of Pharamond, the first king of the Franks; Pharamond begat Clodius Crinitus,[74] from whom the kings of France have the name of 'Criniti;' and Clodius was succeeded by Meroveus, his kinsman, from whom the kings of France received the name of Merovingians. Meroveus begat Childeric, and he begat Clodovius,[75] who was baptized by Saint Remigius. Clodovius begat Clotaire, who begat Chilperic, and he Clotaire the Second. Clotaire begat Dagobert, that most famous king, who begat Clodovius; by Saint Batilda, his queen, Clodovius begat three sons, namely, Clotaire, Childeric, and Theoderic. King Theoderic begat Childebert, and he Dagobert, who begat Theoderic, the father of Clotaire, the last of this line. In succession to him reigned Hilderic, who afterwards received the tonsure, and retired to a monastery, Pepin being made king. In another genealogical line, by the daughter of king Clotaire Ansbert begat Arnold, and Saint Arnold Arnulph, afterwards bishop of Metz. Saint Arnulph begat Anchises, and he Pepin, the mayor of the palace; Pepin begat Charles Martel, and he king Pepin. King Pepin was father of the emperor, Charles the Great,[76] who shone like a constellation among his predecessors and successors. Charles begat the emperor Louis, and he the emperor Charles the Bald, and he king Louis, the father of Charles the Simple. Charles the Simple begat Louis, and he Lothaire, who begat Louis, the last king of that line. After his death, the Franks set over themselves duke Hugh,[77] the son of the great duke Hugh. King Hugh was the father of Robert, a most pious king, which king Robert begat three sons, Hugh, a most beloved duke, and Henry, a most unable king, and Robert, duke of Burgundy. King Henry was the father of king Philip, who, at the close of his life, became a

[74] It need hardly be remarked that this genealogy is for the most part fabulous. Supposing that the Trojan war took place about B.C. 1000, the learned informant of king Henry omits about fourteen hundred years.

[75] More generally called Clovis.   [76] Charlemagne.

[77] Hugh Capet.

monk, and of Hugh the Great, who, with the great army of Christians and many of the chieftains of Europe, laid siege to Jerusalem, and rescued it from the hands of the pagans. In the year from the incarnation of our Lord 1129,[78] king Philip begat Louis, who reigns at the present time; and if he only followed in the footsteps of his ancestors, you would not be remaining so securely in his kingdom." After these things were said and done, king Henry returned to Normandy.

About this time, a certain duke, Theodoric by name, came from the parts of Germany to make certain claims upon Flanders, and leaving with him certain noblemen of that country; and this he did at the persuasion of king Henry. William, earl of Flanders, having collected an army and set his forces in battle array, marched against him, and a fierce battle ensued. By his invincible prowess, earl William made up for the deficiency of his forces, which were few in number. All his arms being stained with the blood of the enemy, he cleared the ranks of the foe with his sword like lightning, and, in consequence, his enemies being unable to bear the terrible might of his youthful arm, in utter dismay, took to flight. Thus did the earl gain a complete victory; but, while he was besieging a castle[79] of the enemy, and was on the morrow to receive its surrender, the foe being now almost annihilated, by the will of God, receiving a slight wound in the hand, he died in consequence thereof. This most noble youth, during his short life, earned endless glory, and, in his praise, a poet has said : "Mars has died on earth, the deities bewail a deity their equal."

This year, also, Hugh de Pains, master of the knights of the Temple at Jerusalem, came to England, and brought many with him from Jerusalem; among whom was Fulk, the brother of Geoffrey, earl of Anjou, who was destined to be king. Ranulph Flambard, bishop of Durham, and William Giffard, bishop of Winchester, departed this life.

In the year 1130, Louis, king of the Franks, caused his son Philip to be made king ; and king Henry, having made peace in all parts with France, Flanders, Normandy, Brittany, Maine, and Anjou, returned in high spirits to England. On the calends of August, he held a great council at London, on the

78 Of course, this date is an error.
79 That of Eu, against king Henry.

subject of prohibiting the priesthood from taking wives. There were present at this council William, archbishop of Canterbury, Turstin, archbishop of York, Alexander, bishop of Lincoln, Gilbert, bishop of London, Roger, bishop of Salisbury, John, bishop of Rochester, Siffrid, bishop of Sussex,[80] Godfrey, bishop of Bath, Simon, bishop of Worcester, Everard, bishop of Norwich, Bernard, bishop of Saint David's, and Hervey, the first bishop of Ely. The bishops of Winchester, Durham, Chester, and Hereford were absent. These constituted at this period the pillars of the kingdom, and the rays of its sanctity. But, through the simplicity of archbishop William, the king deceived them; for they conceded to the king the right of administering justice on the question of the wives of priests; and were deemed imprudent for so doing, as afterwards proved to be the fact, when the matter turned out to their extreme disgrace; for the king received an endless amount of money from priests, and then relieved them from the penalties attendant on so doing. Then, but to no purpose, did the bishops repent of having made this concession, when, before the eyes of all nations, were made manifest the deception practised on the prelates, and the oppression of the king's subjects.

In the same year, misfortunes befell those whom Hugh de Pains, already mentioned, had taken with him to Jerusalem; for, by their sensuality, rapine, and various excesses, the inhabitants of that holy land had offended the Lord. But, as it has been written in the books of Moses and of Kings, their wickedness in those places did not long remain unpunished. For, on the vigil of Saint Nicholas, a multitude of the Christians were overcome by a small number of the pagans, whereas, previously to that, just the reverse used to happen. For, at the siege of Damascus, when a great part of the Christians had gone forth for the purpose of seeking for provisions, the pagans were astonished at the spectacle of a multitude of Christians, most valiant men, taking to flight like women, and, on pursuing them, slew almost countless numbers. But those who took refuge in the mountains, God himself pursued that same night with a tempest, accompanied with drifts of snow and cold to such a degree, that hardly any one escaped.

It also happened that, while the son of the king of the

Franks, who, as previously mentioned, had been graced with the crown of the kingdom, was sportively spurring on his horse, he was met by a pig, which, running against the legs of the horse while in full career, the new-made king fell off, and, breaking his neck, expired. Consider what a dreadful mishap, and how deserving of our astonishment! Behold the loftiness of his position, and by what trivial means it was annihilated!

In the year of the Word become flesh 1131, being the thirteenth year of his reign, king Henry passed the festival of the Nativity at Worcester, and Easter at Woodstock, where Geoffrey de Clinton was accused of treason against the king, and disgraced. During the Rogation Days, the king was at Canterbury, at the dedication of the new church there. At the feast of Saint Michael, the king went over to Normandy. In the same year, pope Honorius departed this life, on whose death a division arose; for two persons were elected to the papacy of Rome, Innocent and Anacletus.

In the year 1132, at Chartres, the king acknowledged Innocent as pope, and rejected Anacletus; for the Romans, dividing into two factions, had made choice of both of them. Innocent being violently expelled from the city by Anacletus, whose previous name was Peter de Leves, was, by the influence of king Henry, received throughout the whole of the Gauls. After this, king Henry returned to England, taking with him his daughter, whom, with the universal consent of the chief men of the whole of England, he afterwards restored to her husband, the earl of Anjou, who then demanded her. In this year died Hervey, bishop of Ely.

In the year 1133, the king passed the festival of the Nativity at Dunstable, and Easter at Woodstock. In the same year died Baldwin, king of Jerusalem, and was succeeded by Fulk, the brother of Geoffrey, earl of Anjou. This Fulk, king of Jerusalem, had by his wife, the daughter of the above-named king Baldwin, two sons, namely, Baldwin and Amauri. Baldwin succeeded his father, Fulk, in the kingdom of Jerusalem, and died without issue. After his death, his brother Amauri succeeded him as king, and reigned eleven years; he was the father of Baldwin the Leper, who was afterwards king, and two daughters, namely, Sibyl and Milicent, of whom further mention will be made in the sequel.

In the year 1134, after Pentecost, Henry, king of England, gave the bishopric of Ely to Nigel, his treasurer, and that of Durham to Geoffrey, his chancellor; the king also created a new bishopric at Carlisle, and gave it to Adelulph, the prior of Saint Oswald. In the same year an eclipse of the sun took place on the fourth day before the nones of August, at about the sixth hour of the day, to such a degree, that the whole of the sun's disk appeared as though covered by a black shield. That same day, the king, although some opposed it, fearing danger, and tried to dissuade him from it, crossed the sea without accident.

In the year 1135, Gilbert, bishop of London, departed this life. King Henry remained in Normandy in consequence of the joy he felt on account of his grandsons, whom Geoffrey, earl of Anjou, had become father of by his daughter, and commanded the earls and barons of all his dominions to swear fealty to the empress Matilda, his daughter, and Henry, her youngest son, naming him king after himself. After this, king Henry frequently purposed to return to England, but his daughter, the empress, detained him in consequence of the various quarrels which, on many occasions, arose between the king and the earl of Anjou, being, in fact, caused by the artfulness of his daughter. By the excitement arising therefrom, the king was excited to anger and rancorous feelings, which by some was said to be the cause of a chill of his constitution, and afterwards of his death. For when the king had returned from hunting, at Saint Dennis, in the wood of Lions, he ate the flesh of some murenæ, or lampreys, a fish which he was always very fond of, and which always disagreed with him. But although the physician had forbidden him to eat of this fish, the king did not obey his wholesome advice, in conformity with the saying, "We always strive for what is prohibited, and desire what is denied."[81]

This food, therefore, was a source of most noxious humours, and a strong exciter of others of a kindred nature, and suddenly caused a deadly chill in his aged body, creating a great disorder thereby. Nature struggling against this, caused an acute fever, in its attempts to resist the attack resulting from this most noxious substance; but the disease gaining the ascendancy, this mighty king departed this life, after having reigned

[81] " Nitimur in vetitum semper, cupimusque negata "

five years and three months, on the first day of December;
relative to whom one of our writers says :—

"King Henry is dead! the glory once, now the grief of the
world.   The Deities lament the death of their fellow divinity:
Mercury, his inferior in eloquence, Apollo, in strength of
mind, Jupiter, in command, and Mars, in might; all bewail
him.   Janus, his inferior in caution, Alcides, in prowess, Pal-
las, in arms, Minerva, in arts; all bewail him.   England,
who, springing from her cradle, had shone exalted on high
beneath the sceptre of this divinity, now sinks in shade.   She,
with her king, Normandy, with her duke, waxes faint; the
one nurtured him as a child, the other lost him as a man."

This happened in the year from the arrival of the Britons
in England, two thousand two hundred and sixty-five; from
the arrival of the Normans, sixty-nine; from the beginning of
the world, five thousand three hundred and seventeen;[82] in
the year of grace, eleven hundred and thirty-five.

On the decease of the great king Henry, as is generally the
case after death, the judgment of the people was freely pronounced upon him.   Some asserted that he shone resplendent in
three particulars ; supreme wisdom, victory, and riches.   In
wisdom, because he was considered most profound in counsel,
remarkable for foresight, and distinguished for eloquence.   In
victory, because, besides other exploits which he had successfully
performed, according to the laws of warfare, he had overcome
the king of the Franks.   In riches, because in that respect he
far outstripped his predecessors. Others again, animated by opposite feelings, charged him with three vices ; excessive avarice,
inasmuch as, while he was wealthy, in order that he might render
all his relatives poor, greedily gaping for their riches, he laid
hold of everything, with the hooks of informers, by means of
taxes and exactions ; cruelty, inasmuch as he put out the eyes
of his kinsman, the earl of Moretuil, whom he had thrown
into prison, (a horrid crime, which was not known until
death had revealed the king's secrets) ; other instances were
cited besides, which we will omit ; and sensuality, because
after the manner of king Solomon, he was continually a slave
to his passion for the female sex.

[82] This is clearly wrong, both according to our present reckoning, and
his own previous mode of calculation, which places the first year of the
Christian era in the year from the beginning of the world 4204.

Such matters as these did the common people freely discuss. In the course of time, however, in consequence of the shocking events which were kindled through the frantic perfidies of the Normans, whatever Henry had done, either in a tyrannical manner, or as befitted a king, seemed most excellent, in comparison with doings still worse. For after this, without delay, Stephen, the younger brother of Theobald, earl of Blois, repaired thither, a man of great activity and boldness; and although he had taken the oath of fealty, in the English kingdom, to the empress and her son Henry, still, like a tempest, he rushed upon the crown of the kingdom of England. William, archbishop of Canterbury, who had been the first to take the oath, oh shame! consecrated him king; in consequence whereof, God pronounced the judgment against him which he had pronounced against the high priest, the smiter of Jeremiah,[82]* namely, that he should not live beyond that year. In like manner, Roger, bishop of Salisbury, who had been the second to take the before-mentioned oath, and had dictated it to the rest, gave him the crown and the support of his assistance; in consequence of which, by the just judgment of God, at a subsequent period, being taken prisoner by him whom he had created king, and consigned to torture, he met with a miserable end.

But why make any further remark? All who had taken the oath, both bishops as well as earls and chief men, gave in their adherence to Stephen and did homage to him. This was, indeed, a bad sign, that thus suddenly all England, without any delay or resistance, as though in the twinkling of an eye, became subject to him.

KING STEPHEN.

In the year of grace 1136, on Saint Stephen's day, king Stephen was crowned, and held his court at London. At his coronation, according to report, the "Pax Domini" [*Peace of the Lord*] was neither said at the mass, nor repeated before the people when this sacrament was performed.

As yet the body of king Henry remained unburied in Normandy; for he had died on the first day of December. His body was brought to Rouen, where his entrails, brains, and

82* Alluding to the fate of Pashur, son of Immer, the priest, who smote Jeremiah. Jer. xx. 2—6.

eyes were buried; but the remainder of his body being cut
asunder with knives in every part, and then sprinkled with a
quantity of salt, was wrapped up and sewed in bull's hides, to
avoid the offensiveness of the smell, which being strong and continued, was overpowering to those who stood near it. In consequence of this, even the person who, in consideration of a large
sum, had opened the head with a hatchet for the purpose of ex-
tracting the brain, which was in a most corrupt state, although
he had wrapped up his own head in napkins, still met with
his death therefrom, and had poor reason for rejoicing at his
bargain. He was the last of the many slain by king Henry.

His attendants then conveyed the royal corpse to Caen,
where, while it was lying in the church in which his father
had been buried, it was steeped in a quantity of salt and
wrapped up in numerous hides, still a black and disgusting
liquid matter coming through the hides oozed forth therefrom,
and being caught in vessels placed beneath the bier, was carried
away by the servants fainting with disgust.

See, therefore, reader, whoever thou art, how the body of a
most potent king, whose head had been decked with a crown,
gold, and the choicest gems, with splendour almost divine,
whose two hands had been radiant with sceptres, the rest of
whose person had glittered all over with tissue of gold, whose
mouth used to be supplied with food so exquisite and delicious,
before whom all were wont to arise, whom all had dreaded, all
congratulated, all admired——See, I say, to what that body
was reduced; how horribly it was put out of sight, how shockingly thrust aside! Behold the result of human affairs,
upon which the judgment ever depends, and learn to have a
contempt for all that thus terminates, all that is thus reduced
to annihilation.

At last, the remains of the royal corpse were brought to
England, and were, in twelve days after, on his birth-day,[83]
buried at the abbey of Reading, which the same king Henry
had founded and enriched with many possessions. Thither,
also, came king Stephen from his court, which, at the feast of
the Nativity, he had been holding in London, to meet the body
of his uncle; and with him, William, archbishop of Canter-

[83] "Natalis" here, is probably a misprint for "Natali." Roger of
Wendover says that he was buried on his birth-day.

Q 2

bury, and many bishops and nobles, and there they buried king Henry with the respect due to a man so great.

King Stephen proceeded thence to Oxford, where he repeated and confirmed the concessions which he had promised to make to God, the people, and the holy Church, on the day of his coronation, which were these : In the first place, he promised on oath that, on the death of bishops, he would never retain the sees in his own hand, but immediately consent to the election and invest them with bishops. Secondly, he promised on oath, that he would retain in his hand the woods of no clerk or layman, as king Henry had done, who had every year impleaded them, if they either took venison in their own woods, or rooted them up or thinned them to supply their own necessities : which kind of unjust impleading was carried to so annoying a length, that, if the supervisors set eye from a distance upon the wood of any person whom they deemed to be a moneyed man, they immediately obtained an injunction against waste thereon, whether it had suffered waste or not, in order that, by some means or other, they might be enabled to mulct him. In the third place, he promised on oath, that Danegelt, that is to say, two shillings on every hide of land, which his predecessors had been accustomed to receive yearly, he would give up for ever. These are the principal things which he promised on oath to God ; there were others besides ; but none of these promises did he keep.

In the meantime, while, at the close of the festival of the Nativity, king Stephen was staying at Oxford, he received tidings which informed him to this effect : " David, king of the Scots, on pretence that he was coming with peaceful intent for the purpose of visiting you, has come to Carlisle and Newcastle, and stealthily taken possession of them both ;" to which king Stephen made answer ; " What he has taken by stealth, I will recover by victory ;" and thereupon, without delay, the king moved forward his army, which was so mighty, so valiant, and so numerous, that none in England could be remembered like it. However, king David met him in the neighbourhood of Durham, and, making a treaty with him, restored Newcastle, but retained Carlisle with the king's consent. David, however, did not do homage to king Stephen ; because he had previously, as the first of the laity, promised on oath to the empress, the daughter of king Henry and his own niece, to maintain her in possession of England after the death of king Henry. However, the son of king David, Henry by name, did homage to king Stephen; on which, the latter presented him with the borough which is called Huntingdon, by way of gift.

After this, the king returned at Lent, and held his court at London during the festival of Easter, amid such dazzling splendour, that there was never one in England more brilliant than it in its multitudes, magnificence, gold, silver, jewels, garments, and luxuries of every description.

At the time of the Rogation Days, the king was seized with a lethargy, and it was currently reported that he was dead. On hearing of this, Hugh Bigod secretly effected an entrance into Norwich castle, and would not restore it to any person except to the king himself on his repairing thither, and then very reluctantly. It was now that the frenzied conduct of the Normans, which has been previously mentioned, began to produce its effects in perjury and treason. The king, therefore, took Badington, the owner of which was one Robert, a traitor, who had rebelled against the king; after which, he laid siege to the city of Exeter, which Baldwin de Redwers[55] held against him; and being long detained there, and constructing many engines of war, consumed a large portion of his treasures in so doing. At length, however, the castle was surrendered to him, and the king, following the most pernicious advice, did not exercise vengeance upon the traitors. But if he had exercised it on this occasion, so many castles would not have afterwards held out against him. The king proceeded thence to the Isle of Wight, and took it from Baldwin de Redwers, previously mentioned, whom he banished from England.

The king, elated at these successes, went to hunt at Bramton, which is one mile distant from Huntingdon, and there he held pleas as to the forests of his nobles, that is to say, with reference to their woods and hunting, and thereby broke the vow and promise which he had made before God and the people.

In the year of grace 1137, being the second year of the reign of king Stephen, the king, at the season of Lent, crossed over into Normandy. Alexander, bishop of Lincoln, and

[55] Or Rivers.

many nobles besides, crossed over with him; and there, the king, who was well versed in martial enterprises, enjoyed brilliant success in all his enterprises; thwarted the strata-gems of the enemy, reduced the fortresses of the foe, and proved himself the most distinguished among the greatest of men. He made a treaty with the king of the Franks, and his son Eustace did homage to the king of the Franks, for Nor-mandy, which is subject to the superior lordship of the Franks. This became known to the earl of Anjou, who was his most in-veterate enemy, inasmuch as he had married the empress of Germany, the daughter of king Henry, who had received the oaths of Stephen with reference to England, and in conse-quence, the husband and wife demanded possession of England, but, in the end, consented to a treaty with king Stephen. For the earl saw that, at present, he could not possibly cope with the king's strength, both by reason of his great military renown, and the money, of which an abundance was still left from the treasures of the deceased king.

In the same year, Louis the Fat, king of the Franks, departed this life, and was succeeded by his son Louis. These two years, in fact, were the most prosperous ones of king Stephen's reign; but the third, of which we shall now make mention, was of a doubtful and varied character, while the two succeeding ones were replete with loss and calamity.

In the year of grace 1138, being the third year of the reign of king Stephen, the king, immediately on his return to England, flew to Bedford, on the vigil of the Nativity of our Lord, and besieged it throughout the whole festival of the Nativity; and, indeed, it was the opinion of many that he incurred the displeasure of God, because the festival of fes-tivals he paid little or no attention to. In the same year, Peter de Leves, the anti-pope, departed this life. Bedford having surrendered to king Stephen, he immediately moved his army onwards to Scotland.

For king David, having sworn fealty to the daughter of king Henry, as though under the veil of respect for his oath, by means of his troops, was perpetrating the most execrable deeds. Pregnant women they ripped asunder, and tore the offspring prematurely from the mother's womb, tossed children on the points of their lances, beheaded the priests upon the altars, and then placed the heads which they had cut off from the

crucifixes upon the bodies of the slain, and, by way of ex-
change, placed the heads of the slain upon the crucifixes.　In
consequence of this, wherever the Scots came, the places were
filled with cruelty and horror, the shrieks of women, the out-
cries of aged men, the groans of the dying, and the despera-
tion of the youthful.

On this, king Stephen aroused himself, and burned and ravaged the southern parts of king David's kingdom, while David
himself did not dare to confront him.　After Easter, however,
the disgraceful fury of the traitors became greatly inflamed.　For
one of the rebels, Talbot by name, held Hereford,[84] in Wales,
against the king; to which, however, the king laid siege, and
reduced it to submission.　Earl Robert,[85] the illegitimate son of
king Henry, held against him a most strongly fortified castle,
the name of which was Bristowe,[87] and another called Slede,[88]
William Lovel held the castle of Kari,[89] Paganel held the
castle of Ludlow; William de Moun held the castle of
Dunster;[90] Robert de Nichole[91] held the castle of Wareham;
Eustace Fitz-John, a one-eyed vile traitor, held the castle
of Malton; William Fitz-Allan held the castle of Salopes-
bury,[92] which last the king took by force of arms, and hanged
some of those who were taken prisoners; on hearing of which,
Walkelin, who held Dover castle, immediately surrendered it
to the queen who was then besieging it.

While king Stephen was thus engaged in the southern parts
of England, David, king of the Scots, led an innumerable
army into England.　By the advice and exhortation of 'Turstin, archbishop of York, the nobles of the north of England
went out to meet him, with William, the illustrious earl of
Albemarle, and planted the standard[93] or royal banner at Al-
verton,[94] on Cutune moor.　As, in consequence of illness, the
archbishop of York could not be present at the battle, he sent
in his place Ralph, bishop of the Orkneys,[95] who, standing
in the midst of the army, on an elevated spot, addressed
them to the following effect:

86 Of Gloucester.　　87 Bristol.　　88 Leeds.

89 Castle Cary, in Somersetshire.　　90 In Somersetshire.

91 Roger of Wendover calls him Robert of Lincoln.

92 Shrewsbury.

93 Hence this is sometimes called the battle of the Standard.

94 North Allerton.　　95 Roger of Wendover says, Bishop of Durham.

" Most illustrious nobles of England, Normans by birth,
(for when about to enter on the combat, it befits you to hold
in remembrance your names and your birth), consider who
you are, and against whom, and where it is, you are waging war;
for then no one shall with impunity resist your prowess. Bold
France, taught by experience, has quailed beneath your valour,
fierce England, led captive, has submitted to you; rich Apulia,
on having you for her masters, has flourished once again;
Jerusalem so famed, and illustrious Antioch, have bowed
themselves before you; and now Scotland, which of right is
subject to you, attempts to show resistance, displaying a teme-
rity not warranted by her arms, more fitted indeed for rioting
than for battle. These are people, in fact, who have no
knowledge of military matters, no skill in fighting, no moderation in ruling. There is no room then left for fear, but
rather for shame, that those whom we have always sought
on their own soil and overcome, reversing the usual order
of things, have, like so many drunkards and madmen, come
flocking into our country. This, however, I, a bishop, and the
substitute for your archbishop, tell you, has been brought about
by Divine Providence; in order that those who have in this
country violated the temples of God, stained the altars with
blood, slain his priests, spared neither children nor pregnant
women, may on the same spot receive the condign punishment
of their crimes; and this most just resolve of the Divine will,
God will this day put in execution by means of your hands.
Arouse your spirits then, ye civilized warriors, and, firmly relying on the valour of your country, nay, rather on the presence of
God, arise against these most unrighteous foes. And let not their
rashness move you, because so many insignia of your valour cause
no alarm to them. They know not how to arm[96] themselves for
battle; whereas you, during the time of peace, prepare your-
selves for war, in order that in battle you may not experience the
doubtful contingencies of warfare. Cover your heads then with
the helmet, your breasts with the coat of mail, your legs with
the greaves, and your bodies with the shield, that so the foeman
may not find where to strike at you, on seeing you thus surrounded on every side with iron. Marching then against them
thus, unarmed and wavering, why should we hesitate? On

[96] This is probably said in allusion to the absence of defensive armour,
with the half-naked Scotch.

account of their numbers perhaps? But it is not so much the numbers of the many as the valour of the few that gains the battle. For a multitude unused to discipline is a hindrance to itself, when successful, in completing the victory, when routed, in taking to flight. Besides your forefathers, when but few in number, have many a time conquered multitudes; what then is the natural consequence of the glories of your ancestry, your constant exercises, your military discipline, but that though fewer in number, you should overcome multitudes? But now the enemy, advancing in disorder, warns me to close what I have to say, and rushing on with a straggling front, gives me great reason for gladness.—I therefore in the place of the archbishop of you who are this day about to avenge the sins committed against the house of the Lord, against the priests of the Lord, and against your king under the Lord's protection, whoever of you shall fall fighting, do absolve him from all punishment for sins, in the name of the Father, whose creatures they have so shamefully and horribly slain, of the Son, whose altars they have polluted, and of the Holy Ghost, whose inspired ones, in their frenzy, they have slaughtered." To this all the troops of the English answered "Amen, Amen;" and the mountains and hills re-echoed with their cries.

At the same instant, the Scots raised the shout of their country, and the cries of "Albany! Albany!" ascended to the heavens; but the shouts were soon drowned in the dreadful crash and the loud noise of the blows. When the ranks of the men of Lothian, who had obtained from the king of Scotland, though reluctantly on his part, the glory of striking the first blow, hurling their darts and presenting their lances of extraordinary length, bore down upon the ranks of the English knights encased in mail, striking as it were against a wall of iron, they found them impenetrable. But the archers of the English, mingling with the cavalry, poured their arrows like a cloud upon them, and pierced those who were not protected by armour. Meanwhile the whole of the Normans and the English, stood in one dense phalanx around the standard, perfectly immoveable. The chief commander of the men of Lothian fell slain, pierced by an arrow, on which the whole of his men took to flight. For the most high God was offended with them, and all their valour was destroyed even as a spider's web. On seeing this, the main body of the Scots, which was fighting with the greatest valour in another part of the field, was alarmed and took to flight. Next, the king's troop, which king David had formed of several clans, as soon as it perceived this, began to drop off, at first; man by man, and afterwards in bodies, the king standing firm, and being at last left almost alone. The king's friends seeing this, forced him to mount his horse and take to flight; but Henry, his valiant son, not heeding what he saw being done by his men, but solely intent on glory and valour, while the rest were taking to flight, most bravely charged the enemy's line, and shook it by the wondrous vigour of his onset. For his troop was the only one mounted on horseback, and consisted of English and Normans, who formed a part of his father's household. His horsemen, however, were not able long to continue their attacks against soldiers on foot, cased in mail, and standing immoveable in close and dense ranks; but, with their lances broken and their horses wounded, were compelled to take to flight. Rumour says, that many thousands[96] of the Scots were slain on that field, besides those who, on being taken in the woods and standing corn, were put to death. Accordingly, the English and Normans happily gained the victory, and with a very small effusion of blood.

In this battle the commanders were the above-named Ralph, bishop of the Orkneys, the illustrious William, earl of Albemarle, of the blood royal, and famed for his military prowess, Walter Espec, a celebrated nobleman, William Piperel of Nottingham, and Gilbert de Lacy, whose brother was the only knight there slain.

On hearing of the result of this engagement, king Stephen and all who were with him gave hearty thanks to God. This battle was fought in the month of August. At the Advent of our Lord, Alberic, legate of the Roman church and bishop of Ostia, held a council at London, on which occasion, with the consent of king Stephen, Theobald, abbat of Bee, was made archbishop of Canterbury.

In the year of grace 1139, being the fourth year of the reign of king Stephen, after the Nativity, the said king took the castle of Slede[1] by siege; and afterwards proceeded to Scotland, where he laid waste the country on all sides with fire and sword, on which the king was obliged to make terms

[96] Roger of Wendover says, eleven thousand.   [1] Leeds.

with him. King Stephen thereupon returned to England, taking with him Henry, the son of the king of the Scots [as a hostage]. He then laid siege to Ludlow, where the same Henry, being dragged from his horse by an iron hook, was nearly taken prisoner, but the king himself valiantly rescued him from the enemy. After this, without accomplishing his object, he returned to Oxford, where a thing took place remarkable for its disgraceful character, and at variance with all civilized usage. For the king, after having received them in peace, violently arrested at his own court Roger, bishop of Salisbury, and Alexander,[1*] bishop of Lincoln, who, so far from refusing to settle matters with justice, had most earnestly entreated permission so to do.

Having thrown bishop Alexander into prison there, he took the bishop of Salisbury with him to his castle, called Devizes, a finer one than which there was not in all Europe. There he tortured him with the pangs of hunger, and tied a halter round the neck of his son,[2] who had been the king's chancellor, as though he were about to be hanged; and by such methods extorted from him the surrender of the castle, far from remembering the benefits which, at the beginning of his reign, beyond all others, he had conferred upon him: such, then, was the reward he bestowed on him for his devotedness. In a similar manner he gained possession of Syresburn,[2*] which was very little inferior to Devizes in magnificence. On obtaining the bishop's' treasures, by means of them he gained Constance, sister of Louis, king of the Franks, in marriage for his son Eustace. On retiring thence, the king took bishop Alexander, whom he had left in confinement at Oxford, with him to Newark, where that bishop had built a castle, near the river Trent, extremely well fortified and most amply supplied. On coming there, the king imposed on the bishop a fast not prescribed by the law,[3] and declared, on his oath, that he should be deprived of all food whatever until the castle was surrendered to him. In consequence of this, with considerable difficulty, by means of prayers and entreaties, the bishop prevailed on his own people to transfer

[1*] Some historians call him the nephew of the bishop of Salisbury, but he was suspected to be his son.

[2] This person, whose name was Roger, was said to be the son of Roger, bishop of Salisbury, by Maud of Ramsbury, his mistress.

[2*] Sherburne.   [3] The ecclesiastical law.

his castle from his own authority into the hands of strangers. In a similar manner, another castle of his was surrendered, called Slaford,[4] not inferior to the other either in appearance or excellence of situation.

Not long after, when Henry, bishop of Winchester, the king's brother, who was now legate of the Roman Church, was holding a council at Winchester, Theobald himself, the archbishop of Canterbury, and all the bishops who were with him, threw themselves at the king's feet, and begged with the most earnest supplications that he would restore their possessions to the above-mentioned bishops, and promised that they themselves would cordially forgive the king for all he had done against them. But the king, listening to the voice of persons evilly inclined, slighted the supplications of so many venerable men of such high station, and would not accede to their requests. In consequence of this conduct, the house of king Stephen was consigned to impending destruction.

For, immediately upon this, the daughter of king Henry, who had been empress of the Romans, and to whom the kingdom of England had been secured by oath, came to England; on which, king Stephen besieged her at Arundel, and, either through listening to perfidious counsels, or else seeing that the castle was impregnable, allowed her to go to Bristowe.[5]

In the same year, Roger, bishop of Salisbury, pined away, being wasted as much by grief as by old age, and ended his life. Let all, then, who read of this, be astounded at so great and so sudden a change of events. For, from his youth upwards, so many blessings had fallen to the lot of the man above-named, and, without interruption, had so wondrously accumulated upon him, that all said that, in his case, Fortune was forgetful of her fickle disposition. Nor did he suffer any adversity during the whole of his life, until at last so vast an accumulation of miseries, befalling him at the same moment, overwhelmed him. Let no one then feel confidence as to the long continuance of his happiness, let no one presume on the stability[6] of Fortune, let no one imagine that his seat can long be firm upon her revolving wheel!

In the year of grace 1140, being the fifth year of the reign of king Stephen, after the Nativity, the said king banished

4 Sleaford.   5 Bristol.
6 " Stabilitate" seems a preferable reading to " instabilitate."

Nigel, bishop of Ely, from his see, as he was the nephew of the above-named bishop of Salisbury; in consequence of which relationship[7] he had become an object of the king's hatred. As to where the king was at the feast of the Nativity, or where at Easter, it matters not to say. For now, courts held in regal state, and the pomp of royalty, handed down from the ancient line of kings, were utterly put an end to, the vast amount of treasures had been entirely expended, there was no such thing as peace in the kingdom, all quarters were threatened with slaughter, conflagration, and rapine. Shrieks, grief, and terror re-echoed in tones like thunder on every side, and in every place there were the tumultuous alarms of depredation and violence. In consequence of this, the following Elegiac lines were composed :—

"Who shall give me a spring, for what else but a spring of tears do I need, that with tears I may bewail the wicked deeds of my native land? A darkness hath come upon it, sent from the depths of hell, which in lowering clouds covers the face of this realm! Lo! frenzy, shrieks, conflagrations, theft, rapine, slaughter, and bad faith, in strict alliance come rushing on! At the present day men act the thief both towards the wealth and the owners of the wealth, and, strange kind of theft! while sleeping in their very castles they surprise them. Perjury is good faith, lying a noble act; even the betrayal of their lords is a deed worthy of men. The band of robbers breaks open temples and tombs, and even—oh shocking deed!—lays hands upon the priests. The anointed of the Lord, and women as well, they torture, and — oh shame!—that they may purchase their liberty, devise how to rack them with torments! Famine, therefore, comes on apace ; their flesh consumed, to skin and bone reduced, they breathe forth their fleeting souls ! Who can give sepulture to crowds so vast of the dying? Behold the face of hell, and a calamity its like !"

In the same year, king Stephen gave Northumbria to Henry, the son of David, king of the Scots. In the same year died Turstin, archbishop of York, on whose decease there immediately arose a division in the church of York, as to the election of an archbishop. For some of the canons made choice of

[7] " Progeniem," in the text, hinting that he was son of the bishop of Salisbury.

William, treasurer of the church of York, who was accordingly
consecrated by Henry, bishop of Winchester, legate of the
Church of Rome. But the other canons chose as their archbishop Henry Murdac, who prevailed, and retained the archbishopric as long as he lived, while archbishop William remained with Henry, bishop of Winchester, who had consecrated
him, until the decease of Henry Murdac.

In the year of grace 1141, being the sixth year of the reign
of king Stephen, that king, before the Nativity, laid siege to
the city of Lincoln, the castle of which, Ranulph, earl of
Chester, had treacherously seized; and there the king took up
his quarters until the Purification of Saint Mary; when earl
Ranulph brought with him Robert, the son of king Henry, his
own son-in-law, and some other valiant nobles, in order to raise
the siege by the king; and the most valiant earl, having
with difficulty crossed a marsh, which was almost impassable,
on the same day, drawing out his troops in battle array, offered
the king battle. He himself, with his own men, formed the
first line; those whom king Stephen had deprived of their
inheritance, the second; and the great earl Robert, with his
men, the third; on the flank there was a multitude of Welchmen, better provided with daring than with arms. After
this, the earl of Chester, a consummate warrior, glittering with
conspicuous arms, thus addressed earl Robert and the other
nobles :—

"With the greatest sincerity, to you, most invincible chieftain, and to you, nobles and fellow-soldiers, do I return many
thanks, who have magnanimously shewn your goodwill towards me at the hazard of your lives. Since then, I am the
occasion of your peril, it is only fair that I should be the first
to expose myself to peril, and be the first to pierce the ranks
of this most faithless king, who, after making a treaty, has
broken the peace. Wherefore, trusting both in the king's
injustice and in my own valour, I will straightway cleave asunder the royal ranks, and with my sword make way through the
midst of the foe. It shall be the part of your prowess to follow me while I, lead the way, and to imitate my example as I
strike. I already seem to myself, in my presaging mind, to be
passing through the royal ranks, trampling the nobles beneath
my feet, and piercing the king himself with my sword."

Thus he spoke; on which earl Robert addressed the youth,

and standing upon an elevated spot, delivered a speech to this effect :—

"It is not without reason that you demand the honor of the first blow, both on the ground of your noble descent, and the valour wherein you excel. But still, if you stand upon noble descent, I am not surpassed by you, being the son of a most noble king, and the grandson of a most mighty monarch : if upon valour, here are many men of most consummate bravery, before whom not a man living can be preferred for prowess. But it is a far different reason that influences me. For, contrary to the oaths which he made to my sister, the king has cruelly usurped the kingdom, and, causing confusion on every side, has been the occasion of death to many thousands,[8] and after his own example, has distributed lands among those who have no right thereto, violently taking them away from those who rightfully possessed them. By those who have been thus wickedly disinherited, with the aid of God, the Supreme Judge, who prepares vengeance, must he be first attacked. He who judges His people in equity, will look down from His habitation on high in the heavens, and will never desert us in this our great necessity, who with justice seek what is just. There is one thing, however, most valiant chieftains, and all you fellow-soldiers, which I desire firmly to impress upon your minds, namely, that by the marshes through which with difficulty you have passed, there can be no way of escape by flight. Here, therefore, we must either conquer or die ; in flight, hope of escape there is none. This alone remains for you, to make a way into the city with your swords. But if my mind presages aught of truth, the fact that you have no possible means of escape is the very thing which, this day, with the help of God, will gain for us the victory. For he must needs have recourse to prowess, who has not any possible means of escape. On the other hand, the citizens of Lincoln, who stand close to their city, with minds quailing beneath the vigour of your onset, you, proving victorious, will see flying for refuge to their homes. Besides, consider who it is against whom you are waging war. Alan, duke of the Bretons, comes forth in arms against us, nay, rather, against God ; an infamous man and one polluted with all kinds of crimes ; who in mis-

[8] The text has "militibus," "soldiers ;" but "millibus," "thousands," seems preferable, and is the reading in Ranulph Highden's narrative.

chief knows not his equal, who has never wanted the desire to do injury, and who would consider it his only and extreme reproach not to be incomparable to any one in cruelty. There is also come out against us the earl of Mellent, crafty in his deceitfulness; a planner of treachery; in whose heart iniquity is rooted, and guile in his mouth; slothful in deeds; presumptuous in heart; magnanimous in words; pusillanimous in acting; the last to attack, the first to run away; tardy in battle, swift in flight. There is also come out against us earl Hugh, to whom it seems a trifle to have broken his oath to the empress, but he must commit perjury a second time in the most glaring manner, by affirming that king Henry gave the kingdom to Stephen and deprived his own daughter thereof. There is also come out the earl of Albemarle, a man of singular constancy in crime, ready for daring evil, and slow to relinquish it; whom his wife, taking to flight, has abandoned by reason of his intolerable filthiness. There is also come out the earl, who has taken away his wife from the last named earl, a most avowed adulterer; of singular impurity, a devotee of Bacchus; a stranger to Mars; wreaking with wine, and unacquainted with warfare. There is also come out, Simon, earl of Hampton,[**] whose deeds consist of words alone; whose only gifts are promises; who when he has said a thing, has done it; when he has promised, has given. There are also come out, other nobles just like their king, accustomed to robberies; enriched with rapines; fattened upon murders; all, in fact, defiled by perjury. You, therefore, most valiant men, whom the great king Henry has advanced, and man has humbled, whom he has raised, this man has depressed, arouse your courage, and trusting in your valour, nay, rather, in the justice of God, take the vengeance thus offered to you by God upon these wicked persons, and confer imperishable glory upon your posterity. If then it is now your determination to be the instruments of this judgment of God, vow that you will press onward, abjure all thoughts of flight, and with one consent raise your right hands towards heaven." Hardly had he concluded, when all, raising their hands towards heaven, with a thrilling shout abjured flight, and getting their arms in readiness for the attack, moved onward against the enemy in splendid array.

[**] Southampton.

King Stephen in the meantime, his mind fluctuating amid mighty cares, had the mass performed with the greatest solemnity. But when, according to the usual custom, he was placing in the hands of bishop Alexander a wax taper, an offering to God worthy of a king, it broke. This was an omen of sorrow to the king. The pix[9] also fell down upon the altar in which was the body of the Lord, the string breaking in the presence of the bishop. This was an omen of the king's ruin. After this, the valiant king went forth, and with the greatest coolness disposed his troops in battle array; he himself on foot ranged in the closest possible order the whole body of his men in armour, dismounted from their horses. The earls with their troops on horse-back[10] arranged to fight in two bodies; but these bodies of horsemen appeared to be very small, as the earls had brought but few with them, though pretended to be more in number. But the king's army was very numerous, and marshalled under only one standard, that of the king; upon which, as king Stephen had not an agreable voice, the speech to the army by way of exhortation was delegated to Baldwin, a man of great nobleness, and a most valiant soldier, who, standing on an elevated spot, when, by a modest silence he had called the attention of all to his words, thus commenced, with the gaze of all intently fixed upon him;

" All those who, when the lines of battle are drawn up, are about to engage, ought to see beforehand to three things: first, the righteousness of their cause; next, the number of their men ; lastly, the prowess of their troops. The righteousness of their cause, lest danger to the soul should be incurred ; the number of their men, lest they should be overwhelmed with the number of the enemy; the prowess of their troops, lest, trusting in a multitude, they should, by relying on the weak, still be overthrown. On all these points we see ourselves suitably prepared in the matter upon which we are engaged. For the righteousness of our cause is this, that, observing what we have sworn to our king before God, we stand facing those who have proved perjured towards him to the peril of death. As to our numbers, in horsemen we are not inferior, in foot more

[9] The box in which the consecrated wafer is kept.
[10] This passage in Roger of Wendover applies to the earls, the antagonists of Stephen, and the liberty has been taken here of adapting the passage to that sense.

numerous. But the prowess of so many earls, so many nobles and knights always accustomed to warfare, who in words can express? Besides, the boundless valour of the king himself will stand for you in the stead of thousands. Since, then, your liege lord is in the midst of you, the Lord's anointed, to whom you have sworn allegiance, perform your vows before God; inasmuch as you shall receive the greater reward from God, the more faithfully and constantly you fight for your king, the faithful against the unfaithful, the observers of the law against the perjured. Then, be of good comfort and filled· with entire confidence. Consider against whom you fight. The might of earl Robert is well known : according to his practice, he threatens much, and does but little, having the mouth of the lion and the heart of the hare—eloquent in words, and always in the back-ground through his slothfulness. As for the earl of Chester, he is a man of unreasonable boldness, ready for plotting, inconstant in performing, impetuous in warfare, unprovided against danger, contriving schemes too lofty for his reach, bent upon impossibilities, and bringing with him few good soldiers : collecting a straggling multitude of strangers, there is no reason why he should be dreaded. For whatever he begins like a man, he always leaves like a woman ; since in all matters in which he has been concerned, he has met with misfortune, either overcome in the encounter and running away, or if, on extraordinary occasions, victorious, sustaining greater loss than those overcome. The Welchmen whom he has brought with him are only objects of our contempt, opposing their unarmed rashness to the front of battle, devoid of skill and all knowledge of the art of war, like cattle running upon the hunting-spears. The others, both nobles and common soldiers, are deserters and vagabonds, and I only wish they had been brought here in greater numbers, for the more they are in number, the worse will they prove in the trial of them. You, therefore, earls and men of noble rank, ought to be mindful of your valour and your dignity. This day elevate your prowess, so inestimable, to the most exalted pitch, and, in imitation of your ancestors, leave to your sons an everlasting glory. The constant success of your arms should be to you an incentive to fight ; the continuance of reverses will be to them a motive for running away. And indeed, already, if I am not deceived, they repent of coming hither, and are at this moment thinking of flight, if the rugged nature of the spot would allow of it.   Since then, it is not possible for them to fight or fly, what else have they done but, by the will of God, offer both themselves and their baggage unto you ?   Accordingly, you see their horses, their arms, and their bodies subject to your determination.   Lift up your hearts, therefore, and stretch forth your invincible right hands, ye warriors ! to receive with extreme joyousness that which God himself has presented to you."

Already, before he had concluded his speech, the shouts of the enemy were heard, the clanging of clarions, the neighing of horses, the re-echoing of the ground.   The troop of the proscribed which formed the van, charged the king's line, in which were earl Alan, the earl of Mellent, Hugh, earl of East Anglia, earl Simon, and the earl of Warrenne, with such fury, that instantly, in the twinkling of an eye, it was routed, and became divided into three parts; some of them were slain, some taken prisoners, while some took to flight. The division which was commanded by the earl of Albemarle and William of Ypres charged the Welch, who were advancing on the flank, and put them to flight.   But the troops of the earl of Chester attacked the body of the above-named earl, and, like the first line, it was scattered in an instant.   All the king's knights took to flight, and with them William of Ypres,[11] a native of Flanders, a man of the rank of an earl, and of great prowess.

In consequence of this, king Stephen was left with his body of foot in the midst of the enemy.   Accordingly, they surrounded the king's troops on every side, and assaulted them in every quarter, just in the way that an attack is made upon a fortified place.   Then might you have seen a dreadful aspect of battle, on every quarter around the king's troops fire flashing from the meeting of swords and helmets,—a dreadful crash, a terrific clamour,—at which the hills re-echoed, the city walls resounded.   With horses spurred on, they charged the king's troop, slew some, wounded others, and dragging some away, made them prisoners.   No rest, no breathing-time was granted them, except in the quarter where stood that most valiant king, as the foe dreaded the incomparable

[11] Roger of Wendover says that William of Ypres " and others, who could not take to flight, were taken and thrown into prison."

force of his blows. The earl of Chester, on perceiving this, envying the king his glory, rushed upon him with all the weight of his armed men.[12] Then was seen the might of the king, equal to a thunderbolt, slaying some with his immense battle-axe, and striking down others. Then arose the shouts afresh, all rushing against him, and he against all. At length, through the number of the blows, the king's battle-axe was broken asunder. Instantly, with his right hand, drawing his sword, well worthy of a king, he marvellously waged the combat, until the sword as well was broken asunder. On seeing this, William de Kahamnes, a most powerful knight, rushed upon the king, and seizing him by the helmet, cried with a loud voice, "Hither, all of you, come hither! I have taken the king!" All flew to the spot, and the king was taken. Baldwin was also captured, who had made the speech for the purpose of exhorting them, pierced with many wounds, and bruised with many blows, while earning undying fame by his glorious resistance. Richard Fitz-Urse was also taken, who in giving blows and receiving them was distinguished by his prowess. After the king was made prisoner, his troop still fought on; indeed, being surrounded, they could not take to flight; but at last were all either taken prisoners or slain. According to the usages of war, the city was plundered, and the king, in a piteous condition, was taken there.

The judgment of God being thus wrought upon the king, he was led to the empress, and placed in captivity in the castle at Bristowe.[13] The empress was recognized as mistress by all the people of England, except the men of Kent, where the queen[14] and William of Yypres fought against her with all their strength. She was first received by the bishop of Winchester, the Roman legate, and, shortly after, by the citizens of London. However, she soon became elated to an intolerable degree of pride, because her affairs, after their uncertain state, had thus prospered in warfare; conduct which alienated from her the affections of almost all the people. Irritated at this, with all the spitefulness of a woman, she ordered the king, the Lord's anointed, to be placed in irons. A few days

[12] "Armatorum" seems a preferable reading to "armorum," as it appears that Stephen was not taken by the earl of Chester alone, but in consequence of being overpowered and borne down by a multitude.
[13] Bristol.   [14] The wife of king Stephen.

after, in conjunction with her uncle, the king of the Scots, and her brother Robert, having collected their troops, she laid siege to the fortress of the bishop of Winchester; on which, the bishop sent for the queen and William of Ypres, and nearly all the nobles of England. In consequence of this, large armies were soon formed on either side. Daily combats took place, not rank meeting rank, but in skirmishes on the exterior of the lines. Their exploits, therefore, were not concealed amid the haze of battle, but the prowess of each was conspicuous, and proportionate renown attended his exploits; so much so, that to all men of prowess this period seemed rich in the dazzling exploits of illustrious men.

At length the army of the Londoners came up, swelled to vast numbers, and, fighting against the empress, compelled her to take flight. Many were taken while flying, and, among them, Robert, the brother of the empress, was captured, in whose castle the king was kept prisoner, and through whose capture alone the king could be ransomed: and, accordingly, they were both set at liberty. Thus then, through the judgment of God, the king was lamentably taken prisoner, and, through the mercy of God, he was mercifully liberated, and received with great rejoicings by the nobles of England.

In the same year, Alberic de Vere was slain at London, in a sedition of the citizens. In this year, also, died Geoffrey, bishop of Durham, and was succeeded in that see by William, dean of the church of Saint Barbara, at York, who was consecrated by Henry, bishop of Winchester, the legate of the Church of Rome.

In the year of grace 1142, being the seventh year of the reign of king Stephen, that king built a castle at Winchester.[15] Just then, an immense multitude of the enemy coming upon him unawares, the king's soldiers, on meeting them, were not able to withstand their attack; on which they forced the king to take to flight. Many of his men, however, were taken prisoners; and, among them, William Martel, the king's sewer, who, for his ransom, gave up the fine castle of Sherburne.

In the same year, the king besieged the empress at Oxford, from after the feast of Saint Michael till the Advent of our Lord; and, shortly before the festival of the Nativity, the

[15] It would appear from Gervase's Chronicle, that this battle took place at Wilton, and not at Winchester, in the year 1143.

empress fled across the river Thame, which was frozen, clothed in white garments. The reflection of the snow and the similarity deceiving the eyes of the besiegers, she escaped to the castle of Wallingford; upon which, Oxford was at length surrendered to the king.

In the year of grace 1143, being the eighth year of the reign of king Stephen, that king was present at a council held at London in the middle of Lent. For, at this period, no respect was paid by those who plundered to either the clergy or the Church of God, and, whether clerks or laymen, they were equally taken prisoners and held to ransom. Upon this, the bishop of Winchester, the Roman legate, held a council at London, which at the time was absolutely necessary for the safety of the clergy. At this council it was decreed, that no one who should violently lay hands upon a clerk could possibly receive absolution from any one, not even from the pope himself, and appearing in his presence. In consequence of this, a slight gleam of serenity, with great difficulty, shone forth at last upon the clergy.

In the same year, the king seized Geoffrey de Mandeville,[16] at his court at Saint Alban's, more in retribution for the wickedness of the earl, than according to the law of nations; more from necessity than from virtuous motives. For, if he had not done so, through the perfidy of this earl, whom from a baron he had created an earl, he would have been deprived of his kingdom. Accordingly, in order that the king might give him his liberty, he surrendered to him the tower of London and the castles of Walden and Plessis. In consequence of this, the above-named earl, being stripped of his possessions, attacked the abbey of Saint Benedict at Ramsey, expelled the monks, and introduced his plunderers, turning the church of God into a den of thieves. He was a man of the greatest prowess, but of the greatest perverseness towards God; of extreme activity in worldly matters, but extremely neglectful towards God.

In this year, shortly before the festival of the Nativity, the bishop of Winchester, and soon after, the archbishop of Canterbury, repaired to Rome, to treat for the legateship, pope Innocent being dead, and having been succeeded by Celestinus.

In the year of grace 1144, being the ninth year of the

[16] His name really was William.

reign of king Stephen, that king laid siege to Lincoln, where, while he was building a fort opposite the castle which the earl of Chester held by force, nearly eighty of his workmen were smothered by the enemy; consequently, abandoning the work, the king retreated in confusion. In the same year, earl Geoffrey de Mandeville greatly harassed the king, and shone forth with great glory in all his exploits. But, in the month of August, the Divine power showed a miracle worthy of its justice : for two persons, who had committed the like offence in expelling the monks, and turning the churches of God into castles, it punished with a similar retribution.

For Robert Marmion, a skilful warrior, had perversely acted thus towards the church of Coventry; while, as already mentioned, Geoffrey de Mandeville had been guilty of the like wickedness towards the church of Ramsey. · Robert Marmion, while attacking the enemy, and in the very midst of a large body of his own men, was slain, singly, before that very monastery, and, having been excommunicated, has death for his everlasting portion.

In a similar manner, Geoffrey, the new-made earl above-named, while amid the dense ranks of his own men, was, singly, pierced with an arrow by a foot-soldier of the lowest rank. He himself at first laughed at the wound; but, after a few days, died in consequence of it, and while excommunicated. Behold here the laudable vengeance of God, similarly attendant upon similar crimes, and worthy to be disclosed to all generations! Also, while the church was held by him as a castle, blood gushed forth from the walls of the church and the adjoining cloisters, in manifestation of the Divine displeasure, and foreboding the extermination of the wicked. This was seen by many persons; and, in fact, I myself[17] beheld it with my own eyes.

Wherefore, because they wickedly said that God was asleep, God was aroused; which is evident from these signs and manifestations. For, in this same year, Arnulph also, the son of earl Geoffrey, who, after his father's death, retained possession of the church as a castle, was taken prisoner and banished the

[17] This is the earliest mention made by the writer of himself in the capacity of witness of what he relates. He must have been very young at the time; consequently it was easy to impose on his credulity. He may, however, be possibly alluding to the extermination of the wicked.

kingdom by reason thereof, and the leader of his troops, falling from his horse at his inn,[18] dashed out his brains and expired.

In addition to this, the commander of his infantry, Reimer by name, whose habit it was to pull down churches or destroy them by fire, was crossing the sea with his wife, when, according to the statements of many, the ship became motionless. The sailors, astonished at this prodigy, made enquiry into the cause of the circumstance, by drawing lots, on which the lot fell upon Reimer. He, however, contradicting, with all his might, that this was the fact, the lots were drawn a second and a third time, and fell upon him still.   Upon this, he was placed in a boat, with his wife and the money which he had most wickedly acquired, and immediately thereupon the ship ploughed the sea with the swiftest speed, just as before.   The boat, however, with these most wicked people, being whirled round by a whirlpool suddenly formed, was sucked in and came to destruction.

In the same year, pope Celestinus having departed this life, Lucius was appointed in his stead.

In the year of grace 1145, being the tenth year of the reign of king Stephen, that king was at first occupied in business relative to the departure of Hugh Bigot.   But, in the spring, earl Robert, and the whole body of the king's enemies, built a castle at Ferendimer;[19] on which, the king, displaying his usual activity, collected his forces and hurried thither, taking with him a numerous and warlike body of Londoners.   After having assailed the fortress for whole days together, while earl Robert and his supporters were not far from the king's army, waiting for additional troops, by a display of military prowess attended with the most laborious efforts, he gained possession of it, though not without great bloodshed.   Then, at length, the king's fortunes began to change for the better, and to soar aloft.

In the same year pope Lucius died, and was succeeded by pope Eugenius.   In this year also, Alexander, bishop of Lincoln, went again to Rome, and was honorably entertained by Eugenius, the new pope, a man worthy of that highest dignity.

[18] "Hospitio."   This may possibly mean the portion of the monastery where the monks were in the habit of entertaining strangers.

[19] "Ferendune" is a various reading, "Ferendimer" being probably a misprint.   Faringdon, in Berkshire, is the place meant.

His mind was always kindly disposed, his discretion always to be relied on, his countenance always not only cheerful but even joyous. The bishop, returning the second year after this to Lincoln, with wonderful taste repaired the church there so skilfully, that it appeared more beautiful than when it was first built.

In the year of grace 1146, being the eleventh year of the reign of king Stephen, that king, having assembled a large army, built an impregnable castle, situate opposite to Wallingford, where Ranulph, earl of Chester, who was now on friendly terms with the king, was staying with a large number of his followers.   But, shortly after, as the earl was coming in a peaceful manner to the king's court, the king seized him at Northampton, while apprehending no such attack, and thrust him into prison until he had restored to him the most famous castle of Lincoln, which he had taken from him by stratagem, and all the rest of the castles which had belonged to himself; upon which, the earl was released from prison and restored to liberty.

In the same year, the noble city of Edessa, in Syria, which is now called Roaise, was taken through treachery by the Saracens, on the night of the Nativity of our Lord, while the bishop and Raymond, earl of Saint Gilles, and innumerable troops collected from the whole kingdom, and the people of the city were engaged in their religious duties; who, on the capture of the city, were put to death by the pagans. In this city the remains of Saint Thomas the Apostle, which were formerly transferred from India, are said to rest.

In the year of grace 1147, being the twelfth year of the reign of king Stephen, that king, at the festival of the Nativity of our Lord, was crowned at the city of Lincoln, which no king had dared to enter, in consequence of certain superstitions[20] preventing them. After the king's departure thence, the earl of Chester came to Lincoln with his troops, for the purpose of assaulting it; upon which occasion, the commander of his troops, a man of invincible bravery, was slain at the entrance of the north gate, and, after losing many of his men, the earl was forced to take to flight. On this, the citizens of Lincoln, being victorious, were filled with extreme joy, and,

[20] It was believed that misfortune and a speedy death would befall the king so doing.

with great pomp, returned thanks, attended with praises, to the
Virgin of virgins, their protectress.

At Pentecost, Louis, king of the Franks, Theodoric, earl of
Flanders, and the earl of St. Gilles, with numberless troops
from the well-peopled kingdom of the Franks, besides many of
the English nation, having assumed the cross, set out for Jerusalem, for the purpose of expelling the pagans, who had
taken the city of Rouise. Conrad also, the emperor of Germany, led a still greater body of troops, and both armies passed
through the dominions of the emperor of Constantinople, who
afterwards betrayed them.

In the month of August, Alexander, bishop of Lincoln, set
out for Auxerre, to meet pope Eugenius, who was then at that
place, having previously been to Paris. He was received by
the pope in the most honorable manner; but, in consequence
of the excessive heat of the weather, brought with him to
England the seeds of disease and death, and died in the following year, having for his successor Robert de Chedney.

In the year of grace 1148, being the thirteenth year of the
reign of king Stephen, the armies of the emperor of Germany
and of the king of the Franks, which, graced by those most
noble chieftains, marched onward with the greatest pomp,
were annihilated, because God utterly despised them. For the
incontinence ascended to the sight of God, of which they were
guilty in acts of fornication and manifest adultery; a thing
which greatly displeased the Almighty, and was aggravated by
the rapine and all kinds of crime of which they were afterwards
guilty. Accordingly, at first they fell, attacked by famine,
through the treachery of the emperor of Constantinople, and
afterwards by the edge of the enemy's sword. The king of
France and the emperor of Germany, upon this, with a very
small number of followers, fled ignominiously, first to Antioch,
and afterwards to Jerusalem. On arriving there, the king of
France, as though about to do something to compensate his loss
of glory, having obtained the aid of the knights of the Temple
at Jerusalem, and gathering forces on every side, laid siege to
Damascus; but having effected nothing there, he returned to
France.

In the meantime, a naval force, headed by no influential
men, and relying upon no mighty chieftain, but only on Almighty God, inasmuch as it had set out in a humble spirit,

earned the favour of God and manifested great prowess. For, though but few in number, by arms they obtained possession of a famous city of Spain, Lisbon[21] by name, and another, called Almeida, together with the parts adjacent. How true is it that God opposes the proud, but to the humble shows grace! For the army of the king of the Franks and of the emperor was larger and better equipped than the former one, which had gained possession of Jerusalem; and yet they were crushed by a very few, and routed and demolished like webs of spiders; whereas these other poor people, whom I have just mentioned, no multitude could resist, but the greater the numbers that made head against them, the more helpless were they rendered. The greatest part of them had come from England.

In the meantime, Geoffrey, earl of Anjou, husband of the above-named empress, the daughter of king Henry, entered Normandy with a great army and ravaged it, and took many castles and fortified cities; and the nobles of Normandy, keeping in mind the oaths they had made to the said empress and her heirs regarding Normandy, readily changed to their side. For Eustace, the son of king Stephen, who had been the duke of Normandy, and had married Constance, sister of Louis, king of France, was now dead, and the king of France had given his sister Constance in marriage to Raymond, earl of Saint Gilles; and from this period the wars so greatly increased against king Stephen in England, that he could give no attention to the defence of Normandy.

At this time, Henry, son of the empress Matilda, being now a youth sixteen years of age, and having been brought up at the court of David, king of the Scots, his mother's uncle, was dubbed a knight by the same king David, at the city of Carlisle, having first made oath to him that if he should come to be king of England, he would restore to him Newcastle and the whole of Northumbria, and would allow him and his heirs to hold for ever in peace, without challenge of their right, the whole of the land which lies between the rivers Tweed and Tyne. After this, the same Henry, by the advice and assistance of David, king of the Scots, crossed over into Normandy, and being received by the nobles, was by them made duke of Normandy.

[21] Great part of Portugal was at this time in the hands of the Moors.

In the year of grace 1149, being the fourteenth year of the reign of king Stephen, Henry, duke of Normandy came into England with a great army, on which many castles were surrendered to him, and a great number of towns; he also coined new money, which they called "the duke's money;" and not himself only, but all the influential men, both bishops as well as earls and barons, coined their own money. But from the time when the duke came over, he rendered null the coin of most of them.

In the same year, Louis, king of the Franks, and Eleanor, his wife, returned from Jerusalem to France.

In the year of grace 1150, being the fifteenth year of the reign of king Stephen, the abbey of Holcoltram was founded, also the abbey of Kinross, in Moray. In the same year, also, the Præmonstratensian order came to Dryburgh, at the feast of Saint Martin

In the year of grace 1151, being the sixteenth year of the reign of king Stephen, pope Eugenius sent by his legate, John Papirius, four palls to Ireland, whither a pall had never been sent before, and appointed archbishops at four places, one at Armagh, another at Cashel, a third at Dublin,[22] and a fourth at Connaught. In the same year, Geoffrey, earl of Anjou, departed this life, and his son Henry succeeded him in the earldom.

In the year of grace 1152, being the seventeenth year of the reign of king Stephen, during this year as also two preceding ones, king Stephen and Henry, duke of Normandy, frequently engaged in battle, and did not withdraw from the combat, except with a great loss of substance and of men; but the duke of Normandy always gained the day. For his resources increased more and more, and became more abundant every day, while the king's power decreased more and more. For the chief men of the kingdom, bearing in mind the oaths they had taken to the empress and her heirs, nearly all gave in their adhesion to the above-named empress and her son, the duke of Normandy. In the same year, Henry, earl of Northumbria, son of David, king of the Scots, and Matilda, his daughter, departed this life.

In the year of grace 1153, being the eighteenth year of the reign of king Stephen, peace was restored to England, a treaty being made between king Stephen and Henry, duke of

[22] Called "Diveline" in the text.

Normandy, whom king Stephen adopted as his son, and appointed his heir and successor in the kingdom, through the mediation of the venerable man Theobald, archbishop of Canterbury, and Henry, bishop of Winchester. The king also appointed the duke justiciary of England under him, and all the affairs of the kingdom were transacted through him ; and from this time forward the king and the duke were of one mind in the government of the realm, so much so that, from this period, no disagreement ever arose between them.

In the same year died David, king of the Scots, on the ninth day before the calends of July, on which, his grandson Malcolm, the son of earl Henry, a boy twelve years of age, succeeded him in the kingdom. In the same year, pope Eugenius departed this life, and was succeeded in the papacy by Anastasius. In this year died Bernard, abbat of Clerville ; William, bishop of Durham, also died in this year, and was succeeded by Hugh de Pudsey,[23] treasurer of the church of York, nephew of the above-named king Stephen. He was consecrated at Rome, by pope Anastasius, on the Lord's day preceding the Nativity of our Lord. In the same year died Henry, archbishop of York, on whose decease archbishop William, whom pope Eugenius had suspended, set out for Rome, and finding grace with pope Anastasius, the archbishopric of York was restored to him.

In the year of grace 1154, being the nineteenth and last year of the reign of king Stephen, Eustace, the son of king Stephen, departed[24] this life. In the same year, William, archbishop of York, was honorably restored to his see ; but shortly after, by the treachery of his clergy, after receiving the Eucharist, during his ablutions, he was destroyed by means of some liquid of a deadly nature ; on which he was honorably interred by Hugh, bishop of Durham, in the church of Saint Peter at York ; and on the presentation of king Stephen, Roger, archdeacon of Canterbury, succeeded him in the archbishopric.

In the same year king Stephen laid siege to many castles, and took them, and levelled many of them with the ground ; almost the very last of which was the castle of Drax ; shortly after

---

[23] Or De Pusat, or Pusar.

[24] There is clearly a mistake here ; as the death of Eustace is mentioned above as having taken place before the year 1148, in which year his widow Constance was given in marriage to the earl of Saint Gilles. 1152 is probably the date of his death.

which, king Stephen died, and was buried at the abbey of Feversham. He was succeeded on the throne by Henry, duke of Normandy, son of the empress Matilda, who was crowned and consecrated king by Theobald, archbishop of Canterbury, at London, on the Lord's day before the Nativity of our Lord.

In the same year, Theobald, archbishop of Canterbury, gave to Thomas Becket, his clerk, the archdeaconry of Canterbury. In this year also, Louis, king of the Franks, caused himself to be divorced from his wife Eleanor, daughter of the duke of Aquitaine, the archbishops, bishops, earls and barons, making oath that she had caused to deserve to be his wife. However, Henry, king of England, took the before-named Eleanor to wife, and had by her sons and daughters. The king of France, however, by his wife Eleanor, had no issue of the male sex, and only two daughters, one of whom he married to Henry, earl of Champagne, and the other to Theobald, earl of Blois, brother of the said earl Henry. After this, Louis, king of the Franks, took to wife the daughter of the king of Spain, by whom he had two daughters only.